AFRICAN HISTORICAL DICTIONARIES
Edited by Jon Woronoff

1. *Cameroon,* by Victor T. LeVine and Roger P. Nye. 1974
2. *The Congo,* 2nd ed., by Virginia Thompson and Richard Adloff. 1984
3. *Swaziland,* by John J. Grotpeter. 1975
4. *The Gambia,* 2nd ed., by Harry A. Gailey. 1987
5. *Botswana,* by Richard P. Stevens. 1975
6. *Somalia,* by Margaret F. Castagno. 1975
7. *Benin [Dahomey],* 2nd ed., by Samuel Decalo. 1987
8. *Burundi,* by Warren Weinstein. 1976
9. *Togo,* 2nd ed., by Samuel Decalo. 1987
10. *Lesotho,* by Gordon Haliburton. 1977
11. *Mali,* 2nd ed., by Pascal James Imperato. 1986
12. *Sierra Leone,* by Cyril Patrick Foray. 1977
13. *Chad,* 2nd ed., by Samuel Decalo. 1987
14. *Upper Volta,* by Daniel Miles McFarland. 1978
15. *Tanzania,* by Laura S. Kurtz. 1978
16. *Guinea,* 2nd ed., by Thomas O'Toole. 1987
17. *Sudan,* by John Voll. 1978
18. *Rhodesia/Zimbabwe,* by R. Kent Rasmussen. 1979
19. *Zambia,* by John J. Grotpeter. 1979
20. *Niger,* by Samuel Decalo. 1979
21. *Equatorial Guinea,* by Max Liniger-Goumaz. 1979
22. *Guinea-Bissau,* 2nd ed., by Richard Lobban and Joshua Forrest. 1988
23. *Senegal,* by Lucie G. Colvin. 1981
24. *Morocco,* by William Spencer. 1980
25. *Malawi,* by Cynthia A. Crosby. 1980
26. *Angola,* by Phyllis Martin. 1980
27. *The Central African Republic,* by Pierre Kalck. 1980
28. *Algeria,* by Alf Andrew Heggoy. 1981
29. *Kenya,* by Bethwell A. Ogot. 1981
30. *Gabon,* by David E. Gardinier. 1981
31. *Mauritania,* by Alfred G. Gerteiny. 1981
32. *Ethiopia,* by Chris Prouty and Eugene Rosenfeld. 1981
33. *Libya,* by Lorna Hahn. 1981
34. *Mauritius,* by Lindsay Rivière. 1982
35. *Western Sahara,* by Tony Hodges. 1982
36. *Egypt,* by Joan Wucher-King. 1984
37. *South Africa,* by Christopher Saunders. 1983
38. *Liberia,* by D. Elwood Dunn and Svend E. Holsoe. 1985
39. *Ghana,* by Daniel Miles McFarland. 1985
40. *Nigeria,* by Anthony Oyewole. 1987
41. *Ivory Coast,* by Robert J. Mundt. 1987
42. *Cape Verde,* 2nd ed., by Richard Lobban and Marilyn Halter. 1988
43. *Zaire,* by F. Scott Bobb. 1988

Historical Dictionary of the Republic of GUINEA - BISSAU

second edition

by
RICHARD LOBBAN
and
JOSHUA FORREST

African Historical Dictionaries, No. 22

The Scarecrow Press, Inc.
Metuchen, N.J., & London
1988

DT
613.5
L6
1988

First edition published as <u>Historical Dictionary of the</u>
<u>Republics of Guinea-Bissau and Cape Verde.</u>

Library of Congress Cataloging-in-Publication Data

Lobban, Richard.
    Historical dictionary of the Republic of Guinea-Bissau /
by Richard Lobban and Joshua Forrest. -- 2nd ed.
        p.   cm. -- (African historical dictionaries ; no. 22)
    Bibliography: p.
    ISBN 0-8108-2086-2
    1. Guinea-Bissau--History--Dictionaries. 2. Guinea-
Bissau--Bibliography. I. Forrest, Joshua. II. Title.
III. Series.
DT613.5.L62   1988
966'.57--dc19   87-32298

This dictionary is dedicated to the people of
Guinea-Bissau, whose tenacity throughout prolonged periods of political upheaval and economic
hardship is no less than remarkable.

CONTENTS

ACKNOWLEDGMENTS

It is something of an embarrassment to put our names as the authors of a work of history to which so many individuals have contributed by their acts: the generations of Africans, the Portuguese explorers, tens of thousands of slaves, and those colonial and anti-colonial forces in the recent war. This collective experience gives us the material for history writing. For the first edition of this book, Richard Lobban would especially like to thank the leadership of the PAIGC for permitting and assisting his travels in the liberated zones in 1973 and then to free Guinea-Bissau in 1975. In the 1980s Joshua Forrest's research was made possible with access to the Republic of Guinea-Bissau.

The first edition was also assisted by Linda Zangari, Jose Aica, Raymond Almeida, and a faculty research grant from the Rhode Island College Faculty Research Fund. Richard's wife, Carolyn Fluehr-Lobban, a busy and productive scholar in her own right, has offered faithful support and sincere interest which is required for a project of this sort. For this, and so many other things, she is thanked.

The second edition was assisted in various ways by Shirley Washington, who helped to bring Richard and Joshua together. Peter Manuel wrote several new entries relating to ethnomusicology, and these are gratefully acknowledged.

In addition, Joshua is particularly grateful to the many dozens of anonymous Guineans whose interviews provided the basis for much important historical data, and he would like to acknowledge the extensive assistance of the directors and archivists of the Arquívo Histórico Ultramarino in Lisbon and the Archives Nationales de Sénégal in Dakar.

vii

EDITOR'S FOREWORD

Guinea-Bissau is not one of Africa's largest countries, nor its most populous, nor its most prosperous. But it has carved a very special place in African history through a long and bloody struggle for independence. How it was colonized, how it escaped from colonialism and what has happened since independence are therefore of special interest to students of African affairs.

However, since the republic is somewhat peripheral and not that easy to visit, and because Portuguese is spoken, less is known about Guinea-Bissau than most African states. That is why we are particularly pleased that this dictionary is not only an updating but also an expansion of the earlier book on Guinea-Bissau and Cape Verde, and that another, enlarged dictionary will soon appear on the latter. Both will provide insight on people, places and events as well as other essential information including substantial bibliographies.

This dictionary is co-authored by Richard Lobban, Jr. and Joshua Forrest with the assistance of several other specialists. Lobban, Professor of Anthropology and Coordinator of the African and Afro-American Studies Program at Rhode Island College, wrote the first edition. One of the few Americans to have seen Guinea-Bissau during the struggle for independence, he visited the liberated zones in 1973, returned in 1975, and has followed events closely ever since. Forrest recently completed a dissertation on "State, Peasantry, and National Power Struggles in Post-Independence Guinea-Bissau." This work grew out of an extended stay in Guinea-Bissau, Senegal and Portugal in 1982-84. The result of these combined efforts is a very comprehensive, informative and fascinating study.

Jon Woronoff
Series Editor

PREFACE TO THE SECOND EDITION

A year ago Jon Woronoff contacted me to ask whether it might be time to update my <u>Historical Dictionary of the Republics of Guinea-Bissau and Cape Verde</u> in view of the facts that seven years had passed since it was first published by Scarecrow Press and that the then unified Republics had been torn asunder following the overthrow of President Luís Cabral. Since I agreed with these observations I accepted the offer, but felt that this would be an excellent chance to include not only major revisions and updating but also to make substantive new additions.

As a result, I contacted Joshua Forrest to suggest that he might include important additions since he was actively writing his Ph.D. at the University of Wisconsin at Madison on modern Guinean politics. I feel most fortunate that he was willing to work on this project as co-author of the second edition. Thus, with this new combination and with very extensive revisions and updating, we present this edition to its readership with the hope that it will be an improvement over the first edition and serve researchers on Guinea-Bissau as a basic reference tool for their studies.

Richard Lobban
Providence, Rhode Island

ABBREVIATIONS AND ACRONYMS

ANP	Assembleia Nacional Popular (Popular National Assembly)
BGB	Bank of Guinea-Bissau
BNU	Banco Nacional Ultramarino (Overseas National Bank)
CEI	Casa dos Estudantes do Império (Imperial Students' Society)
CEL	Comité Executivo da Luta
CONCP	Conferência das Organisações Nacionalistas das Colonias Portuguesas (Conference of the Nationalist Organizations of the Portuguese Colonies)
CSL	Conselho Superior da Luta (Supreme Council of the Struggle)
CUF	Companhia União Fabril
DGS	Direção Geral de Seguranca (General Security Headquarters)
ECOWAS	Economic Community of West African States
FARP	Forças Armadas Revolucionárias do Povo (Revolutionary Armed Forces of the People)
FLGC	Frente de Libertação da Guiné Portuguesa e Cabo Verde (Liberation Front of Portuguese Guinea and Cape Verde)
FLING	Frente de Luta Pela Independência Nacional da Guiné-Bissau (Front for the National Independence of Guinea-Bissau)
FRAIN	Frente Revolucionária Africana para a Independência Nacional das Colónias Portuguesas (African Revolutionary Front for the National Independence of the Portuguese Colonies)
FRELIMO	Frente de Libertação de Moçambique (Front for the Liberation of Mozambique)
GADCVG	Grupo de Acção Democrática de Cabo Verde e da Guiné

JAAC	Juventude Africana Amílcar Cabral (Amílcar Cabral African Youth)
MAC	Movimento Anti-Colonialista (Anti-Colonialist Movement)
MLGCV	Mouvement de Libération de la Guinée "Portugaise" et les Îles du Cap Vert (Liberation Movement of Portuguese Guinea and the Cape Verde Islands)
MLICV	Mouvement de Liberation des Îles du Cap Vert (Liberation Movement of the Cape Verde Islands)
MPLA	Movimento Popular de Libertação de Angola (Popular Movement for the Liberation of Angola)
NATO	North Atlantic Treaty Organization
OAU	Organization of African Unity
PAICV	Partido Africano de Independência de Cabo Verde (African Party for the Independence of Cape Verde)
PAIGC	Partido Africano da Independência da Guiné e Cabo Verde (African Party for the Independence of Guinea and Cape Verde)
PIDE	Polícia Internacional e de Defesa do Estado (International Police for the Defense of the State)
UCID	União Caboverdeana para a Independência e Democracia
UDCV	União Democratica de Cabo Verde (Democratic Union of Cape Verde)
UDEMU	União Democrática das Mulheres (Democratic Union of Women)
UN	United Nations
UPICV	União das Populações das Ilhas de Cabo Verde (Union of the Populations of the Cape Verde Islands)
USAID	United States Agency for International Development

HISTORICAL CHRONOLOGY FOR
GUINEA-BISSAU

ca 4000 BC Expansion of agriculture in the West African savanna.

ca 3000 BC Berbers initiate trans-Saharan trade.

ca 2000 BC Rise of small states in the savanna.

1000 BC Sahelian and Southeast Asian crops penetrate the West African littoral.

500 BC The coastal peoples in the Upper Guinea coast diversify with the penetration of agriculture to the coast.

250 BC Iron-working established in Nigeria.

200 BC Romans occupy the Iberian peninsula.

100 BC Camels enter the Trans-Saharan trade.

ca 300 AD Ghana and Tekrur emerge in the Sahel.

411-660 AD Suevi and Visigoth presence in Portugal.

711 AD Moors begin the occupation of the Iberian peninsula.

800 AD Berbers introduce Islam to the Sahel.

900 AD Savanna peoples penetrate the West African coast.

990 AD Tekrur falls.

1054 AD	Almoravids expand to the West African sahel.
1076	Ghana conquered by the Almoravids.
1135	Almoravid rule of Ghana collapses.
1143	Portugal becomes an independent monarchy.
1230	Formation of Mali.
1248–79	Reign of Afonso III.
1249	The final reconquest of Christian Portugal.
ca 1250	Formation of Gabu.
1325–57	Reign of Afonso IV.
1384	Rise of the Royal House of Avis in Portugal. (Period of Portuguese gold shortage.)
1385–1433	Reign of João I.
1415	The forces of Prince Henry capture Ceuta.
1420–1470	Epoch of Portuguese exploration of the coast of Africa.
1434	Sailing for Prince Henry, Capt. Gil Eannes reaches Cape Bojador.
1436	Portuguese fail in their attempt to take Tangiers.
1438–1481	Reign of Afonso V.
1441	First slaves captured by Antão Gonçalves of Portugal.
1443	Prince Henry monopolizes all trade south of Cape Bojador.
1446	Portuguese reach coast of Guinea-Bissau.
1447	Nuno Tristão killed in Bissagos Islands.

1448	At least 1,000 slaves had been shipped to Portugal from Africa.
1455	Portuguese establish slave trading "factory" at Arguim, Morocco.
1456	Portuguese pilot sights some of the Cape Verde Islands.
1460	Portuguese explorers Diogo Gomes, Antonio de Noli and Bartolomeo da Noli discover the Sotavento group of islands in the Cape Verde archipelago; settlement begins soon afterward.
1462	Diogo Afonso discovers the islands in the Barlavento group.
1466	Early settler from Portugal (Algarve) allowed to trade freely in African slaves and other goods from the coast, but many settlers had left before the end of the decade. Crown administration of Cape Verde officially starts on June 12.
1468-1474	Crown trade monopoly granted to Fernão Gomes.
1469	Songhai becomes dominant on the Niger.
1473	Portuguese explorers reach the West African kingdom of Benin.
1474-1575	Greatest period of Portuguese trade in West African slaves.
1486	Benin sends its ambassador to Portugal.
1490	Formation of Futa Toro.
1497	Vasco da Gama stops at the Cape Verde Islands at the start of his epoch voyage.
1510	First effective and permanent captaincy system established in the Cape Verde Islands.
1514	Expansion of the slave trade to and from the Cape Verde Islands.

1540s	English Captain William Hawkins trades on the Guinea coast.
1546	Fall of the Empire of Mali.
1550s	Dutch seize Portuguese settlements at Arguim, Gorée, and el Mina. English continue to erode the control of Portuguese trade.
1560s	Expansion of English slaving on the west coast of Africa.
1562	John Hawkins begins trade of slaves on Guinea coast as a direct challenge to the Portuguese.
1564	The captaincies of Cape Verde and Guinea revert to being Portuguese crown provinces.
1578	Portuguese defeated in Morocco.
1580-1640	Portugal is ruled by the Spanish crown.
1588	Captaincy system established on the coast at Cacheu; royal governors are subordinate to the governor of Cape Verde. Defeat of the Spanish Armada by the English.
1591	Collapse of Songhai.
1600s	Intensification of the slave trade on the West African coast.
1635	Peace treaty between England and Portugal.
1650-1879	Guinea-Bissau administered from Cape Verde.
1698-1708	One hundred and three ships built in Rhode Island, largely for the West African slave trade.
1775	End of the Denianke dynasty in Futa Toro.
1788	Formation of Futa Djallon as a Fula state.
1800s	European nations begin to abolish slavery.

1808	United States prohibits slave trade.
1836	Portuguese officially abolish slavery; the Governor General of Cape Verde also governs Guinea-Bissau.
1840s and 1850s	The United States establishes the African Squadron, based in the Cape Verde Islands, for the suppression of the coastal slave trade.
1867	Fall of the Mandingo kingdom of Gabu to Fula from Futa Djallon.
1870	U.S. President Grant arbitrates in favor of Portugal in a Luso-British dispute over Bolama.
1878-1936	End of Futa Djallon; Portuguese initiate military "pacification" campaigns to conquer Guinea-Bissau.
1879	Guinea-Bissau gains an administration separate from Cape Verde.
1884-85	Partition of Africa at the Berlin Congress.
1910-20	Portuguese monarchy overthrown.
1926	Rise of Portuguese fascism.
1941	Bissau replaces Bolama as the capital of Guinea-Bissau.
1956	PAIGC formed.
1959	Pidiguiti massacre.
1961	Formation of the CONCP.
1963-1974	Period of the nationalist war in Guinea-Bissau.
1964	First National Congress of the PAIGC inside Guinea at Cassaca.
1973	Assassination of Amílcar Cabral, January 20;

meeting of the first Peoples National Assembly
of the PAIGC, September.

1974   Fall of fascist/colonial Portugal, April 15;
         Guinea-Bissau becomes independent, Septem-
         ber 24.

1975   Cape Verde becomes independent, July 5.

1980   Luís Cabral overthrown by João Vieira in No-
         vember; constitution suspended; PAIGC remains
         in power in Guinea but not in Cape Verde.

1981   PAICV formed in Cape Verde; political union
         between the two nations comes to an end.

1982   Guinea-Bissau and Cape Verde re-establish
         diplomatic relations.

1983   Abortive military coup attempt in Guinea-Bissau;
         widespread cabinet replacements.

1984   Government announces partial economic liberali-
         zation; elections in Guinea-Bissau; Peoples Na-
         tional Assembly reconstituted; new constitution
         adopted.

1985   Attempted military coup led by General Paulo
         Correia fails.

1986   One dozen internal dissidents executed.

INTRODUCTION

Guinea-Bissau is unusual among West African countries in that its history is so closely connected to that of Cape Verde. The Portuguese settled in both areas beginning in the fifteenth century; Cape Verde was used as a port stop and holding station for slaves brought in from Guinea; trade on the Guinean coast was heavily influenced by Cape Verdean lançados; and the two countries shared a common Portuguese administration until the late nineteenth century. Similarly, aspects of African culture are found in Cape Verde, and features of Portuguese and Cape Verdean crioulo culture and language are woven into Guinea-Bissau. In this introduction, while concentrating on the Guinean case, we note the Portuguese Guinea-Cape Verde linkages and include data that are relevant to both countries. At the same time, the history of the two countries is sufficiently distinctive to warrant separate dictionaries for each. We therefore refer the reader to the Historical Dictionary of the Republic of Cape Verde (Scarecrow, 1988) for a full historical accounting of that country.

The name "Guinea" has one of two possible origins: It may be derived from the Berber word "aguinaou," meaning "black," as Portuguese sailors had had extensive contact with Berber peoples before descending below the Sahara; or it may be the name of the first group of Africans that the Portuguese encountered in sub-Saharan West Africa. In the fifteenth and sixteenth centuries, the term "Guinea" referred to the entirety of the West African coast from the Senegal River to the Congo River, although references were sometimes made to Lower and Upper Guinea. Gold from these regions gave the term "guinea" to British Guinea. Thereafter, the term "Portuguese Guinea" referred more specifically to an area including today's Senegal, Guinea-Bissau and Guinea (Conakry), finally coming to refer to the area

1

Guinea-Bissau

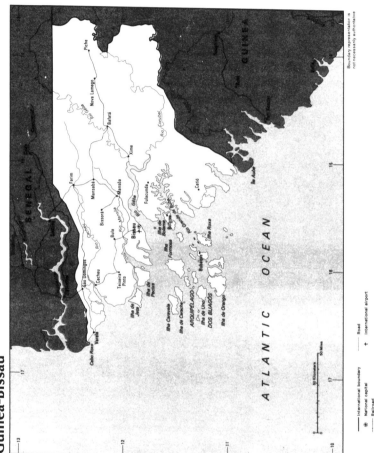

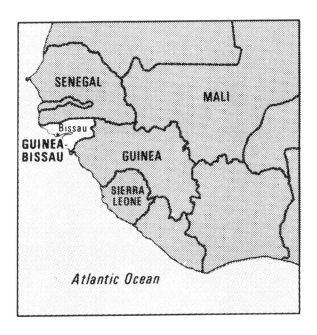

depicted on the above map once the French had consolidated
control of the surrounding region. The name "Guinea-
Bissau" (Guiné-Bissau in Portuguese) was adopted by the
PAIGC at independence in order to distinguish it from both
the colonial appellation and from The Republic of Guinea
(Conakry). We employ the name "Guinea-Bissau" throughout the book, and the term "Guinean" always refers to an
inhabitant of Guinea-Bissau unless otherwise specified. The
terminology for the Republic of Cape Verde may also have
its confusions with Cap Vert, on the coast of Senegal, for
which the archipelago is named. The name literally means
"Green Cape," but with frequent drought, this may be a
misnomer.

Physical Features

    The Republic of Guinea-Bissau lies between 12°40'N
and 10°52'N latitude and between 13°38'W and 16°43'W longi-
tude. Generally the climate is hot and tropical although there
are two seasons. From June to November is the hot and rainy

season during which the bulk of the annual 78-inch rainfall occurs, although the recent Sahelian droughts have slightly diminished the amount of rain in the north and have resulted in uneven rainfall and poorer harvests elsewhere. From December to May is the cool, dry season. Usually the temperatures vary only between 77°F (January) to 86°F (May), 25-30°C. The 13,947.9 square miles (36,125 sq. kms.) of the territory lie on a very broad coastal plain which results in labyrinthine coastal creeks and mangrove swamps. Aside from shallow river valleys and the slightly uplifted Boé hills in the southeast, the terrain is rather undifferentiated and rises only to a maximum altitude to 985 feet. Areas between the coastal swamps contain considerable tropical brush and hardwood forests. Further to the interior the scrub bush gives way to semi-grassland zones. The soil is tropical lateritic or of clay depending upon region; this requires shifting agricultural land use as the soil is exhausted. Along the coastal areas extensive rice paddies are well developed.

The Cape Verde Islands lie about 370 miles off the coast of Senegal, between latitudes 14°48'N and 17°12'N and longitudes 22°41'W and 25°22;W. The archipelago consists of ten major islands and five minor islets. The climate is tropical, but it is extremely dry with less than 10 inches of rain falling on São Tiago annually. The strong prevailing winds and the maritime location result in a temperature fluctuation between 72-80°F (22-27°C) and a notable lack of seasonality. The land is 1,557 square miles (4,033.3 sq. kms.) and is particularly rocky and mountainous owing to the volcanic origin of the islands. Only 1.65 percent (52,688 hectares) of the land area may be cultivated, and much of this is fallow at any one point in time.

Peoples

The 777,214 people who inhabit Guinea-Bissau are essentially derived from the Niger-Congo or Congo-Kordofanian language stock. This group is represented by the West Atlantic and Manding families. Those people of Fula ethnic extraction are descended from an admixture of West Atlantic peoples and from the Berber language family. Except for the Fulas and their subgroups, the other West Atlantic cultures of Guinea-Bissau are known collectively as Senegambians

or Semi-Bantu Littoral peoples. Some of the more numerous
Senegambians include the Balantas, Papeis, Beafadas and
Nalus. The Manding or Nuclear Mande are best represented
by the Mandingos, Susus, and Dyulas.

In general, the coastal Senegambians have acephalous
or slightly centralized political organization. The Manding
inherited a much more complex, stratified system of political
organization from the autonomous Gabu Empire of the pre-
colonial era. An even more stratified and hierarchical system characterized the Fula, who were able to retain many
features of their system through the colonial era as a consequence of their alliance with the Portuguese. Although there
is some debate regarding the term "peasant" in African eth-
nography, one may say that these people are involved with
rural modes of subsistence and cash cropping which have
numerous peasant-like qualities. Such production met domestic needs and yielded agricultural goods for a wider
market.

While agriculture served as the subsistence economic
base for all these groups, many people developed extensive
systems of artisan and handicraft production, while others
became quite successful traders. The Manding djila (or
djula) especially established trade routes that transversed
the country and that intersected with market circuits elsewhere in West Africa and with the Atlantic-based international shipping routes.

Four centuries of slavery brought many Guineans, and
Senegambians in general, to the Cape Verde Islands to work
on slave plantations producing subsistence goods and other
market commodities. The small Portuguese population mixed
extensively with the slaves to produce the rich and varied
cultural heritage which characterizes Cape Verdeans. In
Cape Verde virtually everyone communicates in Crioulo or
Portuguese, however literacy is not high, with about 73 percent of the population unable to read. By comparison, the
illiteracy rate in Guinea-Bissau was far worse at 98 percent,
although the PAIGC educational program has now reduced
this considerably. In the mainland republic, while some 70
percent of the population are able to communicate in Crioulo,
others speak only one of the 25-30 representative languages
of the Fula, Senegambian and Manding stocks. Some effort
is being made to standardize Crioulo as the language of

elementary instruction, but formal and official communication
is carried out in Portuguese.

Population

The 1979 national population census of Guinea-Bissau
places the total population of the country at 777,214.
Throughout this century there has been a relatively low
rate of increase, due largely to the exceptionally high per-
centage of infant mortality. The population's growth rate in
1985 was 1.7 percent. Less than one percent of the populace lost their lives during the war for national independence;
the main demographic impact was that between one fifth to
one fourth of the rural populace left the country, although
most of these refugees have now returned to their region of
origin.

The population of Cape Verde is most likely to be in
the neighborhood of 295,700. Health conditions in Cape
Verde are generally more favorable than in Guinea-Bissau,
but recurrent droughts in the archipelago have a negative
impact on nutrition. The acute limitations on agriculture and
farm labor have resulted in a long history of out migration
(especially to the northeastern coast of the U.S., to Portugal and to Senegal) which has been a significant brake on
domestic population growth.

History

The earliest known human occupation of the West African savanna dates back to Acheulian times of Homo erectus,
about 600,000 years ago or perhaps even much earlier. However, the forested regions closer to the coast may not have
been occupied until about 9000 BC by small groups of hunters and fishermen. There is a possibility of the independent
development of agriculture in the Upper Nile between 5000
and 4000 BC. This spread to the west and other directions
was, no doubt, responsible for the first permanent occupations of the northeastern regions of Guinea-Bissau. Medieval
commercial development was slow since the territory of today's
Guinea-Bissau was at the periphery of the Sudanic states and
the trans-Saharan trade routes. However, the demographic
transformation of the interior brought about by new and

improved crops, camel transport and iron-working had the effect of initiating population pressure on the adjacent territories.

The arrival and slow spread of Southeast Asian tropical crops took place early in the Christian era but later became significant in supporting the diversification of the pioneer peoples in the Senegambian forest littoral. The expansion of trade by the Empire of Ghana and the introduction of Islam to the savanna in about the ninth century lay the basis for the penetration of the forest on a greater scale by people from the interior at the expense of the coastal hunters and gatherers. By the eleventh century the Almoravids had briefly conquered Ghana only to have it re-established in 1205 by the Susu (Soninke), of whom modern descendants are found in southern coastal Guinea-Bissau. The Susu reconquest was maintained only for thirty years, at which point the Keita dynasty of Mali founded its powerful military and trade structure in 1235. The thirteenth-century influence of Mali was felt directly and profoundly in Guinea-Bissau with the creation of the secondary, semi-autonomous kingdom of Gabu. The Senegambians living in Guinea-Bissau and even further to the interior were pushed toward the coast by the growth of Mali and the secondary Mande state of Gabu. In this way, the Senegambians who displaced the hunters and gatherers were themselves displaced by the more dominant local representatives of Mali.

A developing interest in Africa and its valuable resources, and a desire to push Moorish influence out of Iberia, led to the early fifteenth-century moves by the Portuguese to explore, conquer, and claim portions of northwest Africa, beginning with the 1415 conquest of Ceuta by Prince Henry. Throughout the fifteenth century, Portuguese barks and caravels pushed further down West Africa's coast, reaching Cape Bojador in 1434, the Senegal River mouth in 1445, and resulting in the exploration of the estuaries and islands of Guinea-Bissau in 1446 by Captains Gil Eannes and Nuño Tristão. By 1456 the Cape Verde islands were first noted for the Portuguese by Captain Cadamosto. Possibly Phoenician or Malian sailors or Lebou fishermen from Senegal had visited the islands before the Portuguese, but the record is unclear. By 1460, António de Noli and Diogo Gomes claimed official discovery of the Cape Verde Islands for King Afonso V of Portugal. Almost immediately

Portuguese settlers began to arrive on São Tiago, Fogo, and
other islands.

From the very earliest days of exploration one may also
date the initial instances of Portuguese slaving and African
resistance. At first only dozens of slaves were captured,
but by the mid-fifteenth century there were already hundreds of Africans kidnapped annually and sent to work in
Europe. The settlement of the Cape Verde Islands gave
rise to the slave plantation system, and 500-1,000 slaves
reached the islands annually in the second half of the fifteenth century; many of these slaves were exported to
Europe from the islands. The discovery and settlement of
the New World triggered a great intensification of the slave
trade in the sixteenth century, resulting in growing European competition to the point where Portugal was no longer
able to meet the demand. The Portuguese crown issued
slave trade monopolies on the coast, but other European
marauders and African and Luso-African middlemen sought
their own private gains. By 1580 Portugal came under the
rule of the Spanish crown, and English, Dutch, and Spanish slavers and pirates eroded Portuguese control and influence on the West African coast by attacking and looting
Portuguese forts and trading posts.

Portuguese penetration and knowledge of the interior
was superficial at this time, although their slave trading intensified commercial competition among African merchants
who desired to acquire slaves and firearms, producing a rising number of wars throughout the territory. To be sure,
this situation greatly benefited the Portuguese despite their
peripheral location (only on the coast) and their lack of political influence in the interior. For example, when asked by
Mali in 1534 to help them defend against attacks by Songhai,
the Portuguese declined both because their influence was
weak and because slaves would be generated if either side
were victorious. Slaves were brought to the coast on foot
on in light river craft and were then exchanged by middlemen for various merchandise. Aside from the "captaincy"
system in Cape Verde and at such places as Cacheu, Bolama
and Bissau, the Portuguese hold on the African continent
was marginal, although the economic stimulus for slave wars
was penetrating and extensive.

The seventeenth century saw even greater growth of

the slave trade, but the portion of slaves transported on
Portuguese ships steadily declined, and one of Portugal's
main goals in Guinea-Bissau and Cape Verde was to defend
against frequent attacks and encroachments by other European powers. Although attempts at administrative reform
and military consolidation were made in Guinea-Bissau, Portugal's rule on the coast was rather undisciplined and precarious and generally depended upon good relations with
Gabu in the interior and with the Papel king on the coast.
While slaving constituted the economic life-blood of Cape
Verde, it made up only a small sector of economic activity
in Guinea, which remained largely dominated by peasant agriculture and village artisanry of sufficient scope to generate local markets and to allow for participation in long-
distance trading networks with which the Portuguese were
unable to interfere.

Thus, the Portuguese simply perpetuated the political
economy of slavery during the eighteenth century. However,
during this period, the centers of slave trading began to
shift, to some extent, to other parts of West and Central
Africa. The Portuguese crown reasserted its monopoly over
Cape Verdean trade and made some short-lived endeavors to
revitalize slavery in Guinea-Bissau by granting trade rights
to a Brazilian company. Meanwhile, Cape Verdeans often escaped drought and economic uncertainty by joining the crews
of whaling and packet ships. French attacks continued in
the islands, and the British began a protracted campaign to
wrest Bolama from Portuguese rule.

The early nineteenth century saw the widespread abolition of the European slave trade, but the Portuguese were
especially slow to respond. American merchant ships continued to acquire slaves on the coast and in the islands, and
indeed commerce with Americans sometimes exceeded that with
Portugal. The salt and slave trade went on, but as before
a central Portuguese concern was not administrative or commercial reform, but simply the defense of their territories
from British and French expansion. The slave trade drew to
a close as palm and coconut exports came to wield greater revenue on the international market. The American "African
Squadron" based in Cape Verde actively sought to repress
the slave system.

Throughout most of the nineteenth century, the

Portuguese were restricted to their fort-protected coastal
settlements, while the Manding continued to control the
eastern portion of the interior and attempted to repel repeated Fula invasions from the Labé province in what is
now the Republic of Guinea. The Balanta, fortified by a
strong military tradition, were able to fight off the Fula
invaders, while the Fula-Manding wars did not greatly af-
fect the Papeis and other coastal groups. During the last
quarter of the nineteenth century, especially after the Berlin Conference of 1884-5 and the effective delineation of the
territorial holdings of Portugal and France, the Portuguese
unleashed a series of "pacification" drives against the peoples of the coast and of the interior. And in a move toward
bureaucratic efficiency, the administration of Guinea-Bissau
was separated from Cape Verde in 1879 for the first time in
four centuries of Portuguese presence.

An important barrier to the expansion of colonial rule
inland from the coastal ports was the large state of Gabu,
which occupied approximately the eastern half of the territory. As much of Gabu's strength lay in its role in the
slave trade, the state entered into a period of sharp decline
when this trade was curtailed, so that it fell victim to local
Fula uprisings and to a major incursion of Fulas from Futa
Jallon's Labé province. While the new Fula rulers never
really established genuine political and social hegemony over
Gabu, they would soon function as appointed overseers of
the Portuguese in the northeast. The decisive fall of Gabu
to the Fula in 1867, combined with the subsequent Berlin
Conference in 1884-5, provided encouragement to the Portuguese to consolidate their military rule throughout the interior. The "pacification" campaigns, carried out between 1886
and 1936 by the tiny and poorly financed colonial army, were
unable to overcome the tenacious resistance of all indigenous
peoples except for the Fula, who chose to ally with and
serve as military auxiliaries for the Portuguese after some
initial resistance. The hiring of Senegalese mercenaries
combined with the more effective military command of Teixeira Pinto allowed the Portuguese to gain the upper hand
against the rural populace by 1915-16, although serious
armed rebellions occurred in various parts of the country
until 1936.

The establishment of fascist rule in Portugal in 1926
led to a more intensified effort to exploit the colonies. In

Guinea-Bissau this resulted in increased extraction of ex-
portable cash crops such as peanuts, palm oil and coconuts,
which involved the coerced imposition of crop-growing schemes
as well as forced labor. While efforts to upgrade administrative organization and augment bureaucratic efficiency were
made in both Guinea-Bissau and Cape Verde, this was carried out to a much greater extent in the archipelago, which
was more financially self-sustaining (expect in times of
drought) than the mainland, where the administrative institutions were less effectively organized and usually incurred
a debt.

After the formation of the PAIGC in 1956, a series of
peaceful nationalist appeals were made to the Portuguese and
to international political bodies, but a brutal massacre in
Bissau in 1959 impelled the PAIGC toward the path of armed
struggle. The nationalist war, led by party founder and
theoretician Amílcar Cabral, was fought from 1963 to 1974
when, as a consequence of the success of this struggle and
of the nationalist struggles in Mozambique and Angola, discontent within the Portuguese armed forces resulted in the
toppling of the Salazar dictatorship on April 25, 1974.
Guinea-Bissau achieved formal national independence on September 24, 1974, and Cape Verde on July 5, 1975.

Frequently it is said that the achievement of national
independence by Guinea-Bissau and Cape Verde symbolizes
the end of five centuries of colonialism, but this brief account shows that effective colonial rule was not consolidated
until after the first quarter of the twentieth century. Thus,
the PAIGC victory in 1974 represents not so much the ter-
mination of long-lasting Portuguese imperial control as the
re-assertion of indigenous authority after a brief overt colonial tenure.

After independence, both countries were ruled by a
unified PAIGC until 1980, when a locally supported military-
backed coup ousted President Luís Cabral from power in
Guinea-Bissau and placed Commander João Bernardo (Nino)
Vieira into the presidency. In 1981, Cape Verde changed
the nomenclature of its party to PAICV while Guinea-Bissau
retained PAIGC, signifying the separation of leaderships
between the two countries. Both parties claim to be heir
to the ideological legacy of Amílcar Cabral and to the nationalist history of the PAIGC.

In Guinea-Bissau, following the 1980 coup, a PAIGC-
dominated Revolutionary Council consisting of eight army
men and one civilian and presided over by President Vieira
became the country's ruling political organ. An Extraordinary Party Congress held in 1981 resulted in the formation
of a Politburo and Central Committee to serve as the leading
decision-making bodies of the PAIGC. In 1984, the Revolutionary Council was replaced by a fifteen-member Council of
State, approximately half of whom were civilians. Between
1981 and 1986, the PAIGC and the military were marked by
internal ethnic tensions and power struggles among leading
personalities, resulting in several coup attempts and the exe-
cution of a number of military officers in 1986. However,
President Vieira remains in firm political control and appears
to have strengthened his rule by consolidating his power
within the party, army and bureaucracy.

Development and Economics

Both nations are remarkably poor and underdeveloped.
The Gross Domestic Product of Guinea-Bissau in 1982 was
$200 million, while per capita GNP was $170; average life
expectancy is 41 years. Under colonial rule, the exploitation of both human and natural resources was highly ineffi-
cient, and very little infrastructure was built. The main
source of wealth was agricultural surplus. In Cape Verde
this required large numbers of slaves for sugar cane plantation or contract workers for banana and coffee cultivation.
After formal slavery ended, stratified systems of land tenure
and recurrent droughts meant that only a small minority
would possess adequate arable land. Recurrent droughts
and massive erosion provided severe limitations to agricultural productivity. The very low cost of labor in the islands impeded the introduction of any innovations involving
capital expenditure, thus limiting the extent of technical
improvement. Over the years attempts were made to introduce cash crops such as peanuts, cotton, coffee and plant
dyes, but unreliable climatological conditions led to great
difficulties in growing and expanding these crops. Other
products of Cape Verde have included livestock, fruits,
puzzolane (a cement additive) and significant amounts of
salt.

Guinea-Bissau and Cape Verde share a colonial

background that left them both impoverished and without a viable foundation for economic development, but the structure of their economies and the direction of future development differ drastically. While in Cape Verde a limited area of arable land and earlier immersion in a cash market produced an economy mainly organized as a center of international trade, the economy of Guinea-Bissau is based principally on the production of food and cash crops. Thus, the economic future of Cape Verde depends on a continuing expansion of commerce, while the development potential of Guinea-Bissau rests mainly in agriculture.

Most farming systems in Guinea-Bissau have been and continue to be organized mainly around food production, although some cash crop farming has expanded in this century. The country's chief exports from the fifteenth to the nineteenth centuries were slaves, ivory, hides, some gold, spices and wood. In the 1900s exports have consisted of peanuts, palm oil, cotton, wood, coconuts and other tropical fruits, although growers have enjoyed little success in cotton production in either the colonial or post-colonial eras. Rural production, which was decimated during the nationalist war (only 30 percent of the land cultivated in 1953 was still being farmed by 1974), has been to some extent restored, especially as most peasants who fled abroad returned soon after independence, although the uneven impact of the Sahelian drought has caused surplus levels to fluctuate from one year to another. However, despite a return to reasonable production levels, much surplus produce and cash crops are clandestinely transported out of the country and sold in neighboring Senegal or Guinea. This reflects the inability of the government to offer peasants a substantial improvement in the terms of trade; they can obtain a higher price for their goods on the unofficial market. A particularly unfortunate trend has been the selling of rice surpluses abroad, resulting in a lack of rice (the country's staple food) in the non-rice producing areas, including Bissau, and necessitating an increased dependency on imported foods, so that over 40,000 tons of outside foods were needed for Bissau in 1985.

Guinea-Bissau's development potential depends to some extent on the expansion of infrastructure (roads, bridges, ferries, motorized canoes, communications systems, and port facilities), which is necessary for the regularized and orderly

flow of goods and services. Extensive technical training of
local personnel is required in order for the country to be
able to take advantage of the many development projects offered from abroad. At the same time, the government must
continue to improve producer prices in order to shift the direction of agricultural surplus away from unofficial trade and
toward the official markets. Favorable market exchanges and
improved transport could also stimulate increased production
and the eventual export of a variety of tropical fruits and of
rubber, and could generate increased livestock production,
which holds a potential for greater domestic marketing of
meat and for the export of hides. However, augmented agricultural surplus will also depend on government provisioning of seeds, hand tools and plows, some fertilizer, and
equipment for the construction of dikes to stop the flow of
salt from the riverine paddies.

The large number of rivers in Guinea-Bissau, which
contrast sharply with the barren mountains of Cape Verde,
offers some potential for hydro-electric power generation.
There is also an enormous potential for domestic fishing,
with a possible sustainable yield of up to 200,000 tons,
which continues to be exploited by largescale Soviet and
French trawlers under bilateral agreements through which
part of the profits from fish sales go the Guinean government. Successful development will be greatly aided by
shifting government attention away from mass fish trawling
by foreign boats, despite the increase in government revenue this provides, and toward the provisioning of local
fishermen with canoes, motors, nets, hooks, and lines.

There are several untapped mineral deposits, including bauxite ore, phosphates, diamonds and gold, but their
extraction awaits initial investments in the aforementioned
transport infrastructure. Oil deposits have been discovered
offshore and may soon provide a source of government revenue, as agreements with foreign companies for intensified
exploration have recently been signed. Except for a beer
and soft drink facility, there is no substantive industrial
production and little prospects for its development; industrial projects built or proposed in the late 1970s were ter-
minated or sharply curtailed after 1980 following a PAIGC
decision that such investments were premature and uneco-
nomical in light of the country's as yet undeveloped agricultural potential.

Finally, the government will have to make good on its declared intention to shift state spending away from the urban-based public sector and toward the countryside. Indeed, the ratio of energy consumption in Bissau relative to the rest of the country is 24:3, and almost 60 percent of budgetary spending is devoted to civil servants' salaries, 83 percent of whom are located in Bissau. This reflects both an urban-biased colonial legacy and the personal interests of public sector employees, and will therefore be difficult to combat.

For both nations, the attainment of political independence has made it possible for genuine economic growth to take place. While agricultural advance in Guinea-Bissau in the first few years following independence was impeded by the delayed return of migrants, economic damage from the anti-colonial struggle and drought, the rich natural and human resources in the countryside offer reason to assume that successful development remains well within the country's capabilities.

THE DICTIONARY

AFRICAN SQUADRON. In the 1840s and 1850s the United States sought to curtail the trade in African slaves by establishing the African Squadron, a fleet of sailing "cruisers" to further the anti-slavery mission by boarding suspected ships and seizing their human cargoes. Some of these cruisers were based in São Vicente, others at São Tiago, such as the cruiser Jamestown. At times they seized American slave ships which sailed under the Portuguese flag. Commodore Crabbe and Capt. William Perry were prominent officers of the squadron.

AGRICULTURE. Agriculture represents the foundation of the nation's economy as 87.89 percent of the population is involved in agricultural production. Land shortage is not a problem in most areas; many families continue to extend their land holdings or rice fields. While land tenure systems vary notably from region to region, they continue to be regulated by the peasants themselves without outside interference. Unlike other Portuguese colonies, Guinea-Bissau had only a tiny handful of large plantations, and these were placed under state authority after independence. Labor forms vary from individual family units to collective labor teams, to small units organized by sex or by age-group, to single individuals who are at times assisted by task-specific mutual aid groups.

Of the major cash crops, 80 percent of the rice is cultivated by the Balanta in the south, while most of the peanuts are grown in the Fula and Mandingo dominated regions of Bafata and Gabu. However, most peasant farms practice multicropping, integrating various combinations of food and cash crops on their land: rice, millet, fonio grain and beans are a common combination. Other widely cultivated food crops include manioc,

sorghum, white potatoes, yams, maize, sugar cane and
numerous types of tropical fruits. Those food crops
which are not consumed by the household are bartered
or sold in the local market. This is also the case with
products culled from trees or wild fruits, such as palm
oil and wine, cashew nuts and wine, and coconuts.

The anti-colonial war had a massively destructive
impact on agricultural production for two reasons. First,
up to one quarter of the rural producers fled the country, and many more were forced away from their lands
and onto colonially controlled aldeamentos. This meant
not only that a large proportion of the rural work force
was displaced, but that extensive soil erosion occurred
due to the non-use of arable lands; erosion was especially severe where lands were bombed by the Portuguese.
Second, much arable land was lost due to the destruction
by bombing of numerous riverine dikes. These dikes
are necessary to prevent the influx of ocean salt from
the riverines onto the rice fields and arable land plots,
as salt destroys the arability of the land.

After independence, agricultural production was
hindered by the delayed return of peasant refugees, by
the painstaking efforts involved in rejuvenating arable
lands damaged by ocean salt and by bombings, and by
the lack of governmental assistance provided to peasants
in rebuilding the riverine dikes. As a result, less than
half the acreage farmed in 1963, before the beginning of
the war, is presently under cultivation.

Peanut production, which was revived after the
war, fell to 20,000 tons in the drought year of 1980,
recovered to 30,000 tons in 1981 and 1982, but then it
is estimated to have dropped severely in 1983. Rice
production was 29,000 tons in 1972 (during wartime);
67,000 tons in 1975; 45,000 in 1976; 30,000 in 1977;
60,000 in 1978; dropped to 34,000 in 1980; then rose to
80,000 in 1981, and to 100,000 tons in 1982. Inconsistent
rainfall usually accounted for such production fluctuations
in the 1970s, although this has been less of a problem
since 1980. Marketing opportunities also account for
some of the variation in production levels.

Many representatives of the complex of West African crops may be found in Guinea-Bissau. This complex
underlies the establishment of the major Sahelian states
of West Africa. Grains include fonio, sorghum and millet,
some Guinea yam, and okra. Calabash gourds, papayas,

mangoes and watermelons are also important. Sudanic or
Sahelian crops with commercial usages also include cotton,
oil palm and sesame, with special note given to kola nuts
which have been significant as a trade item and in social
relations as an offering among elders.

Millet is one of the more important grains in this
complex of traditional Sahelian crops as it is widely considered to have been at the foundation of the independent
evolution of agriculture in this region in antiquity. There
are various names and a confusing taxonomy, but one may
distinguish bulrush millet (Pennisetum typhoideum), which
is also known as pearl millet, from sorghum (Sorghum
vulgare), also known as durra. These are all known as
milho in Portuguese, with local distinctions in terminology
by varying color of the grains. These tall grasses re-
semble American corn (Zea mays) at a distance, but bul-
rish millet grains grow in clusters like a cat-tail but not
on a unified cob. Sorghum grains grow in a tuft formation by contrast. Bulrush millet is very hardy and requires little rainfall, while sorghum is more often irrigated
but may be grown as a dry-land crop.

Very many of the important West African crops are,
in fact, native to the Americas and were only introduced
in the 16th century. Chief among these is maize, or
American corn, which is well suited to rainy areas or to
places cultivated by irrigation. Lima beans and haricot
beans are common American legumes now frequently found
in Guinean foods. The diet also includes American crops
such as pineapples, pumpkins, squash, tomatoes, and
papaya. Native American crops of great importance to
Africa also include cocoa, red pepper, and tobacco.
See: DROUGHT; ECONOMY; LIVESTOCK.

ALDEAMENTO. Fortified village system used by the Portu-
    guese in Guinea-Bissau to concentrate rural populations
    behind barbed wire, thus denying access of the PAIGC
    to the people.

ALFA MOLO of JIMARA (?-1881). An elephant hunter of the
    Bande family of Futa Jallon who led the successful move-
    ment against King Janke Walli of the Mandingo state of
    Gabu in 1867, thus creating the first Fula state in
    Guinea-Bissau. The conquest of Gabu was achieved in
    association with the general military efforts of Al-Haj
    Umaru of Futa Jallon. Alfa Molo was the son of the

Al-Mami of Timbu, a Fula province of Futa Jallon. The
Al-Mami had married a Gabu princess named Kumancho
Saane. Around the time of Alfa Molo's conquest of Gabu,
he also married into the royal family of Kumba Wude, but
this may have taken place as a result of the conquest.
This marriage resulted in at least two sons, Dikori and
Musa Molo. Upon the death of Alfa Molo in 1881, he was
replaced by his brother Bakari Demba, who was overthrown in 1893 by Alfa Molo's son Musa Molo, who continued the line of Fula dominance of Gabu.

In establishing the hegemony of the new Fula
state, Alfa Molo came into conflict with other Fulas occupying regions north of the Gambia River. After Alfa
Molo's death by disease in Guinea-Bissau, Fulas elsewhere
in the country staged local revolts. Strong measures
taken by Musa Molo temporarily renewed the Fula state,
but after 1931 there was no effective legitimate king.
See: FUTA JALLON; GABU; MUSA MOLO.

ALFA YAYA of LABE. Alfa Yaya was the chief representative of Fula power in Futa Jallon whose rise in power
was simultaneous with French penetration from the coast.
Although Alfa Yaya had a nominally pro-French position,
it appears that he sought to use French rule to consolidate his own position especially between 1891 and 1896.
Alfa Yaya's opportunism led to a revolt by his son, resulting in a decisive battle in which Alfa Yaya crushed
his opposition. In 1897 he served French interests by
the reconquest of other regions in Futa Jallon including
Timbu. In 1904 the relationship between Alfa Yaya and
the French had soured in a series of jurisdictional disputes including the severance of a portion of Labé
province to be transferred to Portuguese control in
Guinea-Bissau. Seeing his power being eroded, Alfa
Yaya planned an armed revolt against the French, but
a spy revealed the plans, leading to Alfa Yaya's arrest
and deportation to Dahomey. After his release in 1910
he made another attempt to organize resistance in 1911,
but this too was blocked by arrest and deportation.

AL-HAJ AL-MAMI UMARU. See: ALFA MOLO; FULA.

ARAUJO, JOSE EDUARDO. PAIGC militant who has served
in various high-ranking capacities including political
commissar of the permanent commission of the Southern

National Committee in Guinea-Bissau during the armed
struggle. Araújo had also been head of the PAIGC Information Section in Conakry and was a member of the
Executive Committee for the Struggle in charge of production. After the reorganization of the CEL, Araújo
became Minister of the General Secretariat. Following
independence he became the organizational secretary for
the PAIGC and a trouble-shooting Minister without port-
folio, after which he was appointed as the Minister of
Education and Culture. See: CEL; CONCP; PAIGC.

ARMAZENS DO POVO (Peoples' Stores). During the period
of the nationalist war, the PAIGC had two main points
in its economic program. On the one hand it sought to
halt the Portuguese use of Guinean exports and to force
a heavier reliance on imports, thereby raising the economic costs of continuing colonialism. On the other
hand the PAIGC aimed at launching a small-scale export
and import economy for the liberated zones. The system
of Peoples' Stores operated to address these two points
and to improve the market system in the liberated zones.
Imported items included textiles, machetes, hoe blades,
blankets, salt, sugar, cigarettes, tobacco, bicycles, pots,
sewing machines, string, matches, flashlights, soap,
needles, thread, paper, sandals, buttons, and fish nets,
to name a number of the more popular items. By 1973
about 32 Peoples' Stores were in operation in many areas
of the countryside and in the frontier regions.
    This integrated economic system strictly excluded
cash but determined fixed exchange equivalents for agricultural produce and other items generated in Guinea-
Bissau. For example, 1 kg. of rice could be exchanged
for 1 kg. of sugar or for clothing which could be tailor-
made at the larger Peoples' Stores; three kilos of rice
would be worth one pair of trousers; a pair of women's
shoes was equivalent to 15 kgs. of rice; or 1 meter of
crocodile skin could be converted to 2 kgs. of rice. Although rice was the main staple exchanged, exports of
the Peoples' Stores also included peanuts, palm oil,
ivory, hides, honey, beeswax, kola nuts, palm nuts,
sesame seeds, and corn. The export of kola nuts was
the greatest export earner by value, but rice was the
major export by volume, which, in 1971, represented
668,511 kgs. In the late 1960s and early 1970s exports
generally increased, with the high in 1971 put at 34.4

million Guinea (C) francs or about 4.25 million escudos
($145,000 U.S.). While this sum was not large in abso-
lute terms, the bulk of trade through the Peoples' Stores
was by barter with no cash flow. Thus the degree to
which the needs of the people of Guinea-Bissau could be
met through the Peoples' Stores denied an additional
market to the colonial economy.

The Peoples' Stores system developed during the
struggle underwent major expansion in the post-
independence period to provide for the state distribution
and regulation of basic commodities. Currently there
are more than 125 Peoples' Stores, and the system has
incorporated the former Casa Gouveia commercial chain
operated for Portuguese interests. See: AGRICULTURE;
ECONOMICS; LIVESTOCK; PEANUTS; RICE.

ARMED FORCES. See: FORCAS ARMADAS.

ARMEE DE LIBERATION NACIONALE GUINEENE (ALNG).
The armed branch of FLING, formed shortly after 1962.
There is little data about the strength of the ALNG, but
it saw combat only on the rarest of occasions and exclu-
sively in the area of Guinea-Bissau near the western
Casamance.

ASKIA MOHAMMAD. Ruler of Songhai (1493-1528). See:
SONGHAI.

ASSEMBLEIA NACIONAL POPULAR (ANP), Peoples National
Assembly. The ANP was first constituted in the liberated territories between August and October 1972, one
year before the end of the armed phase of the independence struggle. The population involved chose 273 regional councillors who, in turn, elected 91 of their peers
to serve as National Assembly deputies. Both voting
procedures consisted of yes/no balloting for a single
candidate who had been previously selected by the party
in the course of discussions with the local populace.
The elected deputies were combined with 21 deputies
appointed by the party and five representatives of the
party youth group to form a total ANP of 120 delegates.
At the first meeting of the ANP in the liberated zones of
Guinea-Bissau during the war it adopted the Constitution
and elected officers and ministers for the Council of
State.

In April 1975 the ANP held its first meeting after
liberation. In December 1976 the same electoral procedures were repeated, but membership of the second ANP
was expanded to 147, with two thirds selected by the
party. This ANP was disbanded immediately following
the 1980 coup d'état of N. Vieira, but a third ANP, with
150 members, was formed through elections held in March-
April 1984.

The Peoples National Assembly is officially the highest political body in Guinea-Bissau, but in fact, from
1972 to 1979 and since 1984 it convened and continues to
meet only once a year for several days. The ANP can
pass laws, ratify decrees and revise the constitution,
but in practice it does not wield substantial political
power, most of which lies with top-level party and state
structures. See: Appendix: Officials of Guinea-
Bissau.

ASSIMILADO. One who was considered during the colonial
period to have "assimilated" Portuguese cultural stan-
dards of literacy, education, financial status or other
criteria in order to gain fuller rights as a Portuguese
citizen. This was a status reserved for Africans, although only a very small number of Africans (fewer than
one percent) in the mainland colonies were ever given
this official recognition.

AZAMBUJA, DIEGO DA. Portuguese knight under the reign
of Dom João II (1477, 1481-95) who was charged with
West African coastal exploration and the rapid construction of the El Mina fortress on the Gold Coast. Materials
and specialist craftsmen were brought from Portugal in
1480 and the project was completed in 1482 to guard the
Portuguese trade in slaves and gold.

AZURARA, GOMES EANES DE. See: ZURARA, GOMES
EANES DA.

- B -

BADIUS. Peasants of the interior of São Tiago who are
primarily descended from runaway slaves and who have

retained a certain degree of cultural distinctiveness in their customs, folklore, religious practices and dialect of Crioulo. Living in remote regions and maintaining a social distance from the rest of the population during the centuries of colonial rule, the badius were the least assimilated to Portuguese culture by comparison with other Cape Verdeans. They were viewed as the primary representatives of an African heritage and, as such, have historically been denigrated by the colonial authorities and looked down upon by other Cape Verdeans. However, the few known instances of slave and peasant rebellions in Cape Verde were often among the badiu populations, giving them a certain notoriety in popular mythology that has engendered a mixture of disdain and admiration toward this so-called primitive social group. Perhaps because of the threat they once posed to the colonial authorities in resisting assimilation, the badius were more likely to have been recruited for contract labor, and they provided the backbone of forced emigration to the cacão plantations in the Portuguese islands of São Tomé and Príncipe. See: BATUCO.

BAIOTES. A numerically small group of the Diola cluster of the Senegambian littoral people. Their concentration is in the Casamance area in northwestern Guinea-Bissau and around the town of Suzanna. The Baiotes are related to the Felupes, the other member of the Diola cluster. The Baiotes depend on rice cultivation and have acephalous political organization although there are instances of local petty chiefs. See: DIOLAS; FELUPES.

BALANTAS (Balantes). The largest single ethnic group of Guinea-Bissau. The Balantas are members of the Senegambian cultural stock, an Atlantic subfamily of the Niger-Congo language stock. The Balanta people are generally egalitarian in socio-political organization but some areas have local chiefs. Today they are found mainly in areas nearer the coast, although they once occupied the interior in such areas as Gabu until the Mandingo expansion. Major Balanta concentrations are in the central northern area west of Farim and in coastal southern areas around Catio. They are, in short, located both north and south of the River Geba. Virtually all Balanta are non-Islamic rice cultivators who are most closely related to the Mancanha ethnic group.

Numerous campaigns of subjugation were directed
against the Balanta in 1883-5, 1891-1910 and in 1912-
1915 until they were brought under nominal Portuguese
control. As one of the most oppressed groups in Guinea-
Bissau, the Balanta were particularly heavily involved in
the nationalist struggle between 1963 to 1974. The 1950
census counted 146,300 people as Balanta, or 29.1 percent of the total population. In 1960 the population of
Balanta was estimated at 250,000, but the 1979 population
census sets the figure at 200,874, representing 27.2 percent of the total population.

BAMBARAS. A relatively large member of the Mande group
concentrated on the Upper Niger in Mali, where they are
often occupied as slightly Islamized fishing people. In
the third quarter of the 17th century the Bambaras revolted against the rule of Mali and created the two independent states of Segou and Kaarta which absorbed the
local remnants of the Malian empire. Between 1670 and
1810 the Bambaras controlled Djenne, and they briefly
held Timbuktu. The Bambara influence declined after
this period, and from 1854 to 1861 Fulani jihads destroyed the Bambara states. In Guinea-Bissau there
are very small concentrations of these animistic peoples
in the vicinity of Gabu (Nova Lamego).

BANCO NACIONAL DA GUINE-BISSAU (BNG). The BNG
was originally established as the BNU (Overseas National
Bank), a major Portuguese banking organization set up in
Lisbon in 1864 and in Cape Verde in 1868, which monopolized banking in Guinea-Bissau during the colonial
period. The BNU Board of Directors was in intimate
association with the colonial administration, having two
former colonial secretaries as well as major shareholders
associated with CUF and its overseas linkages. In addition, the BNU had significant association with finance
capital in Paris, Madrid, and London. Net profit during
a typical colonial year (e.g. 1963) was some US $3 mil-
lion, with dividends commonly at 9 percent from colonial
investments. The BNU was also associated with the major
insurance firm, Companhia de Seguios a Mundial. In
Guinea-Bissau the BNU was represented by the Sociedade
Comercial Ultramarina, which was second only to the António Silva Corporation, the affiliate of CUF which dominated trade and commerce in Guinea. With such extensive
connections, the BNU had an important influence in

agriculture, transport, petrochemicals, oil-processing and rice-processing in Guinea-Bissau and Cape Verde. After independence there were deep divisions between Lisbon and Bissau over the terms of repatriating BNU capital. Guinea-Bissau nationalized the BNU in February 1975 and ended the escudo currency, which was replaced by the new peso of Guinea; thereafter the name of the bank was changed to the BNG. See: COMPANHIA UNIÃO FABRIL.

BANYUNS (Banhuns). This very small Senegambian group is closely related to the Cassangas and the Cobianas and may be found in the southern Casamance area. During the period of Mandingo expansion the Banyuns were pushed toward the coast and were largely absorbed by the Diolas, Manjacos, and Balantas. While the Banyuns are acephalous agricultural animists, the related Cassangas developed a secondary kingship structure with its capital at Birkama. The term "Casamance" is said to be derived from Kassa-Mansa, the Cassanga ruler at Birkama. The Banyuns and Cassangas are known as skilled weavers and dyers. In the late 16th century the Cassangas became active slave hunters and expanded into Banyun territory, assimilating many of these people.

BARBOSA, RAFAEL (1924-   ). Barbosa was born in the Safim section of Bissau of a Guinean mother and Cape Verdean father. He was employed in Bissau as a public works foreman when he and Amílcar Cabral and several others joined to form the PAIGC in 1956. Barbosa operated under the nom de guerre of Zain Lopes as the President of the Central Committee of the PAIGC until his arrest by the Portuguese on March 13, 1962, in Bissau where he was carrying out his revolutionary activities. Barbosa was initially tortured and then released by the Portuguese on August 3, 1969, after seven years of imprisonment. His confinement led him to take positions viewed as compromising and, finally, treasonous by the PAIGC, which expelled him from the party in April 1970. He had still been considered as the President of the PAIGC until February 1964.

    After independence, Barbosa was charged with high crimes against the state and party, having been directly implicated in the assassination of Amílcar Cabral. At the conclusion of his trial on October 8, 1976, he was

sentenced to death for his anti-PAIGC and pro-Spinola
statements and activities. On March 4, 1977, his death
sentence was commuted to fifteen years at hard labor.
See: CABRAL, A.; PAIGC; SPINOLA.

BARRETO, COL. HONORIO PEREIRA. Barreto is believed to
have been the first Cape Verdean Governor of Guinea-
Bissau. This ambitious representative of Crioulo culture
was appointed superintendent of the Portuguese fortress
at Cacheu in 1834 and was the governor of Cacheu and
Bissau in 1837. Barreto's importance also lies in his defense of Portuguese colonial interests against the intru-
sions of the French and British.

BATUCO, BATUKO, BATUQUE. Batuco is a musical genre
with accompanying dance of the badius (rural Cape Verdeans of African slave origins), especially on the island
of São Tiago. The term batuco derives from the Portuguese verb "to beat." The traditional batuco is performed exclusively by women, generally at night. A
lead singer (who may be either amateur or professional)
improvises secular, topical verses, while several other
women, arranged in a rough circle, sing choral responses
and execute rhythms by clapping hands and beating on
cushions held between their legs. One or more women
dance vigorously inside the circle, each wearing a shawl,
or pano, around her waist.
    Batuco and the related finançon are the only Cape
Verdean musical forms to employ a true polyrhythm,
superimposing (in Western terms) 6/8 and 3/4 time in a
manner similar to much of West African music. Indeed,
batuco's percussive intensity, use of polyrhythms, call-
and-response singing, and its dance style all strongly
suggest African derivation.
    Batuco has traditionally incurred the disapproval
of the Catholic Church for its sexually suggestive dance
styles. At the same time, the colonial rulers intermittent-
ly repressed the genre for its obliquely militant texts,
while the middle classes have tended to disparage it as
vulgar. Since independence, however, it has been celebrated as folklore by the state and promoted, in styled
and modernized form, by rock-oriented groups. (Peter
Manuel) See: BADIUS; PANOS.

BAUXITE. See: COMPANHIA LUSITANA DO ALUMINIO DA
GUINE E ANGOLA.

BEAFADAS (Biafadas). This non-Islamic Senegambian group
    once occupied the Gabu area until their expansion in the
    14th or 15th century by the Mandingo. The Beafadas
    acquired many Mandingo characteristics including the
    system of secondary kingship, especially in the 16th
    century when they paid tribute to the Empire of Mali.
    In the 19th century the Beafadas resisted the incursions
    of the Futa Jallon Fulani under Coli Tenguella and forced
    him to divert to the northeast of the Beafada territory.
    The period of Portuguese colonial penetration was met by
    numerous instances of Beafada resistance in 1880-82,
    1886, 1900, and in 1907-08 before they were considered
    "pacified." Today the major concentrations of the
    Beafadas are in the region just north of Bambadinca
    and mainly in the area near a Fulacunda-Buba axis.

BERLIN CONGRESS. Between 1884 and 1885 the major Euro-
    pean powers of the time met in Berlin to organize the
    colonial partition of Africa. The Congress was dominated
    by France and England, but claims to African territory
    were made by Portugal, Germany, Italy, Spain, and Bel-
    gium. This meeting launched the "scramble for Africa"
    which triggered an era of military conquest and subjuga-
    tion by European powers in order to support claims of
    occupation and control.
        Before the Congress, the European ruling classes
    had, in general, neglected Africa as too expensive for
    permanent settlement, and there was remarkably little
    knowledge of the people and resources of the interior at
    that time. The age of European exploration of Africa
    took place mainly in the period just prior to and after
    the Berlin Congress. The basic configuration of modern
    African national boundaries has largely descended from
    the Berlin Congress with various local adjustments made
    throughout the colonial era. Many of the present-day
    African conflicts have roots in the arbitrary borders
    drawn a century ago.

BIKER, JUDICE. Early 20th-century governor of Guinea-
    Bissau, best known for his 1903 documentation of the
    slave labor conditions of São Tomé. Biker's articles un-
    leashed a major political scandal showing that 2,000 to
    4,000 "contract laborers" went to São Tomé each year
    but few ever returned to Angola from where they origi-
    nated. See: SÃO TOME.

BISSAGOS (Bujagos, Bojagos, Bijagos). This ethnic stock
   is the principal group which occupies the islands (11°15'N,
   16°05'W) on the Atlantic coast of Guinea-Bissau. The
   Bissagos archipelago is sometimes confused with the Cape
   Verde Islands since they were all under Portuguese colonial administration. The Bissagos people are animists
   with petty chiefdoms, probably derived from the adjacent
   mainland since they have certain affinities with the Diolas,
   Cocolis, Nalus, Padjadincas, and Papeis. At present
   their economy is largely based on fishing and palm products.
       The fiercely independent Bissagos peoples were
   not "pacified" by the Portuguese until as late as 1936
   and were distinguished among the peoples of Guinea-
   Bissau for the persistence of their opposition to foreign
   penetration and colonial rule. The earliest resistance
   dates to the very first Portuguese explorer, Nuno
   Tristão, who reached the islands in 1447 and was killed
   during his attacks on the Bissagos people. A Portuguese
   attack on Ilha Roxa in the Bissagos likewise failed in
   1550. The Bissagos people were famed for their large,
   ocean-going canoes holding up to 70 people. These
   fast-moving canoes enabled them to conduct liberal slave
   raids on the coast with little fear of retaliation.
       In the period between 1840-50 the Bissagos again
   mounted a stiff resistance against European intrusion,
   and they were certainly not under effective Portuguese
   control. The British and French called on the Portuguese to suppress these people, but the Portuguese
   were unable to meet this request. In 1849 the British
   and French organized a joint "punitive" raid on the islands with three ships and more than 50 soldiers. After
   meeting with strong opposition they too withdrew. Additional recorded instances of largely unsuccessful attempts
   to suppress the Bissagos "tax revolts" occurred in 1900,
   1906, during the Pinto campaign of 1913-15, in 1917,
   1918, 1924, and in 1936. See: PINTO, T.; TRISTÃO, N.

BISSAU. Capital city of the Republic of Guinea-Bissau at
   the broad estuary of the Geba River on the north shore
   (11°51'N; 15°35'W). The area has been occupied by a
   concentration of Papeis people. The first European to
   reach the area was the Portuguese explorer Nuno Tristão in 1446, who was killed the following year in the
   Bissagos Islands. In the 16th century Bissau became

a modest coastal base for slave-trading lançados and
other Luso-Africans who continued in this capacity
through the late 19th century.

Following attacks by European powers and virtual
anarchy in the slave trade, Bissau was appointed as a
captaincy-general in 1692 in order to strengthen the
Portuguese monopoly coordinated from the Cape Verde
Islands. This was designed to make a more meaningful
coastal presence between Cacheu to the north and Bolama to the south. By 1696 Bissau town held a fort,
church and hospital and controlled trade on the Geba
and Corubal Rivers. The trade remained largely in the
hands of sometimes independent lançados. About a
dozen settlers were assigned there each year in the
early 18th century; later this number was raised to 40
per year. A high death rate from tropical diseases and
frequent attacks by neighboring Africans on ports and
forts strongly discouraged expanded colonization. In
1869 Bissau became one of four administrative comunas
in order to create a more effective local administration,
although the Governor's residence was still at Geba, a
small town much further east in the interior. When the
administration of Guinea-Bissau was fully separated from
Cape Verde in 1879, the capital was transferred to Bolama. The first three decades of the 20th century saw
almost continuous resistance by the Papeis in the Bissau
area, but in 1941 the colonial capital was moved to Bissau from Bolama. After independence in 1974 there was
some discussion about moving the capital to a central
place in the interior, but it remains at Bissau.

On August 3, 1959, the Pijiguiti dockyards in
Bissau were the scene of bloody repression against the
rising nationalist movement. The Pijiguiti massacre, as
it became known, caused the leadership of the nascent
PAIGC to determine that a path of armed struggle rather
than negotiation would be necessary to achieve independence. Bissau itself was attacked in 1968 and June 1971
during the nationalist war (1963-1974).

The population of Bissau rose from approximately
25,000 to 80,000 in the course of the war as a result of
the dislocation of the rural populations from military activity. The 1979 national population census showed that
Bissau had swelled to 109,214 by that year, mostly from
young migrants attracted to city life and dependent upon
salaried relatives.

Regarding urban planning, some progress has been
made regarding port expansion, piped water systems and
electric power, but major difficulties remain in the areas
of inadequate housing, insufficient supplies of fuel oil
for electric power, lack of spare parts for the electric
and water systems and massive unemployment. See:
BARRETO; BOLAMA; CACHEU; LANÇADOS; PIJIGUITI.

BNG. See: BANCO NACIONAL DA GUINE-BISSAU.

BOLAMA. From the very earliest times in the Portuguese
colonial administration the area of Guinea-Bissau was
ruled from Cape Verde. Bolama, or Bulama, was thereby a Guinea town under the direct administration of Cape
Verde. This island town (11°35'N, 15°28'W) faces the
tidal estuary of the Fulacunda flood basin. The Portuguese navigator Nuno Tristão reached Bolama in 1446
when he explored the Geba River. Throughout the
period of the Cape Verdean slave trade, but especially
in the 18th and 19th centuries, Bolama offered an ideal
defensive position with easy access to the riverine interior. In 1753 Portugal claimed official ownership of
the island, but their authority was weak and control
fell back to local African leaders who in turn sold a portion of Bolama to the British trader Philip Beaver and
others. By the end of the 18th century all of these
ventures had failed.
    In 1828 the Portuguese returned to fortify the
town and to restore their control. The British pro-
tested and in 1837 sent the naval brigantine The Brisk
to cut down the Portuguese flag and hoist the Union
Jack. For more than thirty years the conflict continued, with various acts of violence and ownership shifting back and forth. The British occupied Bolama again
in 1858 and claimed the Bissagos Islands as well. In
1860 the British declared that both territories were
considered incorporated within the administration of
Sierra Leone. The Portuguese rejected this claim and
the entire matter was sent to U.S. President Ulysses
Grant for final arbitration. Grant ruled in favor of
Portugal, and the British withdrew in January 1869.
In order to improve their restored administration, the
Cape Verdean authorities gave Bolama the status of a
comuna (one of four in Guinea-Bissau) so they could
intensify the effort to pacify and colonize the local

population. Finally, in 1879 the administration of Cape
Verde was separated from Guinea-Bissau, which began
to be ruled as a distinct colony. Bolama was the first
capital of this colony.

BOLANHAS. Riverine marshes typical of coastal Guinea;
areas suitable for rice cultivation given proper drainage
and irrigation.

BRAMES. These representatives of the Senegambian stock,
Atlantic subfamily, are located in the area between
Canchungo and Bula on the right bank of the Mansoa
River. Related to the Papel, Manjaco and Mancanha
peoples, the Brames are hardly Islamized and are mainly
animist. Their economy is based on slash-and-burn
agriculture with limited hierarchical political organization. The 1950 census showed 16,300 Brames, while the
1960 estimate indicated that the population of Brames
rose to 35,000, and the 1979 census indicates 26,026,
or 3.3 percent of the total population.

BULL, BENJAMIN PINTO. Historian and secondary school
teacher in Dakar who was President of the UNGP which
sought independence from Portugal without revolution.
He held talks in Lisbon in July 1963 to achieve this end.
Bull's brother is Jaime Pinto Bull, who was the UNGP
Vice President. See: UNIÃO DOS NATURAIS DA
GUINE PORTUGUESA.

BULL, JAIME PINTO. One of the few Africans from Guinea-
Bissau who served as a deputy in the Portuguese National Legislative Assembly (NLA) in Lisbon in 1964.
Bull was also the Inspector of Administration and Secretary General of the colonial administration in Guinea-
Bissau. He served as the Vice-President of the UNGP
and later as President of FLING after 1966. In 1969
Bull was re-elected as the only African representative
of Guinea in the NLA in Lisbon. He was killed in a
helicopter crash in July 1970 while on a tour of the
territory. See: BULL, B.P.; FLING; UNGP.

- C -

CABRAL, AMILCAR LOPES "ABEL DJASSI" (Sept. 12, 1924-

Jan. 20, 1973). Cabral was born in Bafata in Guinea-
Bissau of a Cape Verdean father, Juvenal Cabral, and a
Guinean mother. Because his father was educated,
Amílcar was sent to the Liceu Gil Eanes in São Vicente
for his secondary education. At the age of twenty-one
he entered the University of Lisbon Institute of Agron-
omy, from which he graduated with honors in 1950. In
the early 1950s he was associated with the Lisbon Casa
dos Estudantes do Império where he met revolutionary
intellectuals from other African colonies. While in Lisbon he met and married his Portuguese wife, Anna Maria,
who was herself a dedicated revolutionary. With his
training complete, in 1950 Cabral entered the colonial
agricultural service where he applied soil science, demography and hydraulics engineering. During the period
1952-54, Cabral traveled very extensively in Guinea to
conduct its first agricultural census and to gain an intimate and detailed knowledge of the land and people
which would become a great asset in organizing the
PAIGC, the nationalist revolutionary party.

Cabral's first effort in mobilizing a nationalist
movement in Guinea was in 1954 with the "Recreation
Association," which was parallel to the movement MING
also founded by Cabral in the same year. In the mid
1950s Cabral met with his revolutionary friends from the
CEI and they formed the Movimento Anti-Colonialista
(MAC). Finally, on September 19, 1956, Cabral, his
brother Luís, Aristides Pereira, Rafael Barbosa and two
others met secretly in Bissau to form the PAIGC. Cabral
could not remain in Bissau at the time as he had to return to Angola where he was at work with a private
sugar company. In December 1956 Cabral, Agostinho
Neto and other Angolans met secretly to form the Movimento Popular de Libertação da Angola (MPLA). The
clandestine organizing continued and sought to mobilize
the workers of Bissau. On August 3, 1959, a nationalist
dockworkers' strike was met with savage colonial repression while Cabral was at work in Angola.

Following this event Cabral returned to Bissau to
discuss a change in tactics and to prepare for a protracted armed struggle to win independence for Guinea-
Bissau and the Cape Verde Islands. In 1960 Cabral
secretly left Bissau to continue organizing and to form
the FRAIN in Tunis; this was soon replaced by the
CONCP in April 1961. These organizations sought to

unify the struggles in the different Portuguese colonies
in Africa.   After 1963 the PAIGC launched its war.
Within a decade the PAIGC had gained control of two
thirds of the countryside.   During that period (1962-
1973), Cabral served as Secretary General of the PAIGC,
directed the liberation struggle, and wrote a number of
brilliant works on African liberation and culture, African
and Guinean history and class formation for which he
received worldwide acclaim.   (See: The Bibliography.)
     In 1973 the PAIGC was able to declare itself as the
government of an independent Guinea-Bissau.   Such actions severely demoralized a Lisbon regime which was already financially and politically exhausted from the end-
less wars in Africa.   The April 1974 overthrow of the
regime in Lisbon brought an end to decades of fascism
in Portugal and to the Portuguese colonial presence in
Africa and elsewhere.
     In an abortive anti-PAIGC plot, Cabral was assas-
sinated in Conakry on January 20, 1973.   He did not
personally live to see all of his objectives fulfilled only
a few months later.   Achievements of such a scale for a
man of such modest beginnings earned Cabral many international awards and honors.   He received the Nasser
Award, the Joliot-Curie Medal, and honorary doctorates
at Lincoln University (U.S.) and from the Soviet Acad-
emy of Science.   Today Cabral is widely recognized as a
major African revolutionary theoretician in both analysis
and practice.   He is survived by his brother, Luís, who
became the first President of Guinea-Bissau until his
overthrow, as well as his three children and his wife,
who has worked in the Ministry of Health and Social Welfare.   September 12, Cabral's birthday, is now celebrated
as a national holiday. See: BARBOSA, R.; CABRAL, J.;
CABRAL, L.; CONCP; FRAIN; MAC; MING; PAIGC;
PEREIRA, A.

CABRAL, JUVENAL (1889-?).   Father of Amílcar and Luís
     Cabral and author of Memórias e Reflexões (1947).
     Cabral studied at the Seminary of Viseu in Portugal and
     had a deep understanding of the cultural aspects of
     Portuguese colonial rule, which caused him great per-
     sonal frustration.   Such a family context played an im-
     portant role in the formation of the revolutionary nation-
     alist ideology of his two sons. See: CABRAL, A.;
     CABRAL, L.

CABRAL, LUIS DE ALMEIDA (1931–   ).   One of the six
   original founders of the PAIGC and first president of
   Guinea-Bissau.   Born in Bissau, Cabral's training was
   as an accountant for CUF.   He left for Guinea-Conakry
   soon after the PAIGC was formed in 1956 because the
   Portuguese secret police were seeking his arrest.   In
   1961 Cabral became the founding Secretary General of
   the pro-PAIGC trade union group, the UNTG.   By 1963
   he was in charge of the strategic Quitafine frontier zone,
   which was militarily active at that time.   In 1965 he became a member of the PAIGC War Council.   Following reorganization of the PAIGC in 1970, he became a member
   of the Permanent Commission of the CEL with the responsibility for national reconstruction in the liberated zones.
   Independence of Guinea-Bissau followed his brother's
   assassination, and Luís Cabral became the first president
   of that new nation as well as the deputy secretary of the
   PAIGC.   In November 1980 he was overthrown by "Nino"
   Vieira and was jailed until his negotiated release from a
   death sentence.   Following his initial exile to Cuba and
   then to the Cape Verde Islands, Cabral fled to Lisbon,
   where he now lives.   Recent efforts by Guinea-Bissau
   and Cape Verde have restored diplomatic relations, but
   Cabral's overthrow fractured unity between the republics and the original goals of the PAIGC.   See: CABRAL,
   A.; CABRAL, J.; CEL; CUF; PAIGC; UNTG.

CABRAL, PEDRO ALVARES.   Portuguese sea captain whose
   fleet reached the Cape Verde Islands on March 22, 1500.
   Rather than travel along the West African coast, he went
   far to the southwest and accidentally discovered Brazil
   in April 1500.

CABRAL, VASCO (1924?–   ).   Cabral was born in Guinea-
   Bissau but was one of the very few Africans to study in
   Lisbon University in 1950.   In 1954 he was arrested for
   his political views and was held in prison for almost six
   years including two years in solitary confinement.   Upon
   his release in 1959 he completed his degree in economics
   and met with Amílcar Cabral, who was also in Lisbon at
   that time.   Vasco Cabral fled from Portugal in July 1962
   with A. Neto of the MPLA and soon joined the PAIGC to
   serve on its central committee and on the War Council.
   Cabral also served on the Executive Committee of the
   Struggle with his specialty in party ideology.   He served

as Minister of Economic Coordination and Planning from
1974 to 1982, devoting himself to full-time party work
since that time as well as serving as economic planning
advisor to President Vieira since 1984. See: CEL;
CONCP; PAIGC.

CACHEN RIOS E COMERCIO DA GUINE. See: CACHEU.

CACHEU. Town in Guinea-Bissau (12°10'N, 16°10'W) located
on the south bank of the Cacheu River in an area populated by the Manjaco and Cobiana ethnic groups. The
Cacheu River was first reached by the Portuguese explorer Nuno Tristão in 1446. In the early 16th century,
slaving became the notable activity at Cacheu where salt
and horses from Cape Verde were traded for slaves cap-
tured and sold by lançados along the coast and from the
interior tributary kingdoms of Mali. In 1588 Cacheu became an official Portuguese captaincy under the regional
authority of Cape Verde. As a captaincy it was to regu-
late the slave trade and establish a post for regular trade
and supplies. As Cacheu's prosperity grew, a special
crown agreement with Jewish merchants (ladinos) in 1601
gave them permission to settle and trade in the Cachen
Rios area and to establish a capitão e ouvidor which was
subordinate to the Governor of Cape Verde. In the 17th
century the slave trade was intensified, and in 1624 the
Dutch temporarily seized the Cacheu captaincy. In 1630
Cacheu was fully returned to Portuguese control as it began to be developed as the economic nucleus for the
province of Guinea. Security remained a problem, and
Cacheu was fortified in 1641 against attacks by Luso-
African lançados and various European powers.
   The 1660s brought the creation of the Cape Verdean-
based slaving company Cachen Rios e Comércio da Guiné,
which had a slave trade monopoly from Senegal to Sierra
Leone including the rivers of Guinea. In 1676 this company was reorganized as the Companhia do Cacheu Rios
e Cabo Verde, but its main slaving activities were still
based at Cacheu, which continued to dominate the slave
trade in Senegambia. The Companhia do Cacheu Rios e
Cabo Verde enjoyed relative prosperity until the close of
the 17th century, when it lost its monopoly on the slave
trade to Spanish America. With locust plagues and some
reduction in slaving itself, the importance of Cacheu declined into the early 18th century as Bissau's importance

increased and as the slave trade expanded further south
along the West African coast.

In the 19th century European rivalries for African
territory were intensified; the District Officer at Cacheu
had to battle for Portuguese control of Northern Guinea-
Bissau in the 1830s. Honório Barreto gained some promi-
nence for his stalwart defense of Portuguese interests.
In administrative reorganization in 1869, Cacheu was
given the status of one of the four colonial comunas, but
when the government of Guinea-Bissau was separated
from that of Cape Verde in 1879, the first capital became
Bolama rather than Cacheu. Portuguese efforts at settlement and "pacification" of the Cacheu area were sharply
resisted by the Papeis people in 1891-4 and in 1904. Today Cacheu is a small Guinea town of modest importance.
See: BARRETO; BISSAU; BOLAMA; LANÇADOS.

CADAMOSTA, ALVISE. Venetian navigator in Portuguese
service who sailed in the Senegambian area between 1454
and 1456 in a 90-ton vessel. In 1455 Cadamosta and
Usodimare, a Genoan, separately reached the estuary of
the River Gambia. In 1456 the two navigators sailed on
a joint two-ship mission two miles up the Gambia River,
where the ships were forcefully attacked by the local
population and their ship crews mutinied. On the same
voyage they reported active trade of merchandise and
slaves at Arguim Island in Mauretania. Three or four
armed caravels attacked coastal fishing villages in the
Gulf of Arguim to capture slaves for the return voyage.
Still, in 1456 Cadamosta and Usodimare reached the Rio
Geba (Grande) and the Bissagos Islands.

CADERNETA. Labor passbook system started in 1920s in
conjunction with the contratado labor system. Similar to
the South African system of passbooks of African labor
registration. See: CONTRATADO.

CAETANO, DR. MARCELLO. Prime Minister of Portugal
from September 1968, following the incapacitation of
Prime Minister Salazar, until April 25, 1974, when he
was overthrown by the Armed Forces Movement (MFA).
Caetano was a professor of public law and the main
author of the 1933 Constitution which institutionalized
Portuguese fascism. He was the Minister of Colonies
from 1944 to 1949 and was also instrumental in the 1951

revisions of the Portuguese constitution which maintained Portugal's colonies in Africa. As head of Portugal during the key years of the nationalists in Guinea-Bissau, Mozambique, and Angola, Caetano presided over Portugal's historically doomed, though unyielding, efforts to retain direct imperial ("overseas") control of its African and Asian holdings, which led to massive discontent within the Armed Forces Movement (MFA) in Portugal and the final overthrow of Portuguese fascism.

CANARY CURRENT. Southerly ocean current off the Atlantic coast of Morocco enabling early Portuguese sailors to pass easily down the coast in the epoch of great maritime exploration. Because these navigators were without tacking vessels that could sail close to the wind, the Canary Current sometimes made the return trip slow and difficult.

CANCHUNGO (12°04'N; 16°02'W). Town in northwestern Guinea-Bissau formerly named Teixeira Pinto during the colonial era in honor of the colonial militarist who was infamous in Guinea for his brutal "pacification" program which brought 20th century Portuguese colonialism. After independence Guineans changed the name to Canchungo.

CÃO, DIOGO. Born in the mid-15th century, he was a Portuguese navigator who in 1482 was the first to explore the west coast of Central Africa just south of the equator. He reached the Kongo kingdom in 1483. Christopher Columbus sailed along the Guinea coast between 1482 and 1484, possibly meeting Cão. Both Cão and Columbus sought to go around the Muslim world in the Middle East and secure an alternate route to India. Cão was thus the forerunner to the voyages of Bartolomeu Dias and Vasco Da Gama. See: COLUMBUS; DA GAMA; DIAS.

CAPITACÃO. Head tax; a key source of state revenue during the colonial era.

CASABLANCA GROUP. African organization formed in January 1961 which sought to unify the socialist oriented states such as Egypt, Guinea-Conakry, Mali, Algeria, and Ghana in opposition to the moderate Brazzaville Group formed in December 1960. The Casablanca Group was

officially disbanded in 1963 upon the formation of the
OAU. As a result of the emergence of the Casablanca
Group, the Conference of Nationalist Organizations in
the Portuguese Colonies (CONCP) was formed in April
1961. This represented a major African effort to unify
the three leading nationalist movements then fighting in
the Portuguese colonies. See: CONCP.

CASA DOS ESTUDANTES DO IMPERIO (CEI). This semi-
official African student center in Lisbon was a locus for
African assimilados and intellectuals including figures
such as Marcelino dos Santos of Mozambique, Amílcar
Cabral of Guinea, and Mario de Andrade of Angola.
From the CEI, revolutionary thinkers formed the MAC
in 1957. In 1965 the CEI was finally closed by the Salazar government, which termed it subversive. See: MAC.

CASAMANCE. Region and river in southern Senegal forming
a portion of the general area known as Senegambia. The
trade and administrative center of Casamance is at
Ziguinchor, which was a portion of Portuguese Guinea
until the late 19th century. French traders became quite
numerous in the 1820s and 1830s and they pressed for
the inclusion of the Casamance region within French
Senegal. Following the Berlin Congress in 1886, Portugal agreed to give up its claims to the Casamance Basin
and Ziguinchor. Meanwhile France withdrew its claims
on Cacine in southern Guinea-Bissau. Other minor
changes were made in the 1890s and early 1900s in order to settle claims between France and Portugal, the
two colonial powers of the immediate area. During the
nationalist war the PAIGC had important offices and military bases in the southern Senegalese parts of the Casamance just across the border with Guinea-Bissau. Today
the Casamance harbors the largest single portion of exiles
from Guinea-Bissau, most of whom emigrated for economic
reasons. Many hundreds of Guinean peasants temporarily
migrate to the Casamance for trading purposes, and
Crioulo is widely spoken in dozens of Casamance villages. See: BERLIN CONGRESS; GABU.

CASSANGAS. See: BANYUNS.

CENTRO DE INSTRUÇÃO POLITICO MILITAR (CIPM). In
order to develop ideological unity with the PAIGC cadres,

Amílcar Cabral founded the CIPM in 1961 during the
earliest period of the operation of an exile base in
Conakry when a number of the leading figures such as
João Vieira, Francisco Mendes, Domingo Ramos, Constantino Teixeira, and others attended this seminal party
school. One of the center's functions was to link ideological and military training in the formation of "bi-
grupos," the basic guerrilla army unit. The CIPM also
trained those returning from abroad and offered basic
education. In the early 1970s, 200-300 students in groups
of 25 were trained through a series of formal, informal,
and role-playing exercises during a program of several
months. The curriculum included national and world
history, a PAIGC code of behavior, lessons on the party
program and organization, military and political tactics,
decolonization and foreign relations. Participants were
expected to develop a strong sense of national unity and
purpose; and their training emphasized the political
rather than military dimensions of the struggle.

CHAMPALIMAUD. One of the major financial and industrial
conglomerates of Portugal with ties to the BNU and extensive colonial interests. Champalimaud virtually con-
trols the Portuguese steel industry although it is, in
turn, dominated by West German finance capital.
Champalimaud operated a variety of firms in Guinea-
Bissau. <u>See</u>: BANCO NACIONAL DA GUINE.

CLASS STRUCTURE. For a small, largely rural nation the
class structure of Guinea-Bissau is rather complex in its
diversity but remains overwhelmingly geared toward agricultural production. Essentially, one may apply the
term "peasant" or subsistence farmer to describe the
mode of production in Guinea-Bissau. This reflects the
dominance of agriculture, a cultural heritage of African
values but with a peripheral participation in the "Great
Tradition" of Portugal. In Guinea the systems of plantation agriculture, sharecropping and absentee landlords
were very limited by contrast to Cape Verde. The farming classes in Guinea include, on the coast, largely
stateless rice farmers and, in the interior, more centralized peanut growers and cattle herders of the northeast. The acephalous peoples may be exemplified by the
Balantas, who have village-level authority and who are
primarily animist in religious outlook. The most prominent

centrally governed people are the Fulas, who have local
and regional leaders who traditionally commanded the
respect of large numbers of their people, especially when
the colonial authorities supported the local Islamic religious hierarchy of chiefs, local nobility and traditional religious leaders.

The working class proper is quite small and gener-
ates rather little surplus value; it is centered around the
few light industries which process agricultural, animal
and fish products, the small lumber and dairy industry,
and some relatively well organized workers in the transport and port services. Service sector positions of driv-
ers, repairmen, mechanics, street vendors, secretarial
and clerical jobs, and domestic servants are to be found.
Some traditional artisans such as weavers, blacksmiths,
leatherworkers and musicians are also active.

During wartime the urban areas under Portuguese
control also saw a sizeable minority of "lumpen" or déclassé
strata of criminals and prostitutes, although in the period
since independence the government has sought to curb
such elements with innovative social programs. The military of Guinea-Bissau during colonial times and during
the war was largely derived from Portuguese conscripts,
but today the Guinean armed forces are made up of volun-
teers, many of whom fought during the war of independence.

There is also a small mercantile strata including
various shopkeepers, hotel operators, bankers, and those
from the road and water transport industries. Industrial
capitalists in Guinea are extremely few indeed. In the
past a large portion of the mercantile group was made up
of Portuguese and some Lebanese merchants. Since independence a number of the larger firms have come under
state control. High-ranking civil servants, government
officials and functionaries are also associated with the upper classes. The colonial class structure in Guinea-
Bissau followed rather sharp racial and rural-urban
differences. Aside from the military, almost all Portuguese were found in the several larger towns, with most
in Bissau itself. Likewise the top positions, including
those as government officials and bureaucrats, were monopolized by Europeans or some Cape Verdeans. This
group also predominated among traders and businessmen,
managers, and representatives of foreign firms. Social
mobility or innovations in class formation under colonialism

were very limited. The majority African population was
generally excluded from these occupations and was overwhelmingly rural in location and agricultural in occupation.

At various points in the history of Guinea-Bissau,
the Dyulas, a Mandingo-derived, itinerant trading group,
controlled the trade to the interior, with Afro-Portuguese
lançados working along the coast. Similarly, there are
traces of the traditional class structure of Gabu and of
the subsequent Fula who are present today.

With the departure of the Portuguese colonial authorities, top positions in Guinean society were vacated,
resulting in a sharp struggle for power between the
PAIGC cadres and a relatively weak petit-bourgeoisie.
Since independence, the leadership has consciously
sought to attack the remnants of the traditional and
colonial class structure. The cephalous, feudal-like,
traditional authorities have lost considerable power, and
most foreign monopolies, financial interests, and commercial sectors have either been nationalized or brought under strict control. The new leadership has formed a new
state bureaucracy, and limited large-scale private ownership has been abolished and placed in the state sector.
This socialist program has also resulted in notable urban
unemployment and difficulty in attracting foreign investments.

During Portuguese colonial rule the process of
local class formation was very much repressed and ab-
breviated except for those traditional hierarchies which
could be brought into the colonial administration. Thus,
with the rather sudden exit of the Portuguese, the
PAIGC initially moved into positions of power to block
the formation of a local bourgeoisie based on private
ownership of the means of production. However, since
independence, the privileges of salary and status associated with government positions have allowed for the
precipient formation of a state bourgeoisie, even though
its members' material advantages are quite modest in comparison with their counterparts elsewhere in Africa.

COBIANAS. See: BANYUNS.

COCOLIS (KOKOLIS). This small Senegambian group is
derived from the Bissagos peoples and occupies coastal
stretches at the mouth of the Geba River near the Nalus
peoples. See: BISSAGOS; NALUS.

COLI TENGUELLA. See: TENGUELLA, COLI.

COLUMBUS, CHRISTOPHER. Credited as the first European navigator to reach the New World. Between 1482 and 1484 Columbus visited the Guinea coast, which prompted a 1484 audience with King João II to gain financing for further voyages. João II turned down his request, although Columbus visited him again in 1493 after his epic voyage across the Atlantic. Some reports indicate that Columbus stopped in the Cape Verde archipelago before making his crossing in 1498.

COMISSÃO PERMANENTE. See: PERMANENT SECRETARIAT.

COMPANHIA DO CACHEN E CABO VERDE. See: CACHEU.

COMPANHIA GERAL DO GRÃO PARA E MARANHÃO. This Brazilian slave company was formed in 1753(5) to supply the labor needs of the two northern coastal Brazilian states of Grão Pará and Maranhão. Initially the company held a 20 (25?) year lease on the slave trade in Guinea-Bissau, and there are indications that such trade continued well into the 19th century. This company revived a dying slave trade in Guinea. The Portuguese Marquis of Pombal was instrumental in arranging the charter of this company. See: BISSAU; BOLAMA; SLAVERY.

COMPANHIA LUSITANA DO ALUMINIO DA GUINE E ANGOLA. This Dutch firm was founded on August 16, 1957, to discover and process bauxites in Guinea-Bissau and Angola. The Portuguese government and Billiton Maatschappig N.V. of the Netherlands, with an initial investment of US $172,000, agreed to prospect in the Boé area for an estimated 200,000 tons of bauxite related to the same field of aluminum-bearing ore in neighboring Guinea-Conakry. Regular productive exploitation is not yet underway.

COMPANHIA UNIÃO FABRIL (CUF). CUF was one of the very largest Portuguese conglomerates with large investments in Africa and with approximately 10 percent of Portugal's total corporate capital. CUF is a multinational concern involved in textiles, agriculture, petrochemicals, steel and shipbuilding. It has its own merchant ships and tens of thousands of employees. CUF is primarily

owned by the powerful Mello family, which in turn has
links to the BNU and the Champalimaud conglomerate
that share CUF's dominance of the Portuguese, and formerly the colonial, economies. CUF has important ties
to American and French capital as well.

In Guinea-Bissau, the two major CUF affiliates
were Casa Gouveia, exporting palm and peanut oil, and
the António Silva Corporation, which had significant investments in shipping, insurance, light industry, and
import-export concerns central to Guinea's colonial economy. Until 1928 CUF was one of seven foreign firms in
Guinea-Bissau; although it was the only Portuguese firm
in the colony, it played a relatively minor role. As of
that year, with Salazar's "New State" having been proclaimed, Portugal more forcefully asserted its economic
interests in its African territories, ousting the non-
Portuguese firms and thereby allowing CUF to monopo-
lize trade in Guinea for the remainder of the colonial
period. Furthermore, Portugal bought into CUF, so
that part of the profits went directly to the Guinean
colonial state. The fact that peasants could only sell
to CUF companies partially monetarized their economy,
providing them with cash with which to pay colonial
taxes, but also resulted in depressed rural living stan-
dards. See: BNU; CHAMPALIMAUD.

CONFERÊNCIA DE ORGANIZAÇÕES NACIONALISTAS DAS
COLONIAS PORTUGUESAS (CONCP). Founded in April
1961 in Casablanca, Morocco, the CONCP maintained a
Permanent Secretariat at Rabat under Marcelino dos
Santos, who was to become a central leader of FRELIMO
in Mozambique. The CONCP replaced the former umbrella
organization FRAIN. The Second CONCP Conference was
held in Dar es Salaam, Tanzania, in October 1965. In
addition to other liberation movements and organizations,
the PAIGC sent a five-person delegation consisting of A.
Cabral, V. Cabral, V. Maria, A. Duarte, and J. Araujo,
as well as representatives from the UNTG and UDEMU.
See: CASABLANCA GROUP.

CONHAQUES. These small, isolated clusters of Senegambian
people manifest considerable Mandingo acculturation as
they were separated from the main coastal Senegambian
groups during Mandingo expansion. They are now found
in the hilly areas in the extreme southeast of Guinea-
Bissau; some small pockets reside in the Madina Boé area.

CONSELHO DE GUERRA (WAR COUNCIL). See: CONSELHO
    EXECUTIVO DA LUTA; CONSELHO SUPERIOR DA LUTA;
    PERMANENT SECRETARIAT.

CONSELHO EXECUTIVO DA LUTA (CEL), Executive Council
    of the Struggle. After the 1964 PAIGC Party Congress,
    a 20-member (15 regular members and five alternates)
    Political Bureau was organized and functioned until it
    was replaced and enlarged by the CEL in 1970. During
    the close of the nationalist war (1970-73), the Council
    was central to the regulation of political and military
    affairs. This was especially the case as the CEL con-
    tained the seven-member Conselho de Guerra (War Coun-
    cil) and the powerful PAIGC three-member Permanent
    Secretariat. From 1970 to 1981, the CEL was elected
    during the annual meetings of the CSL and functioned
    between CSL meetings, acting as the PAIGC's Political
    Bureau. It met at least every four months or more of-
    ten if needed; members of the CEL made up about one
    third of the CSL. Both councils were abolished in 1981
    and replaced with a Politburo and Central Committee.
    See: CONSELHO SUPERIOR DA LUTA; PAIGC.

CONSELHO SUPERIOR DA LUTA (CSL). The High Council
    of the Struggle functioned within the PAIGC as an or-
    gan roughly equivalent to a Central Committee, that is,
    it was the highest body except for the irregular meetings
    of the Peoples National Assembly (ANP). Within the CSL
    were the CEL, the War Council, and the Permanent Com-
    mission. The CSL met annually since its first session in
    August 1971 when it replaced the PAIGC Central Commit-
    tee (65 members) that emerged from the Second Party
    Congress. In 1964 the Central Committee has seven de-
    partments, but these were reduced to five by 1967. In
    1970 the Central Committee was initially enlarged to 70
    members and was newly named the CSL, with about one
    third of its members also being on the CEL. At the time
    of the 1973 Second Party Congress, the CSL increased
    its membership from 81 to 85. The membership was
    raised to 90 at the 1977 meeting of the Peoples National
    Assembly. During the CSL meetings, members of the
    CEL were elected to serve between the yearly CSL meet-
    ings. See: CONSELHO EXECUTIVO DA LUTA; PAIGC.

CONTRATADO. A contract laborer who agrees to sell his
    labor power for a proscribed period of time to a specific

employer. The system was used extensively in Cape
Verde to reduce the population of the poor, desiccated
islands and to generate remittances to be sent back to
the islands. Often the contratado system was used for
agricultural production and for public works.

CORUBAL, RIO (CORUBAL RIVER). This major river of
Guinea-Bissau has its headwaters in the vicinity of Labé
in the Futa Jallon plateau of Guinea-Conakry. Before it
reaches Guinea-Bissau it is known as the Koliba River
until it enters the eastern frontier of Guinea-Bissau,
south of Buruntuma, curving back south through the
Gabu and Boé areas before swinging northward again
to empty into the upper portion of the Geba estuary.
The Corubal is about 280 miles long and once provided
a convenient route for the export of slaves to the coast.
See: GEBA, RIO DE.

COUP D'ETAT. See: PAICV; PAIGC.

- D -

DA GAMA, DUARTE LOBO. Da Gama was the first Governor
of Cape Verde, appointed in 1587. This appointment
ended the captaincy system which had prevailed in Cape
Verde from 1460.

DA GAMA, VASCO. Da Gama was the first Portuguese
soldier-navigator to round the Cape of Good Hope and
travel up the east coast of Africa to India. He initiated
the Portuguese trade monopoly of the region. With relatively advanced navigational equipment, Da Gama sailed
directly from the bulge in West Africa to the South African Cape on his trip to the region during the years 1502-
1504. On his first trip, 1497-99, Da Gama rounded the
Cape with three ships. In 1498 he encountered Muslims
at Quilemane on the east coast, then sailed to Malindi
and on to Calicut and Malabar, India. On the 1502 trip
he subdued Kilwa at gunpoint, opening the era of early
16th-century rivalry between the Portuguese and Moslems
for East African coastal trade.

DEGREDADOS. Exiled Portuguese criminals, often charged
with political crimes, who settled in the Cape Verde

Islands or were confined there for a period of punishment
or exile. Some degredados formed a permanent settler
population where they were sometimes considered as
lançados. See: LANÇADOS.

DEMOGRAPHY. The demographic data for Guinea-Bissau are
relatively limited. Under the best of conditions, unknown
numbers of people avoided tax collectors, census-takers
and agents of the colonial government who sought military
or labor conscription. Disruption during war years
caused large-scale emigration and population movement.
As a consequence all of the data offered must be considered approximations.

A census in 1926 put the population of Guinea-
Bissau at 434,000. The census in 1950 was one of the
better demographic studies taken in this nation; it
showed a total population of 510,777 of whom 502,457
(98.3 percent) were "uncivilized natives" or basically
the rural agricultural population. "Mestiços" were numbered at 4,568 (0.8 percent of the population). These
were often of Cape Verdean origin and were involved in
small-scale commerce and some local government administration. The same census reported 2,263 Europeans
(0.4 percent), a mere 1,478 "assimilados" (0.2 percent),
and finally 11 Indians. In the following years the population statistics show greater variation for the same period
and cannot be considered precise, but one may assume
that the socioeconomic and ethnic composition of the population stayed relatively similar until 1974.

Population estimates have ranged as high as 800,000
but this figure seems unlikely. Most statistics did not
include the 25,000-30,000 Portuguese soldiers stationed
in Guinea-Bissau during the war years, and only in 1976
did some 70,000 refugees from Senegal and Guinea-Conakry
begin to return to their homes in Guinea-Bissau. The
main demographic effects of the war were the relocation
of some people to secure areas across the borders and
substantial migration from rural areas to the cities and
towns. Combatant deaths in the irregular war were perhaps something more than 1,000 per year but were not of
major demographic significance. By the mid-1960s the
population had probably reached about 530,000. The
1979 census shows a total population of 777,214 with a
national population density of approximately 21 inhabitants per square kilometer; this is up from 18 per square

kilometer about ten years ago. A 1982 estimate gives
the population figure as 594,000 so it is difficult to determine which figure may be closer to reality. The respective percentages of the largest ethnic groups are:
Balantas, 27.2%; Fulas, 22.9%; Mandingas, 12.2%;
Manjacos, 10.6%; Papeis, 10.0%.

The infant death rate in Guinea-Bissau is put at
149/1,000 although other sources give the rate of
80/1000. In either case the rate is substantially higher
than these in Europe or North America. For the period
between 1970 and 1975, the overall crude birth rate is
25.1/1,000 resulting in a rate of natural increase of 1.5%
per year, which is somewhat low for Third World nations.
Health conditions are generally poor in Guinea-Bissau,
but life expectancy has risen to about 41 years on the
average, with men living somewhat less than the average
and women living somewhat longer.

The most densely populated areas of Guinea-Bissau
are in the east along a Bafata-Gabu axis and in the vicinity of Cacheu. The capital city of Bissau has the
largest urban population with 14.6 percent of the nation,
up from 8% a decade ago. Nevertheless, the country remains overwhelmingly rural despite increasing rates of
urbanization. The least populated concelhos are to be
found in Bolama and in the Bissagos Islands.

DE NOLI, ANTONIO. De Noli was a Genoese navigator in
Portuguese service. In 1457, at Arguim, de Noli and
Gonçalo Ferreira traded slaves for horses from Diogo
Gomes. De Noli and Gomes are considered to be the
first Portuguese navigators to set foot in the Cape Verde
Islands. In the early 1460s de Noli was in charge of
one of the captaincies on São Tiago island, from which
trade on the Guinea coast could be regulated.

DGS. See: PIDE.

DIALONKES (DJALONKES, JALONCAS, JALLONKES). This
small group appears to be of Senegambian stock but with
very pronounced Mandingo acculturation, so that it is
sometimes placed in the latter category. They are partly
Islamized as a result of the 18th-century Fula migrations
from Futa Jallon and are now located east of Duas Fontes
(Bangacia). The Dialonkes are the neighbors of the
Quissincas, a Manding group.

DIAS, BARTOLOMEU. Portuguese navigator who rounded
the Cape of Good Hope, South Africa, in 1488 and returned along the Guinea coast to Portugal in December
of that year.

DIAS, DINIZ. Portuguese navigator who "discovered" the
mouth of the Senegal River and the Cap Vert of Senegal
in 1444-5.

DIOLAS, DJOLAS. This group of Senegambian cultural stock
is related to the Senegalese Serer and is thought to have
split from them in about the 14th century with the creation of the Sine and Salum kingdoms of that period.
These animistic rice cultivators are found between the
Casamance and Cacheu rivers in the northwest and
coastal portions of Guinea-Bissau, and they have absorbed some of the Banyun population living to the east.
The term Diolas must be distinguished from the Manding-
derived Dyulas. The Diolas were frequent targets of
Manding slave raiders who sold their captives to the
lançados and other Portuguese traders. See: DYULAS.

DONATORIOS. The system of property holding and local
rule in Cape Verde and Cacheu in Guinea-Bissau and
some other colonial holdings in which a capitão was
given a royal grant to adminsitration with a high degree
of local authority. The local captain was appointed under crown authority and was subject to inspection, review, and appeal by Lisbon. It was normal to farm the
donatório by slave labor. See: CAPITÃO.

DROUGHT. The Sahelian drought in Africa is a continuation
of centuries of desiccation of the Sahara and the Cape
Verde archipelago. Drought in Cape Verde has been
accompanied by major demographic transformation of the
population of the islands. On the one hand, resultant
famines have commonly cut the population by 10-40 percent. Statistics have been kept from 1747 to 1970 which
show 58 years of famine and over 250,000 related deaths
in some dozen drought periods. Drought cycles have
also caused massive loss in crops and livestock. The
drought in 1832 was associated with a severe famine in
which 10 percent of the population died. It is estimated
that about 25 percent of the population perished in
1854-56, with the number of islanders falling from over

120,000 to less than 100,000. Famine and drought are
also recorded for 1902-03, in the 1940s and in the late
1970s.

On the African mainland, especially in such countries as Senegal, Mali and Chad, the situation has been
parallel to that in the Cape Verde Islands. Tens of
thousands of people have died or have been improperly
nourished, while hundreds of thousands of heads of
livestock have perished. Those traditional people dependent upon pastoral economies have been shattered
and forced to change their mode and social relations of
production, sometimes irreversibly. The unpredictable
role of agriculture has forced massive migration from
those regions most severely affected in search of cash
employment elsewhere.

A large factor in the drought and desiccated conditions has been a lack of proper land management and
water conservation. Guinea-Bissau's southern regions
are forested and rainfall remains adequate, but in the
northeast areas with Fula concentrations drought resulted
from less than average rainfall and low production of ani-
mals and agricultural commodities. An extensive slash-
and-burn crop rotation system has offered some protection from drought at least in comparison to the far more
severe effects in the Cape Verde Islands and in regions
further north in the Sahel proper.

DYULAS, DIULAS, JOOLAS. This economically important
ethnic group of Manding derivation must be distinguished
from the Senegambian Diolas. The Dyulas are mainly
from the Soninke branch with some Fula admixture.
Functioning as a specialized class of itinerant traders,
the Dyulas integrated coastal Portuguese economic concerns with those of the interior peoples, especially in the
early 16th century until the arrival of the colonial era.
During the decline of Mali, the influence of the Dyulas
appeared in a series of petty chiefdoms on the shores of
the Gambia and Cacheu Rivers and at the Dyula commercial center at Kankan. The Dyulas stimulated local production of gold, kola nuts and the exchange of slaves
for imported products such as salt, textiles and firearms
during the pre-colonial times. These items were traded
throughout Guinea-Bissau and in much of the Upper
Niger River. The Dyulas often worked in close association with Mali and various Mandingo subkingdoms. Most

Dyulas were Muslims, but they did not carry out con-
versions or jihads. The penetration of the interior by
the Portuguese broke into Dyula commerce, subsequently
helping to cause the Dyula revolts from 1835 to the 1880s
in the Upper Niger and in Guinea-Conakry. During
these revolts the Dyula tried to re-establish their commercial authority. Their trading networks functioned
clandestinely during the colonial period and have expanded markedly since independence. See: ECONOMICS;
GABU; MANDE; SONINKE.

- E -

EANNES, CONSALO. As a representative of the Portuguese
crown, Eannes was sent to visit the Prince of Tekrur
and the Lord of Timbuktu in the last quarter of the 15th
century in order to establish commercial and political relations. See: MALI.

EANNES, GIL. Sailing for Prince Henry in 1434 and 1435,
Eannes made two trips in a cumbersome 50-ton square-
sailed barca. More efficient caravels were operational
after 1441. After returning to Lisbon in 1435, he later
set sail with Afonso Gonçalves Baldaia and went south of
the Tropic of Cancer. These voyages were the first recorded in that region since the time of the Phoenecians
in 813 BC. In subsequent expeditions, Eannes made
three consecutive trips in 1444, 1445 and 1446 using the
more advanced caravel-type of ship.

ECONOMICS, TRADE, DEVELOPMENT. The vast majority of
trading in Guinea-Bissau occurs through barter and cash-
purchased exchanges carried out between individual
peasant producers or at village, regional and urban markets. Among items bartered and sold are food surpluses,
fish caught locally by village fishermen, small-scale livestock (chicken, pigs, goats, sheep) as well as large livestock (cattle), wild fruits (bananas, coconuts, cashews),
firewood, and artisanal products. Artisanal products
are fabricated within villages and include soap, pots,
calabashes, baskets, palm oil, peanut oil, cashew wine,
cloths and clothes made by weavers and tailors, iron
farm tools wrought by blacksmiths, and salt extracted
from brackish riverine paddies. While weaving, tailoring,

blacksmithing, and large-scale herding are carried out by men, the remainder of the artisanal activities are undertaken by women, and it is the women who also do most of the barter and cash trading.

Although cash was introduced into the rural economy during the colonial era, mainly by coercing peasants to pay colonial taxes and through the introduction of some imported goods in urban areas, trade remained dominated by barter exchanges. Some 50 to 70 percent of rural exchange is still carried out through barter trading, but the economic crisis that emerged during and after the independence struggle did force rural people to rely more heavily on monetary exchanges. This had not only stimulated greater efforts at cash crop and surplus food production, artisan production, fishing, livestock raising, and fruit and firewood gathering, but has also generated an enormous amount of seasonal migration such as young men traveling to Senegal and Guinea-Conakry during the agricultural off-season to labor for wages or to sell products grown or fabricated in Guinea-Bissau.

To a large extent, the continuing predominance of barter and local cash trading reflects the failure of the state to construct a viable official marketing structure in the post-colonial period. After independence, the government set up two state-owned retail/wholesale companies, Socomin and a network of Armazens do Povo (Peoples' Stores), together totaling 216 official trading centers. There was especial cause for optimism because the Peoples' Stores had expanded successfully during the anti-colonial struggle, providing peasants with foreign supplied goods (such as sugar and lamps) in return for cash crops. However, large-scale difficulties emerged during the independence era, including a lack of trained and competent managers, the inability to distribute basic grains to needy sectors of the population during periods of food shortage, and a lack of foreign exchange with which to purchase imports that could have stimulated peasants to bring their cash crops to these state stores. As a result, not only did the traditional local trading continue to predominate, but a long-distance unofficial trade network carried out by Dyula and Senegalese merchants has emerged. This trade is based on foreign currency, such as the French West African franc, and it has expanded through the late 1970s and early 1980s.

In addition to these problems, the few industrial enterprises that had been constructed operated at far-from-productive capacity, and they generated substantial investment losses. Macro-economic statistics indicate the depth of the difficulties: between 1975 and 1979, the external debt tripled. The external debt in 1983 was $200 million, as exports barely covered one-fourth of imports; the 1982 balance of payments showed a $32 million deficit. The country remains highly dependent on overseas aid, requiring a predicted $110 million a year of such aid to keep the economy afloat in 1983-86. In recognition of all these difficulties, radical reforms were carried out in 1984 with the specific goals of reviving officially sanctioned trade and of boosting the level of marketed agricultural surplus. Large-scale industrial projects were discontinued or radically reduced in scale, and the state trading companies, especially the Peoples' Stores, were privatized in order to encourage the flow of consumer goods to the countryside. Producer prices were raised 76 percent for rice, 72 percent for groundnuts, 84 percent for cashew nuts, and 92 percent for palm kernels, and export earnings for all these crops increased as a result of these price rises. These reforms, combined with a 50 percent devaluation of the Guinean peso and price rises for basic food, were viewed positively by the World Bank and the IMF, which made loans in 1984 totaling U.S. $26 million. It is expected that budgetary and external deficits will be reduced.

Between 1980 and 1984, production of groundnuts rose from 20,000 to 30,000 tons, although only 17,600 and 19,000 tons, respectively for 1980 and 1984, were sold to the official market, with 6,800 and 10,000 tons being exported. In 1980, 8,800 tons of palm kernels were marketed and 6,000 tons were exported, with the figure rising in 1984 to 11,000 tons marketed and 10,600 tons exported. In the same four-year period, the amount of cashew nuts marketed rose from 1,000 to 7,000 tons, with 900 tons exported in 1980 and 6,000 tons in 1984.

The most significant exports are groundnuts, palm kernels, and palm oil, together comprising $6.1 million in exports; shellfish and fish, totaling $5.5 million in exports; industrial products, with $1.7 million of exports; and timber, with $0.7 million. While the exported agricultural commodities are the same as under colonial rule, the development of fish exports is a post-colonial

development, as fish exports grew from $0.3 million in
1976 to $5.5 million in 1982. Regarding imports, food,
especially rice, and beverages constitute the largest
single item, followed by industrial and commercial supplies, petroleum, and capital goods. While this represents a shift from most of the colonial period, when the
country exported rice and peanuts and its largest import
item was textiles, it is the logical consequence of the
agricultural destruction which occurred during the anti-
colonial struggle and which forced Guinea to begin rely-
ing on food imports by the mid-1960s.

Portugal monopolized 90 percent of trade during
the colonial era, but since independence Guinea-Bissau
has accumulated an extraordinary diversity of trading
and, especially, development partners. Portugal remains
the largest single source of imports, providing 43 percent of Guinea-Bissau's imports in 1982, followed by
France with 9 percent, Sweden with 7 percent, the U.S.
with 6 percent, the Netherlands and the U.S.S.R. with
5 percent each, and Burma with 2 percent. Portugal is
also Guinea-Bissau's principal purchaser of exports, buy-
ing 34 percent. Spain buys most of Guinea-Bissau's
caught fish, followed by Senegal and China.

Guinea-Bissau receives international aid from the
World Bank, the EEC, the IMF, COMECON, and OPEC,
and enjoys bilateral development funding from Abu Dhabi,
Saudi Arabia, Kuwait, Canada, Norway, Sweden, Den-
mark, France, West Germany, England, Italy, Spain,
Greece, Luxembourg, Belgium, Austria, the United
States, Brazil, Chile, China, India, Pakistan, Burma,
Thailand, Japan, South Korea, the U.S.S.R., East
Germany, Hungary, and Yugoslavia. As a result of
this diversity, Guinea-Bissau is able to avoid economic
dependency on any one political block or superpower and
to uphold an international political stance of genuine nonalignment.

EDUCATION. Portugal was notable in Europe for a particularly low level of public education. For example, in 1960
in Portugal only 9.8 percent of the population was enrolled in primary school, while the comparable statistic
for Holland was 13.0 percent, the U.S.S.R., 14.2 percent, and the U.S. 18.4 percent. In Portugal's African
colonies the situation was expectedly even worse. Only
3.8 percent of the population of Guinea-Bissau was

enrolled in primary school in these late years of colonialism. Such low rates were typical of the European colonies in Africa, but following independence this proportion has changed markedly.

The main function of the colony of Portuguese
Guinea was for primary production and some labor recruitment. Formal mass education was deemed unneces-
sary or even counterproductive to these goals. Judging
from a rate of 98 percent illiteracy in 1950, in the heyday of colonialism, one may easily see the educational
policy of Portugal in Guinea-Bissau. Even mission education, which sometimes played an important role in other
African countries, was virtually negligible in Guinea-Bissau.
Even as late as 1972 the educational budget for Guinea-
Bissau was an absurd 42 cents per student per year.

The available educational statistics are also unclear
as they do not indicate whether students were simply
enrolled, actively attending, or had completed a given
level of education. Just prior to independence, the
1973 Provincial Report on Educational Services of Guinea
Bissau offered the following data, which should be considered as maxima for the various categories:

Education in Guinea-Bissau

	Primary		Secondary	
Dates	Students	Teachers	Students	Teachers
1962-63	11,827	162	987	46
1963-64	11,877	164	874	44
1964-65	12,210	163	1,095	45
1965-66	22,489	192	1,293	42
1966-67	24,099	204	1,039	43
1967-68	24,603	244	1,152	40
1968-69	25,213	315	1,773	111
1969-70	25,854	363	1,919	147
1970-71	32,051	601	2,765	110
1971-72	40,843	803	3,188	158
1972-73	47,626	974	4,033	171

Source: Repatição Provincial do Serviços de Educação,
Província da Guiné, February 1973.

To the credit of Portugal, it is clear that in the last decade before departing Guinea-Bissau they not only quadrupled the number of primary students but also improved the student-teacher ratio from 73:1 in 1962 to a far better 48:1 in 1973. The level of adult literacy in the 1970s was 25 percent for men and only 13 percent for women. This inequality by sex is also expressed at the primary level, with almost twice the number of boys as girls enrolled in school.

In 1960, the Portuguese policy had resulted in only 14 university graduates in the entire country, while between 1964 and 1973 the PAIGC itself arranged to send some 422 students overseas for advanced education, and by 1973 there were some 35 PAIGC-supported university graduates. During the nationalist war the PAIGC also constructed its own educational system in the liberated areas. This effort to achieve mass primary education did not surpass the Portuguese in numbers given the great adversity of air attacks by Portuguese fighter-bombers and security problems for the young students. However, because of this context it was a remarkable achievement nevertheless. Enrollment fluctuated during periods of Portuguese counterinsurgency when the simple school buildings were moved to new locations while new air attack trenches were dug and supplies were carried from place to place.

The leading PAIGC facility was the Pilot School in Conakry, which usually had about 120 students (about 80 boys and 40 girls). This secondary school was very disciplined and was often a source of direct recruitment into the PAIGC through the operation of the Pioneers of the Party youth organization which operated within the PAIGC educational system. A kindergarten for absent PAIGC-party officials and war orphans was also located in Conakry. Each of the three regions inside liberated Guinea-Bissau also had a boarding school as well as more than 200 primary day schools under the forest canopy. For primary students (ages 7-15) the data on PAIGC schools during the war are shown on page 57.

Since independence, the PAIGC claims to have achieved a 23 percent decline in illiteracy, to about 75 percent, as the educational facilities have been able to operate openly under peaceful conditions. Needless to say, there is a very long way to go. The most recent statistics in the 1980s suggest that there is still forward

PAIGC Primary Schools in Liberated Zones

Year	Students	Teachers	Schools
1965	13,361	191	127
1966	14,380	220	159
1967	9,384	284	158
1968	8,130	243	134
1969	8,559	248	149
1970	8,574	251	157
1972	14,531	258	164
1972	20,000	251	200
1975	60,000	---	400

Source: PAIGC Document

progress, with 89,720 students enrolled in primary school; 6,236 in secondary schools; 135 students in technical and higher-level courses; and 1,130 students receiving secondary, university or specialized training in such areas as medicine, vocations, and administration in a variety of foreign countries.

Aside from those institutions that support formal education, there are now mass circulation newspapers, radio programs, community organizations, and adult literacy programs which play an important role in the goal of upgrading and constructing expanded educational services.

EXXON EXPLORATION OF GUINEA. See: MINERALS.

- F -

FARIM-CACHEU, RIOS (Farim and Cacheu Rivers). With headwaters to the north on Contuboel on the Geba River, the Farim River flows almost directly west until it reaches the town of Farim. At this point it begins to widen and proceed westward until it becomes known as the Cacheu River since it is in the vicinity of the town of that name. As with the other rivers penetrating the coastal swamps, the Farim and Cacheu rivers were important corridors for the export of slaves and for

commerce with the interior through lançados and Dyula
traders. The combined length of these rivers is about
160 miles, although ships of 2,000 tons are only able to
navigate about 62 miles to the interior. See: CACHEU;
DYULAS; LANÇADOS.

FEITOR, FEITORIA. Portuguese royal trade monopolies and
private mercantile concerns were usually represented by
a feitor or local business agent, sometimes with very
considerable powers. A feitor occupied a feitoria, or
(sometimes) fortified trading outpost.

FELUPE. A minor Senegambian group most closely related
to the Balantas and Baiotes. They have a limited hierarchical structure, but there are some reports of a small
tributary kingdom of Mali among the Felupes in the 15th
century, although this may have just been imposed by
Mali itself. The Felupes are famed rice cultivators using
flood irrigation techniques. They are mainly located in
the northwest corner of Guinea-Bissau, especially south
of the Casamance but north of the Cacheu River and
reaching the ocean coast in that region. During the
period of aggressive Portuguese colonization, military
reports show acts of resistance by the Felupes in 1878-
90, 1901, 1903 and finally in 1915 when they were repressed in the campaigns of Teixeira Pinto. See:
BAIOTES; CACHEU; CANCHUNGO; DIOLAS.

FERNANDES, GIL VICENTE VAZ (May 10, 1937-). Born
in Bolama, Guinea-Bissau, Fernandes attended high
school in Bissau. Because of his early affiliation with
the PAIGC, he fled to Senegal in September 1960. With
plans to study in Poland, he was recruited to attend the
University of New Hampshire from which he earned a
B.A. degree in political science in 1965. Later he received an M.A. from American University in Washington,
D.C. Fernandes is a pioneer of the PAIGC on the international scene. From 1970-72 he was the party representative in Cairo; in 1973-74 he served in Scandinavia.
At the time of independence he was a roving ambassador
of the Foreign Affairs Commission. He has played a
significant role in representing the party at the United
Nations and was the first ambassador of the Republic of
Guinea-Bissau to the United States. See: CSL; UNITED
NATIONS.

FERREIRA, ANTONIO BATICA (Dec. 25, 1939-). Ferreira
is one of few Guinean poets of African origin. The son
of a village head in the Canchungo area, he spent seven
years in Dakar, then lived and studied in Lisbon and
Paris and went on to study medicine in Switzerland. His
poetry has been published in Portuguese, French, Senegalese and German journals. Most notable are his poems
in Poetry and Fiction, published by the Society of the
Portuguese Language in 1972. His best known poems
are Infancia and Pais Natal. See: LITERATURE.

FONIO. This important cereal grain is native to West Africa
as a member of the Sudanic food complex. The scientific
name is Digitaria exilis; in Portuguese it is known as
fundo. A hardy plant needing little rain or cultivation,
fonio was a basic foodstuff in the Empire of Mali and
surrounding secondary kingdoms.

FORÇAS ARMADAS REVOLUCIONARIAS DO POVO (FARP).
The regular armed forces of the PAIGC during the war,
FARP was formed in 1964 in order to wage a more aggressive war against Portuguese colonialism. The function of civilian defense was then handled by the PAIGC
local militia units, Forças Armadas Locais (FAL). The
present armed forces of Guinea-Bissau are derived from
FARP but are now separate from those in Cape Verde
following the 1980 coup d'état in Guinea. The total
armed forces of Guinea Bissau number about 6,250 with
a ratio of 1:131 in the military versus the general population.

FORCED EMIGRATION. See: SÃO TOME.

FOREIGN AFFAIRS. While diplomatic contact and economic
exchanges between colonial Portuguese Guinea and other
nations were mainly restricted to England, France and
Germany, Guinea-Bissau has, since independence, enjoyed diplomatic relations and economic support from
nearly one hundred nations located in all world areas
and representing a wide cross-section of ideological and
superpower blocks. This reflects the enormously popular appeal of PAIGC ideology as articulated by Amîlcar
Cabral during the independence struggle and the respect
gained by the PAIGC during that struggle for its battle-
field and diplomatic successes. The continuing reassertions

by the PAIGC and government leaders that development
is to be based on the peasantry and on the agricultural
sector more generally has enabled Guinea-Bissau to garner
outside economic assistance from numerous countries, and
the extraordinary diplomatic skills of the PAIGC leaders
combined with their insistence on maintaining a staunchly
nonaligned foreign policy has gained them the respect of
a striking diversity of nations. Guinea-Bissau receives
specific development aid from, and maintains solid diplomatic relations with, the Soviet Union, most of Eastern
Europe, Yugoslavia, China, Pakistan, India, Thailand,
Burma, South and North Korea, Arab nations, Chile,
Brazil, Argentina, Mexico, Cuba, Canada, the United
States, virtually every Western European and Scandinavian nation, and many African nations.

Diplomatic relations with Portugal in particular,
while rather strained in the first several years of independence, have warmed markedly since 1978. Economic
aid from Portugal has risen so that the ex-colonizer is
now by far Guinea-Bissau's largest supplier of external
assistance, providing 35 percent of Guinea-Bissau's imports and purchasing 34 percent of its exports in 1983.
Diplomatic ties between the two countries have progressed
to the point where Portugal's President Ramalho Eanes
visited Bissau with great political fanfare in 1983. Portugal has expanded large-scale economic, cultural and
educational exchange projects that have further deepened
the ties between the two countries.

Guinea-Bissau has consistently sought to expand its
links with its Lusophone counterparts. This effort began
in 1965, when Amílcar Cabral and others founded the
CONCP (Conference of Nationalist Organizations of the
Portuguese Colonies) on the basis of commonalities among
the liberation movements of Guinea-Bissau, Cape Verde,
Mozambique, Angola, São Tomé and Príncipe. CONCP
meetings took place until 1975, by which point all these
countries had achieved their independence and the CONCP
was effectively disbanded as the respective ruling parties
focused their attention on domestic political and economic
problems. In 1978, President Luís Cabral set in motion
efforts to form a new organizational vehicle for reconsol-
idating ties among the five nations, known colloquially as
Os Cinco (The Group of Five). To this purpose, the
respective heads of state met in Luanda in 1979, in
Maputo in 1980, in Praia in 1982, in Bissau in 1983, in

Maputo in 1983, in São Tomé in 1985, and in Luanda in 1986. The 1983 summit was by far the most productive, and accords were reached regarding the establishment of a common bank, joint air and sea traffic, trading links and joint training of personnel. However, the economic difficulties of all five nations, combined with the strains of war in Mozambique and Angola, have so severely limited these governments' fiscal and organizational capacities that the actual implementation of the 1983 accords has been very limited. Still, the diplomatic, political and cultural solidarity among Os Cinco remains strong, providing a sense of community and a potential base for more concrete economic exchanges in the future.

Diplomatic relations between Guinea-Bissau and its African neighbors--Senegal to the north and Guinea-Conakry to the south--have alternated repeatedly between mutual support and hostility both before and since independence. During the anti-colonial struggle, after initial hesitation these two countries allowed the PAIGC to operate largely free of interference in regions bordering Guinea-Bissau. Guinea-Conakry was especially helpful in providing strategic and administrative support. However, tensions between the PAIGC and Presidents Senghor (Senegal) and Touré (Guinea-Conakry) flared periodically, with some observers believing that Senghor and Touré became jealous of the international status gained by Amílcar Cabral and the PAIGC. After independence, economic exchanges with Senegal and Guinea-Conakry have been carried out in a number of areas, mostly regarding agriculture, water resource management, trade and migration policies. Formal diplomatic relations are emphatically mutually supportive. However, hostilities between Guinea-Bissau and its two neighbors have broken out on occasion and largely center on territorial disputes regarding fishing rights and access to offshore oil deposits. The worst such flare-up occurred in January 1984, when in a dispute regarding fishing vessels, Senegal and Guinea-Bissau each massed troops and tanks on their borders before diplomats succeeded in peacefully resolving the immediate problem. Intensifying such tension is the feeling in Bissau that Guinea-Bissau's political independence and cultural identity would be threatened by allying too closely with its francophone neighbors.

Diplomatic, economic and cultural relations and

exchanges with the United States have been widened
dramatically in the 1980s. This reflects the particular
diplomatic skills of U.S. Ambassador Jon de Vos, the
genuinely open and receptive cultural and political pos-
ture of the people of Guinea-Bissau, as well as Guinea-
Bissau's growing need for U.S. economic support. As a
result, the United States has become Guinea-Bissau's
fourth largest provider of imports, and bilateral U.S.
development aid totaled over U.S. $4 million by 1983-84,
not including a program instituted by the U.S. Agency
for International Development through which approximately two hundred Guineans have attended colleges and
training schools in the United States since 1978. See:
CONCP; PAICV, PAIGC.

FRENTE DE LIBERTAÇÃO DA GUINE (FLG). In 1961 the
FLG was created with the merger of the MLG of François
Mendy and the RDAG. By 1962 the FLG had combined
its forces with the moderate FLING. See: FLING; MLG;
RDAG.

FRENTE DE LIBERTAÇÃO DA GUINE PORTUGUESA E CABO
VERDE (FLGC). The FLGC emerged in 1960 under the
leadership of Henri Labery, the founder of the União
Popular da Guiné in 1957. Essentially the FLGC replaced the MLGCV of Dakar and its three constituent
organizations. The FLGC included the MLGP and the
MLICV so as to broaden the base of support to provide
more effective opposition to the growing PAIGC founded
four years earlier. While the FLGC united new groups,
it lasted only one additional year until it was replaced by
FUL following factional divisions within the FLGC. FUL
and some former FLGC members led to the formation of
FLING in 1962. See: FLING.

FRENTE DE LUTA PELA INDEPENDÊNCIA NACIONAL DA
GUINE-BISSAU (FLING). FLING was the only serious
rival of the PAIGC during the period of anti-colonial
nationalism. The principal differences lay in FLING's
moderate program, ethnic allegiances, and exclusion of
Cape Verdean unity and independence, versus the
PAIGC's social reforms, anti-tribal program, and pro-
jected unity of Guinea-Bissau and Cape Verde. FLING
emerged in a July-August 1962 meeting in Dakar, Senegal, which formed a coalition of seven ethnically-based

groups such as the MLG, UPG, and RDAG under the leadership of Henri Labery. In 1966, Jaime Pinto Bull became the President of FLING, and the main operation continued from a Dakar office.

FLING undertook some military activities shortly after being founded but not after 1963. Some members of FLING were openly hostile to Cape Verdeans due to the role of Cape Verdean merchants during the period of slavery and the presence of some Cape Verdean administrators during colonialism. Between 1963-1967 the OAU sought to merge FLING and the PAIGC with active encouragement by Senegal's moderate President Senghor. After 1967, Senghor reluctantly accepted the supremacy of the PAIGC, although Senegal's support for FLING continued quietly from 1967 to 1970. It was long assumed that the Portuguese PIDE and the American Central Intelligence Agency (CIA) favored FLING in order to divide the supporters of the PAIGC. The most militant members of FLING were the former MLG members, while most of the other member groups held reformist, rather than revolutionary, goals.

In 1970 FLING was reorganized with Domingos Joseph Da Silva as the new Secretary General of FLING-UNIFIE. As the successes of the PAIGC mounted, FLING undertook direct actions against the PAIGC and was implicated in the assassination of Amílcar Cabral in January 1973. In 1973 the leadership passed again to Mário Jones Fernandes. FLING was charged with creating disturbances in Bissau, Bolama and Bafata in May 1974, and FLING members were arrested by the Guinea-Bissau government in April 1976. Since then there has been no reported activity of FLING in either Guinea-Bissau or Senegal.

FRENTE REVOLUCIONARIA AFRICANA PARA A INDEPENDÊN-CIA NACIONAL DAS COLONIAS PORTUGUESAS (FRAIN). This umbrella organization was formed in Tunis, Tunisia, in 1960 to link the PAIGC and the MPLA of Angola in their common programs against Portuguese colonialism. The first leader of FRAIN was Mario de Andrade of the MPLA. Just as FRAIN replaced the MAC (Movimento Anti-Colonialista), it was replaced in 1961 by the CONCP, which continued the same function but included FRELIMO of Mozambique as well. See: CONCP.

FRONT UNI DE LIBERATION (de Guinée et du Cap Vert),
    FUL. In July 1961 Amílcar Cabral again sought to unify
    the PAIGC with Henri Labery's FLGC and some other
    groups. This attempt to create a united front failed
    because of the hesitating support of the FLGC and the
    refusal of the MLG to participate because of its concern
    about the role and future of Cape Verde. The effort to
    create FUL was the last attempt to develop a united front
    for national independence. Once FUL became moribund,
    Cabral returned in 1962 to organize the PAIGC in Conakry.
    The other leaders agreed to form FLING, which subse-
    quently proved to be the only substantial rival to the
    PAIGC during the years of armed struggle. See:
    FLING; PAIGC.

FULA (Fulbe, Fulani, Peul, Fellani, Ful, Foulah, Fellata).
    The Fula are known by a variety of names depending
    upon local usage. They are members of the West-Atlantic
    subbranch of the Niger-Congo language stock, but their
    history is quite different from the other Senegambians.
    The Fulani language is much closer to that of the Serer
    of Senegal from which they originated, although some
    scholars have attributed Fula origins to the Nile valley
    in prehistoric times with westward migration across the
    Sahel or southern Sahara. Fula-like people are shown
    in Saharan rock paintings drawn during periods when
    the Sahara region was much wetter. This effort at re-
    constructing Fula cultural history is still considered
    speculative.
        The Fulas may be subdivided into two main cate-
    gories: the sedentary and more fully Islamized Fula,
    versus those who still practice a degree of pastoral no-
    madism and have syncretic belief systems which mix Is-
    lam and animism. The sedentary Fula were rather strong-
    ly hierarchical in socio-political organization and were in-
    fluential in the spread of Islam through much of the sub-
    Saharan region. In the southward migration to and
    through Guinea-Bissau, some Fula adopted some Man-
    dingo cultural patterns and became known as the Fulas
    pretos or Fulacundas, who are much less cephalous than
    the Fulas of Futa Jallon or Futa Toro. Where the Fulas
    did not establish their own local rule, they often served
    as herdsmen for the various kingdoms in the western
    Sudan.
        The more immediate origins of the Fula are now

clearly traced to Tekrur and Futa Toro in the Senegal
River valley. The Fula are related to the Berber,
Tukulor, Wolof and Serer peoples. The 1950 census of
Guinea-Bissau put the Fula population at 108,400, or
21.5 percent of the total population. In 1960 the
Fula population was estimated at 100,000, but clearly
this is a major ethnic group of Guinea-Bissau; because
of their numbers there are a variety of local names, but
these are often overlapping and ambiguous rather than
reflecting more substantial differences.

In any case, there are, first, the most numerous
Fulas pretos, or "Black Fulas," concentrated in a wide
area between Gabu and Bafata and in scattered groups
in the southeast of Guinea-Bissau. The Fulas pretos
also include the Fulas forros (Free Fulas) or Fulacundas
(Futacundas, Foulacoundas) found in the northeast and
with sizeable groups in the vicinity of Aldea Formosa
and in the south central areas. The large numbers and
wide distribution of this major Fula grouping attest to
the centuries of admixture with local Malinke people long
before the conquest of Kansala by the Futa-Jalonkas.
The second Fula grouping is known as the Futa-jalonkas
(Foutajalonkes) including the Futa-fulas of the north-
central Gabu-Pitche area. Sometimes the Futa-fulas are
known as Quebuncas since it was these Fulas from Futa
Jallon (Labe province) who brought about an end to the
Mandingo kingdom of Gabu (Quebu). The Futa-jalonkas
also incorporate the Boencas, just to the north of Gabu,
and the Futa-fulas pretos in the extreme southeast near
Madina Boé and adjacent to the former Labé province
from which they originated. The third group of Fulas
is considered to have had its origins in Futa Toro in
Senegal. They are known by several local names such
as Torancas, Futancas, Tocurures, Fula-forros or
Vassolancas, depending again upon local usage. Members of this group are found in the northeast and especially in scattered groups in the southeastern regions
which they share with the Futa-fulas pretos.

Some non-Islamic pastoral Fula may have spread
into remote eastern parts of Guinea-Bissau as early as
the 12th or 13th centuries. More significant numbers
of cattle-herding Fula arrived in Guinea-Bissau in the
15th century from Futa Toro. From the 15th to 18th
centuries the Fulacunda (Fulas pretos) population was
in formation, although there was continued peaceful

settlement of other Fula peoples who arrived and mixed with the Mandingos. Another wave of Fula migrants came from Massina after Fula and Mande peoples became allied in their joint efforts to destroy Songhai in 1591. These migrants paved the way for the open Fula conquest of Futa Jallon during the later period of the formation of revivalist theocratic states based on local Islamic brotherhoods. Such migrants were especially involved in the group of sedentary town Fula. This epoch was filled with religious and military campaigns against the Wolof and Serer of Senegal; against the local peoples of Futa Jallon; and against the various secondary states of Mali including Gabu in Guinea-Bissau.

Still another wave of migration took place when the Fulacundas and others left Futa Toro between 1650 and 1700 to settle among some Mandingo populations in Futa Jallon and eastern Guinea-Bissau. In general Fula have been either cattle owners or pastoralists, while Mandingos were more committed to agricultural pursuits.

The policy of Fula settlement in Guinea-Bissau was endorsed by the 15th and 16th century Fula leader, Coli Tenguella. Fula migrations were stepped up in the 18th century, although the Fula of Guinea-Bissau were still subordinate to the Mandingo state of Gabu at that time. Until then, the Fula were essentially stateless pastoralists, although they were the most extensive and numerous of such groups in West Africa. By the 19th century Fulas (Fulani) were expanding everywhere in Sahelian West Africa, as noted by the important jihads in northern Nigeria in 1804-1820 and the arrival of the Fulani as far east as Cameroon in about 1900.

From the mid-18th century until 1867, the Fulas from Futa Jallon and especially from Labé province frequently attacked Gabu until it finally collapsed. This long-term Fula offensive against Gabu may have received some Portuguese support, or at least little opposition, since the on-going presence of Gabu was a barrier to the consolidation of Portuguese penetration and control of the interior. Following the fall of Gabu in 1867, the entire eastern portion of Guinea-Bissau was administered from Labé province. This development excluded the remaining fragment of Mandingo rule at Braco, but Fula influence reached as close to the coast as areas south of Buba. However, with the power at Gabu removed the Portuguese colonial authorities began to carry out military

expeditions in 1880-82 and in 1900 against the Fula themselves. The Portuguese finally brought them under control by means of the Fula's increasingly hierarchical political system which they had developed for the administration of their conquered territory. Later, under Portuguese colonial rule, the now centralized Fula society
proved to be well suited to a form of indirect colonial
rule which reinforced a chiefdom structure by paying
them and giving them social privileges within colonial
society. See: ALFA MOLO; ALFA MUSA; COLI
TENGUELLA; DIALONKES; FUTA JALLON; FUTA TORO;
GABU; TEKRUR.

FUNANA. Funana is a music and dance genre associated
with the badius of São Tiago in Cape Verde. Typically,
a vocalist improvises verses in a fast quadratic rhythm
while playing a simple chordal ostinato on the concertina-
like gaita. Another musician provides rhythmic accom-
paniment on the ferro, or ferrinho, a strip of metal which
is scraped, like a rasp, with a small peg. Others present may sing loose choral responses to the lead vocalist's
lines. The harmonic pattern usually consists of a simple
alternation between two adjacent chords. Funana accom-
panies informal couple dancing, which may be erotic and
often resembles Caribbean dances like the merengue.
Like batuco, funana has been enjoying a folkloric revival
since independence in Cape Verde and has been incorporated, in modernized form, into the repertoires of some
popular dance bands. (Peter Manuel) See: BADIUS;
BATUCO.

FUTA JALLON (Fouta Djallon, Djalonkes, Jalonke, Dialonke,
Jaalo). A plateau area of the interior of Guinea-Conakry
which has served as the homeland for a portion of the
Fula people of Guinea-Bissau and as a major source for
the regional spread of Islam.
        Fula peoples arrived in Guinea-Bissau at least by
the 15th century, particularly as an effect of the movements of Coli Tenguella (I), but the greatest period of
Fula migration took place between 1654 to about 1700.
The Fula were disorganized and nomadic and at first
lived peacefully with Mande and Dialonkes peoples but
paid tribute to the Mandingo state of Gabu. In 1725
the first Fula jihad against the Dialonke of Futa Jallon
took place but was indecisive at this time. By the

mid-18th century Gabu was increasingly under attack by
the Labé branch of the Fulas from Futa Jallon. This
period of intense and complex local conflicts was also
related to the heavy demand for slaves and the widespread introduction of firearms. Whichever group was
the victor in any given battle, there was a ready market for prisoners of war to be sold or exchanged as
slaves at such places as Cacheu, Bissau, or on the
Casamance or Gambia Rivers.

Late in the 18th century the Fula peoples had
conquered the Dialonke branch of Mali in Futa Jallon.
As a result, nine Fula leaders drew up a constitution
of this theocratic military state. The influence of this
state in Futa Jallon was widely felt as, for example, in
the formation of Labé province adjacent to Guinea-Bissau.
By 1788 the Fula ruling aristocracy had been stabilized
and such former residents of the region, like the Susu,
had been pushed toward the coast in Guinea-Conakry
and into southern Guinea-Bissau where they assimilated
coastal cultural patterns. Islamization of many neighboring peoples increased considerably in extent if not in
depth. At the close of the 18th century a holy war had
been declared against the nonbelievers in Gabu, and
while the Mandingo state lasted another seventy years
it underwent rather steady weakening. In one case in
1836-37 the Mandingo state of Braco in Guinea-Bissau
attempted resistance and defeated Almami Bubakar of
Labé, but this represented only a short-lived halt in the
deterioration of Gabu.

Throughout the first quarter of the 19th century,
the Fula jihads intensified and the power of Gabu continued to decline. No fewer than a dozen military missions were carried out against Gabu from Labé. The
holy war was justified by the fact that the Mandingo
were mainly animists even though some had converted
to Islam as early as the time of Coli Tenguella. Ironic-
ally, even the Fula founder of Labé, Kalidou, was not a
Muslim himself although he was not opposed to Islam.
One of the most prominent 19th-century jihad leaders was
Al-Haj Al-Mami Umaru, a Tukulor from Futa Toro who had
joined a Tijaniya religious brotherhood during his pilgrimage to Mecca. Upon his return he revitalized the
holy war movement in Futa Jallon, prepared his disciples,
and entered into full-scale trade on the Atlantic coast to
acquire firearms. In 1848 Al-Haj Umaru declared his

hijira, or holy emigration, from Futa Jallon to Dinguiray,
a small kingdom near Futa Toro. On the way north he
passed through Guinea-Bissau and killed the king of
Gabu, Yangi Sayon, in 1849. Gabu was also suffering
internal weakness from various revolts of indigenous Fula
peoples such as the 1850 upheaval which led to the creation of the small Fula state of Forrea on the Corubal
River. In 1862 Al-Haj Umaru initiated his major jihad,
first against Futa Toro where he met defeat, but his
army still grew in size and later went on to capture Segu
and Masina.

In 1865 Al-Haj Umaru made preparations for the
final conquest of Kansala, the capital town of Gabu. In
direct association with Alfa Yaya Maudo of Labé and Musa
Molo of Jimara, a siege by Al-Haj Umaru was laid against
Kansala from 1866 to 1867 when the governor, Mansa
Dianke Walli finally capitulated and conceded the collapse
of Gabu. This shift in power brought about relocation
of many of the peoples of Guinea-Bissau. On the one
hand it represented the start of still another wave of
assimilation by Fula migrants from Futa Jallon; on the
other hand, the fall of Kansala also stimulated Malinke
migrations to the Gambia area, where their town of Braco
remained unconquered, even though some Fulacunda in
Braco drove Malinke peoples out of the lower Casamance and lower Gambia regions. In addition, Beafadas
and Nalus who had been living under the control of Gabu
were driven further west to the coastal river lowlands
where they resettled, with some Portuguese aid, at the
forts at Geba and Buba.

With the end of the military campaign, Gabu was
placed under the authority of Alfa Yaya, the Fula leader
of Labé. When Al-Haj Umaru went back to Futa
Toro, he was engaged in battle with the French under
General Louis Faidherbe who blocked his advance into
the middle sections of the Senegal River valley. In 1878
Faidherbe completed his task and dealt Al-Haj Umaru his
final defeat. At the height of his conquests (1862-78),
Al-Haj Umaru briefly controlled an area about as large
as the former Empire of Mali. See: ALFA MOLO; ALFA
YAYA; BEAFADAS; FULAS; FUTA TORO; GABU;
MANDE; NALUS; TEKRUR; TENGUELLA, C.

FUTA TORO. Geographically adjacent to the Senegal River
valley is the plateau region of Senegal known as Futa

Toro, which is also the name usually given to the Fula
state built upon Tekrur, itself known from ancient times.
By the 11th century the Islamic state of Tekrur at
Futa Toro was ruled by peoples from the mergers of
Berber, Tukulor and Soninke ethnic stocks who controlled local Wolof and Serer populations. During the
11th century some Serer left Futa Toro to resist the
Islamization of and by Tekrur, and they moved to the
Sine and Salum areas of Senegal where they set up their
own small but powerful states. Between the 13th and
15th centuries Sine and Salum assimilated local Malinke
and Serer culture and society, which was highly stratified with Malinke warriors in the dominant positions.
The Malinke penetration of the upper reaches of the
Gambia was limited to that area because it was at the
frontiers of control from Futa Toro. Some Wolof also
left Futa Toro in the mid-14th century in opposition to
the Tekrur rulers, thus starting some small Wolof states
in Senegal.
From Futa Toro, the Fula peoples spread widely
in the 12th and 13th centuries as the most important
pastoralists of West Africa. As Mali grew in power and
influence in the 13th and 14th centuries under Sundiata
and his followers, the Fula ruling class of Futa Toro was
composed mainly of Fula refugees from the kingdom of
Kaniaga, which had already fallen to the Malian Keita
dynasty. Under the rule of Mansa Kankan Musa (1312-
1337?) of Mali, the Wolof and Tekrur areas were maintained as tributary states, thus extending the rule of
Mali virtually to the Atlantic coast. When Mali declined
in the 15th century, both Tekrur and Wolof states re-
emerged. The best known Fula leader of this period
was Coli Tenguella, who established the new Denianke
dynasty of Futa Toro in about 1490 when he attacked
the western flanks of Mali. The Denianke dynasty of
Futa Toro lasted until the 1770s. During the period of
this dynasty the Portuguese made some of their first
contacts with the peoples in the interior of Africa.
King João II sent missions to Mali in 1494 and under
the reign of João III another mission was undertaken in
1534. Portuguese trade to the African interior between
the 15th and 16th centuries was largely conducted on
the Senegal River for slaves, gold, and ivory from Mali
and Futa Toro and on the river systems on the Gambia
and the Geba which gave some access to the Futa Jallon

plateau region to which some Fula from Futa Toro had
already migrated.

Throughout the 15th century, Fula from Futa Toro
drifted eastward and southward to Guinea-Bissau, where
they settled peacefully with the existing Mande-speakers
and other Senegambians. Between 1654 and 1694(?), the
greatest wave of Fula and Dialonke migration left Futa
Toro. In 1750 the theocratic state in Futa Toro launched
a jihad against the animist Dialonke located, in small
part, in Guinea-Bissau and against various Senegambians
inhabiting Futa Jallon. This jihad resulted in a cultural
admixture known as Futa-jalonke. A second major period
of Fula migration and jihad left from Futa Toro in about
1770. Then between 1770 and 1818 two additional jihads
were initiated in Futa Toro.

With this pattern clearly established, it was Al-Haj
Umaru, originally from Futa Toro, who began his own
series of jihads against Futa Toro which brought an end
to the Denianke dynasty. Despite his final defeat by
the French general Faidherbe, Al-Haj Umaru and his
army briefly held an area about the equivalent of former
Mali, reaching as far east as Jenne. During these migrations and holy wars, the Fula people crossed over
eastern Guinea-Bissau and added to the already existing
regions of Fula population concentration. See: FULA;
FUTA JALLON; MALI; TEKRUR; TENGUELLA, C.

- G -

GABU (Kaabu, Quebu). A tributary kingdom of the Mandingo Empire of Mali, Gabu was founded in the mid-13th
   century by Tiramakhan Traore, a general under the fa-
   mous Malian King Sundiata. It was at this time that
   Traore brought his soldiers to regions around northeastern Guinea-Bissau and the Casamance to lay the
   foundations of Gabu, then a secondary kingdom of Mali.
   Subsequently, local Mandingos were appointed to serve
   as regular administrators. The first king (Mansa) of
   Gabu, Mansa Sama Coli (Kelemankoto Baa Saane) was
   said to have been the son or grandson of Traore. Some
   historical accounts consider that Gabu formally began
   with Mansa Sama Coli rather than with his ancestor.
   Early in the history of Gabu there were three royal
   provinces: Pachana (Pathiana) on the headwaters of

Geba; Jimara (Djimara) in Senegal, south of the headwaters of the Gambia River; and Sama on the Casamance.
The capital town of all of Gabu was at Kansala in northwestern Guinea-Bissau just south of today's border with
Senegal. Mali used the well-situated Gabu to secure the
trade in salt, gold, and slaves on the coastal river estuaries. The Mande-derived Dyulas were important links in
this early trade with the Portuguese. Gabu's influence
extended from the Gambia to the Corubal Rivers, that is,
most of the upper Casamance and virtually all of eastern
Guinea-Bissau.

During the period of subordinance to Mali, each
provincial Farim (Faren) or governor had considerable
local authority and was accorded his own administrative
council, symbolic war drums, and personal army. On
the other hand, the rule of the Mansa was considered
sacred and even followed the matrilineal line of succes-
sion rather than the patrilineal descent for the Farims
and ordinary people. The Mansa of Gabu was selected
from the eldest of the leaders of the royal provinces.
Each provincial capital town was fortified and had a regular guard. Some of these armed forces could be supplied to the Mansa in time of war.

The degree of centralized control of the Empire of
Mali slipped away in the late 15th and early 16th centuries
as it increasingly fell to the attacks of Songhai after
1546. At this time Gabu gained full autonomy and was
able to expand and maintain its own kingdom until 1867.
Between the mid-16th century until the 18th century,
Gabu was still ruled from Kansala, but it also included
some 20 to 30 royal trading towns and several additional
royal provinces, e.g., Manna, Payinko, Paquessi, Kusara,
Badora, Tumanna, and Koliba. Gabu became the most important and strongest of these, and under its direct
stimulation it launched the growth of the small but strong
Serer states of Sine and Salum when they came under the
authority of Gabu's Guelowar (Gelwar) dynasty. Salum
was just north of the River Gambia and Sine was to the
northwest of Salum, in Senegal. However, Mandingo rule
from Gabu did not last out the 16th century, and the
Guelowar dynasty was assimilated by the Serer who restored independence to Sine and Salum as small centralized Senegalese states.

Also coming under the control of Gabu were the
provinces of Oio and Braco, which maintained a greater

degree of local autonomy than the other provinces. Oio
was south of the headwaters of the Cacheu River and
Braco to the north of the headwaters. Just beyond
Braco's control farther north lived the Cassangas with
their capital at Birkama. The Cassangas, who are related to the Banhun of Guinea-Bissau, formed their own
secondary Mandingo kingdom on the south bank of the
Casamance River. The Cassanga king was called Cassa
Mansa in the Mandingo tradition, and it is from this that
the term Casamance is derived. These various Mandingo
kingdoms were all under the general Malian authority at
Niani until its fall in 1546.

In the 17th and 18th centuries various military
operations augmented Gabu's power and produced many
slave captives for the export trade. Perhaps as many
as half of all African slaves in the late 16th and early
17th centuries were generated from Gabu's wars. Later
the state became quite stable and this role ceased.

As Gabu gained in power, the Fula pastoralists
and farmers with whom the Mandingo lived became a subordinate, subject population. At times there was comparative harmony between the ruling Mandingos and the
Fulas, however other periods were marked by struggle,
conflict, insult, and oppression by the ruling classes of
Gabu. These precarious socio-political relations led to a
long pattern of Fula revolts. At the end of the 18th
century Gabu was increasingly the victim of Fula attacks from Futa Jallon, sometimes in local alliances with
the Fula of Guinea-Bissau. Into the 19th century the
Fula pressed their attacks, and at least one Farim of the
royal Province of Paquessi was converted to Islam, while
the Fula jihad leader Al-Haj Umaru killed Farim Yangi
Sayon in 1849. The following year local Fulas in Guinea-
Bissau broke away to form their own small states. In
the mid-19th century King Siibo ruled Gabu, but he died
with no clear successor. The Gabu throne was contested
by Saama, Tumanna, and Waali groups, and Mansa Janke
(Djanke) Waali finally prevailed. In 1867, Mansa Waali,
then at Kansala (the capital), capitulated to the Fulas
under a purported force of 12,000 soldiers beholden to
Alfa Molo and led by the Fula marabout of Timbo, Abdul
Khudus. After three days of siege, Waali realized the
futility of his resistance and blew up his powder magazine with many family members inside.

Six centuries of the Gabu empire had come to an

end, although some small Mandingo states lingered on
into the 19th century. Taking advantage of this condition of internal disorganization and the Mandingo-Fula
rivalries, the Portuguese initiated a series of protracted
military campaigns between 1891 and 1910. They concentrated their attacks on the Oincas (Oio Mandingos
and Balantas) in 1897, 1902, and in 1912-15. With such
aggression, first from the Fula and then by the Portuguese, the Mandingos were stripped of their former
glory and power. The eastern city of Guinea-Bissau
once known as Gabu was renamed Nova Lamego to com-
memorate the Portuguese military conquest. See: ALFA
MOLO; FUTA JALLON; MALI; MANDINGO; PINTO; SAMA
KOLI; SERER; TENGUELLA; TIRAMAKHAN.

GEBA, RIO DE (Geba River). The Geba River has its
headwaters in northernmost Guinea-Conakry but then
curves through regions of the upper Casamance area of
Senegal before turning back toward the southwest and
into Guinea-Bissau through the northeast. At the town
of Bafata the Geba is joined by the small Colufe River
flowing from Gabu town. The river remains relatively
narrow flowing by Geba town and Bambadinca, but at
Xime it broadens very widely, joined by the Corubal to
become, ultimately, a huge estuary with a mouth of
about 10 miles across near Bissau. The Geba was an
important route for commerce and slavery to the interior
and gave an axis around which the Gabu state was
formed. The Geba is about 340 miles in total length,
but it is only navigable for ships up to 2,000 tons for
about 93 miles. See: CORUBAL.

GOMES, DIOGO. Portuguese navigator and pilot. In 1455,
along with the Venetian Cadamosta, Gomes established
commercial relations with the Wolof people at the mouth
of the Senegal River and with the Malinke states on the
Gambia, thereby strengthening early Portuguese relations
with Mali. In 1457 Gomes reportedly arrived at Arguim
with four horses, where one horse usually brought 10 to
15 slaves. Gomes found Gonçalo Ferreira and the Genoese António de Noli already trading at Arguim at that
time. By exercising the royal Portuguese trade monopoly,
Gomes gave de Noli and Ferreira seven slaves per horse,
but received 14 to 15 slaves per horse from the African
traders. Gomes is credited with being one of the dis-

coverers of the Cape Verde Islands. This occurred when
he was blown off course while returning from a coastal
exploration in 1460. He landed at what is now São Tiago
and he also visited Fogo. Since he landed on São Tiago
on May 1, he named it in honor of that saint's day.
Later he reported on Boa Vista, Maio, and Sal islands
as he sailed northward. In 1461 Gomes sailed to coastal
Liberia and Sierra Leone. See: DE NOLI.

GOMES, FERNÃO. In 1468 Gomes, a Lisbon merchant, received a five-year lease for Guinea trade from King
Afonso V (1438-1481) for the price of 200 milreis a year
on the condition that he explore 100 leagues of West
African coastline to the east of Sierra Leone. This
lease excluded land opposite the Cape Verde Islands.
Gomes was also required to sell ivory to King Afonso V
at a fixed price. Between 1469 and 1475 Gomes carried
out his explorations, and he is credited with the discovery of the Gold Coast (Ghana) during this period.
In 1477 Gomes reached the Bight of Biafra. In 1482 a
Portuguese fort was constructed at El Mina as a result
of Gomes' travels and reports. The Portuguese crown
granted Gomes a trading monopoly along the Guinea
coast, but the operation was based in the Cape Verde
Islands, which had only been settled a few years
earlier.

GONÇALVES, ANTÃO. With Nuno Tristão, Gonçalves was
the first to capture Moorish slaves at Cape Blanc and
thus begin the age of slavery in 1441. Africans were
initially seized for information and ransom. With this
cargo of slaves and gold dust, Gonçalves returned to
Portugal to stimulate further exploration. Gonçalves
made at least five voyages in 1441, 1443, 1444, 1445,
and in 1447 to the upper Guinea coast in West Africa.
See: HENRY.

GRIOT. The term for a greatly respected poet, oral historian, itinerant musician, arbitrator, and keeper of
lineages, especially in Senegambia and points east in
the Sahel.

GROUNDNUTS. See: AGRICULTURE.

GRUMETTAS, GRUMETES. African ship crews occupying

low ranks of irregular forces in the navy. Other reports suggest that they were Christianized slaves, especially as private slave armies of the lançados. See:
LANÇADOS.

GRUPO DE ACÇÃO DEMOCRATICA DE CABO VERDE E DA
    GUINE (GADCVG). The Democratic Action Group of Cape
    Verde and Guinea-Bissau emerged in the period after the
    fall of the Caetano government in Lisbon and essentially
    represented the position of the PAIGC regarding the unity
    of Guinea-Bissau and Cape Verde. The GADCVG rapidly
    became a mass organization which blocked the organizing
    efforts of the UDCV and the UPICV, particularly in mid-
    November 1974 when it organized a 24-hour general strike
    to back the PAIGC demand that it would be sole repre-
    sentative in the independence negotiations with Portugal
    in 1975.

GUINEA-CONAKRY. See: FOREIGN AFFAIRS.

- H -

HAWKINS, SIR JOHN (1532-1595). Like his father, William
    Hawkins, John was an English merchant adventurer, but
    the main items of commerce for John Hawkins were Afri-
    can slave captives. In 1559 Hawkins moved from London
    to the port town of Plymouth, where he married the
    daughter of Benjamin Gonson, Treasurer of the Navy,
    an office that Hawkins was later to hold. Backed by
    English merchants, Hawkins left for Africa in 1562 in
    three small ships named Salomon, Swallow, and Jonas.
    This first adventure in English slaving was sufficiently
    profitable that it attracted the secret financial backing
    of Queen Elizabeth I and several of her Privy Council-
    lors as secret stockholders. The second voyage took
    place in 1564 and met Portuguese armed resistance which
    was forcefully broken by Hawkins, who seized several
    Portuguese ships. For these successes Hawkins was
    knighted by the Queen and given a royal emblem show-
    ing an African slave in chains. The rapid gain in popu-
    larity in Europe of sugar as a sweetener encouraged a
    third voyage in 1566 under a different captain and in
    1567 with Hawkins again in charge. On his last trip
    Hawkins was attacked and defeated by Spanish ships,
    thus ending this first period of English slaving.

HEALTH.   In 1972 the Portuguese health budget for Guinea-
Bissau was 10 million escudos (2.7 percent of the total
budget); the processing industries received 56 percent
of the budget while transport was allocated 26 percent
of these revenues.   These proportions suggest the limited
concern for African health by the colonial government,
and they demonstrate the financial base for the extremely
low level of the health delivery system.   In all, during
one of their last years as the colonial power, the Portuguese spent about U.S. $350,000 or 66 cents per person
for health, and the vast majority of health services were
located in the capital city and were geared to the white
and "assimilated" sectors of the populace.

In Guinea-Bissau there are numerous debilitating
tropical diseases such as malaria, bilharzia, filariasis and
various gastrointestinal disorders.   Tuberculosis and nu-
tritional deficiencies are also common problems.   To meet
these needs in 1959 there was about one doctor for every
20,000 inhabitants.   Although thousands of people never
saw a doctor, there were some gains in the colonial health
services in the closing years, as the following data indicate.

	1960	1961	1963	1966	1971
Doctors	25	26	34	48	46
Nurses	100	150	202	---	285
Hospitals	10	---	31	34	---
Beds	300	---	839	850	1027

By 1964 the doctor-to-inhabitant ratio had improved
to one doctor for every 15,400 people, and the per capita
expenditure had risen to U.S. $1.45 per person annually.
Obviously the improvements were still hopelessly inadequate, and many of the increased services were simply
involved with the treatment of war-related injuries as
the anti-colonial war intensified.

During the course of the nationalist struggle, the
PAIGC began to develop its own health and military facilities to treat war casualties and to serve the increasing numbers of people in the widening liberated zones of
the country.   In the midst of guerrilla warfare, services
were crude and decentralized but relatively effective

given the combat environment. Each village committee
had specific health assignments and close personal contacts, so that by 1970 the number of sanitary posts
(dressing stations) of the PAIGC exceeded those of the
Portuguese. Throughout the war the PAIGC sent people overseas for nursing and medical training while some
foreign doctors, especially those from Eastern Europe
and Cuba, came to serve as doctors in the liberated regions. In addition to the village health committees, the
PAIGC organized traveling health brigades.

By 1972 there were five PAIGC hospitals in the
south, two in the north, and two in the east. These
primitive facilities were concealed under the tree canopy
and were sometimes moved several times a year for security reasons. Operations such as Caesarean sections,
amputations, and appendectomies were performed using
blood plasma, local anesthetics, and antibiotics to which
there was an unusually good response. The main goal
in these field hospitals was to get patients ambulatory
so they might be transported to the 123-bed PAIGC
hospital at Boke, Guinea-Conakry, or to the 50-bed
facilities at Koundara or Ziguinchor in Senegal to the
north. In 1972, Boke processed 5,000 outpatients. By
the same year the total number of doctors working with
the PAIGC was 41, thereby approximating the number
used by the Portuguese at that time.

Since the conclusion of the war the PAIGC has
inherited the colonial facilities and has further expanded
health services. In absolute terms these services are
still very underdeveloped and much further growth is
still required, since existing health services continue to
suffer chronic shortages of medicines, hospital facilities,
and medical personnel. As illustrative of the poor health
environment, the following statistics are appropriately
revealing: life expectancy at birth is only 41 years,
and the infant death rate is extremely high at 149/1,000;
the average caloric intake is just 74 percent of the mini-
mum daily requirement.

HENRY, PRINCE (1394-1460). Prince Henry "The Navigator"
was the son of King João I (1357-1433) and Philippa,
daughter of an Englishman, John of Gaunt. Henry was
responsible for organizing about one third of the early
Portuguese exploration of the West African coast during
the great age of Portuguese maritime innovation in the

first half of the 15th century. Henry led the military
expedition against Ceuta, Morocco, in 1415 for the Royal
Portuguese House of Avis. Stimulated by reports of the
mysterious Christian, Prester John, and lured by the
knowledge of gold mines feeding trans-Saharan trade,
Prince Henry sent ships along the coast of Morocco looking for an easier route to the interior of Africa. Because Moors were still ruling considerable portions of
the Iberian peninsula and all of north Africa, they controlled the trade to the east and had blocked Portuguese
and European penetration of Africa. In 1434 ships of
Prince Henry reached Cape Bojador (Saharan Arab Democratic Republic/Morocco), the furthest point reached by
Portugal until that time due to the limitation of prevailing winds, navigational skills and equipment. In 1436
Prince Henry led an unsuccessful military effort against
Tangiers. Five years later a ship captained by Antão
Gonçalves, sailing for Prince Henry, returned to Portugal with the first documented African slaves (Moors
from an area probably along southern coastal Morocco).
Prince Henry usually received 20 percent of slave cargos.

In 1453, Gomes Eanes da Zurara, a well-known
chronicler for Prince Henry, wrote "Cronica de Guiné,"
which described some of the aspects of this early exploration and slave trading. In 1456 the Genoan captain
Usodimore and the Venetian captain Cadamosta both
sailed under Prince Henry's flag when they reached the
Geba River in today's Guinea-Bissau. During the period
1419-1460 there were at least 35 voyages under the Portuguese flag. Of these, eight were initiated directly by
Prince Henry and two were co-sponsored by him, although
at his death in 1460 he had never actually participated in
an exploration mission as it was not considered appropri-
ate for a man of his status. See: ZURARA; CADA-
MOSTA; GONÇALVES, A.

- I -

ILHAS DE BARLAVENTO. Northern, windward islands of
    Cape Verde including Santo Antão, São Vicente, Santa
    Luzia, São Nicolau, Sal, and Boa Vista.

ILHAS DE SOTAVENTO. Southern, leeward islands of Cape
    Verde including Maio, São Tiago, Fogo, Brava, and the
    islets of Grande, Luis Carneiro, and Sapado.

INDIGENA. See: ASSIMILADO.

INDIGO. Indigo (Indigofera, Sp.) and urzella (Litmus
    roccella) are both plant dyes, originally from the Rio
    Nuno area on the Guinea coast, which have been ex-
    ports from Cape Verde. They were planted to help
    revive stagnant agriculture, but the commerce in these
    dyes was controlled by the British to the disadvantage
    of Cape Verdeans. While indigo and urzella were used
    to dye Cape Verdean textiles, especially panos, used in
    the slave trade, they never became significant cash crop
    exports, and today this role is largely taken over by
    coffee production. See: AGRICULTURE; PANOS.

                        - J -

JEWS. While there was not a formal Jewish synagogue in
    Guinea-Bissau or Cape Verde and a Jewish population is
    not currently active, historically there was a very defi-
    nite Jewish presence amongst early Cape Verdeans. In
    late 15th century Portugal Jews were sometimes known as
    Marannos or Judeus Segredos (Secret Jews), and there
    is reason to believe that Jews were a very large minor-
    ity, but when the Spanish and Portuguese crowns were
    merged from 1580 to 1640 Jews were expelled or fled
    elsewhere. The Portuguese Marannos were largely con-
    verted to Christianity and absorbed.
        In this context, Jews first came to the island of
    São Tiago as refugees from religious persecution during
    the Inquisition. They were shunned by the wider soci-
    ety of the islands at that time and they were confined
    to a separate ghetto-like community in Praia. During
    the early nineteenth century, Jews came to settle in the
    mountains of São Antão where there are still traces of
    their influx in the three Jewish cemeteries on that is-
    land and in the name of the village of Sinagoga. Some
    of the Jewish settlers migrated to Boa Vista, trading in
    pelts and hides. Jewish-derived surnames can be found
    amongst the inhabitants of these islands and elsewhere.
    See: LADINOS; LANÇADOS; RELIGION.

JOÃO II (ruled 1477, 1481-1495). Portuguese king during
    the later period of the Age of Maritime Exploration. He
    was the son of King Afonso V. During his reign, settlers

began arriving in the Cape Verde Islands.   Under João
II, chartmaking began in Lisbon, including the work of
Bartolomeu Columbus, brother of Christopher Columbus.
In 1484 João II turned down a request by Christopher
Columbus to finance further voyages after he had visited
the Guinea coast between 1482 and 1484.   Columbus
visited João II again in 1493 after his historic voyage
to "India" (the New World).   See: COLUMBUS, C.

JUVENTUDE AFRICANA AMILCAR CABRAL (JAAC).   See:
PIONEERS OF THE PARTY.

- K -

KANSALA (CANSALA).   See: GABU; FULA.

KUSSUNDE.   Kussunde is a traditional Balanta festivity that
is realized when agricultural harvests have been especially plentiful.   The entire village population participates
in ceremonial activities related to this festivity.   Special
dances and songs leading up to a religious ceremony are
performed repeatedly from October or November to February or March, when the rice is harvested and the festival begins.   The festival itself involves singing, drum-
ming and acrobatic dancing, an enormous meal in which
a variety of dishes are served, and a ceremonial plant-
ing of seeds.   The point of the ceremony is to gain the
favor of certain spirits, re-legitimizing the villagers'
acceptance by deceased ancestors and securing the op-
timum conditions for continued agricultural success.
Depressed crop outputs, migrations, and bombings of
rice fields by the Portuguese did not allow kussunde to
be carried out during the nationalist struggle, but the
ceremony was recommenced after independence, varying
in intensity and duration from year to year depending on
the output of each year's harvests.

- L -

LABERY, HENRI.   Founder of the UPG in 1957 which led to
his direct involvement of the founding of the FLGC in
1960.   Some elements of the FLGC appeared in 1961 as
FUL.   In 1962 Labery emerged as the head of FLING.

Labery is of Cape Verdean extraction and was an early associate of Amílcar Cabral. He went to schools in Lisbon but lived mainly in Guinea-Bissau. Labery's program was less clear than that of Cabral on ideological matters and was essentially concerned with the independence of Guinea. See: FLING.

LADINOS. This ethnic group constituted a portion of early migrants to the Cape Verde Islands. They may be remnants of some Sephardic Jews from the Iberian peninsula who at one time spoke an archaic form of Spanish. Exiles, out-groups such as the lançados, and political prisoners were often sent to Portuguese possessions in Africa and its offshore archipelagos. See: JEWS.

LANÇADOS. Portuguese settlers, including fugitives, known for having courage and initiative; also, half-caste traders living on or near African coastal communities who maintained semi-autonomous control of local coastal communities. They often had African wives from the local groups and were intermediaries or middlemen for the Portuguese or Cape Verdeans. Literally, out-caste. See: JEWS.

LANDUMAS. A very small Senegambian grouplet inhabiting the area immediately around the southern town of Catio.

LANGUAGES. According to the 1979 national census, 54.4 percent of the total population speak only one of the approximately 15 languages of Guinea-Bissau, while 45.6 percent are bilingual or multilingual. Of the latter group, 30 percent speak two languages, 12 percent are conversant in three languages, and three percent speak four or more languages.

This polyglot complexity of languages is tempered by the fact that almost half of the populace (44 percent) speak Crioulo, which serves as the lingua franca of the country. Crioulo is based essentially on a combined Portuguese morphology and African phonetic system with words borrowed from both sides. Although used mainly by the urban population for most of the colonial period, Crioulo developed on a more national basis during the nationalist struggle in order to facilitate intercommunication among the various ethnic groups, and it has continued to expand since independence. Crioulo is today the major language of discourse among both the general

population and the elite in urban areas, while its usage
in the rural areas varies from 18 percent in Gabu (where
Fula predominates) to 79 percent in Bolama on the coast.
Thus, while Portuguese is the official national language
and while official documents are usually composed in
Portuguese, it is Crioulo that is usually spoken within
government ministries and by party members. Crioulo
is the de facto dominant language in Bissau, and most
educated Guineans grew up speaking Crioulo before they
learned Portuguese.

Regarding the other principal languages, Balanta
is the second most widely spoken language (spoken by
24.5 percent of Guineans), followed by Fula (20.3%),
Portuguese (11.1%), Manding (10.1%), Mandjack (8.15%),
and Papel (7.2%). These percentages essentially reflect
the relative size of the respective ethnic groups, although
it is also the case that many Guineans of one ethnic
group have learned the language of others. Portuguese
is spoken almost exclusively by educated Guineans located
in and near the capital of Bissau and, to a lesser degree,
in Bafata, Bolama, Gabu, and other smaller semi-urban
centers. This reflects the fact that the Portuguese colonial population resided mostly in or near the center of
these urban areas and that the national educational system has not yet effectively disseminated Portuguese in
the countryside. See: NIGER-CONGO LANGUAGES.

LEGISLATIVE ASSEMBLY. The 130-member Legislative Assembly of Portugal provided for two representatives from
Cape Verde and one from Guinea-Bissau. In the two
colonies there were separate Legislative Assemblies replacing the former legislative councils. In Guinea-Bissau
the assembly consisted of 17 members: five elected representatives, three traditional chiefs, three administrative representatives, two commercial representatives, two
members from workers' organizations, and two members
representing "cultural and moral" concerns. In Cape
Verde there were 21 members of the assembly, expanded
from the 18-member council. The composition included:
11 representatives elected by vote, four administrative
appointees, two commercial representatives, two workers'
representatives, and two members representing "moral
and cultural" concerns. After 1971 both Guinea and
Cape Verde were designated as "Overseas Provinces" of
Portugal with subdivisions of concelhos (municipalities)

and civil parishes (administrative posts). In Guinea-Bissau a provision was made to have traditional ethnic group leaders meet in an annual Peoples' Congress, which had no real power.

LIGA DA GUINE. The first modern African voluntary association in Guinea-Bissau, this proto-nationalist formation emerged in 1911 under the leadership of Oliveira Dugu. The Portuguese government forced it to disband in 1915.

LITERATURE. The literature and folklore of Guinea-Bissau have three main sources. Cape Verdean and Crioulo culture; Portuguese culture; and a diversity of African sources. The deep Cape Verdean ties to Guinea-Bissau have helped result in the development of Crioulo as the lingua franca of Guinea-Bissau. Crioulo, particularly in Cape Verde, has rich traditions in literature, poetry, and music in such forms as the mornas and coladeras. Crioulo has incorporated African elements especially among the populations of badius, as seen in the batuko and funana. These, in turn, resonate back in Guinea-Bissau in many ways, but especially with those many Guineans of Cape Verdean extraction born or residing in Guinea, such as the following writers: Fausto Duarte, Terencio Anahory, João Alves das Neves, or Jorge Miranda Alfama.

European Portuguese residing in Guinea-Bissau were relatively few in number, but those who wrote usually used paternalistic or romanticized images of Africans as derived from a colonial psychology. An example of this may be found in the work of Fernanda de Castro.

The vast majority of Guineans belong to the Mande, Senegambian and Fula ethnic groups, which have great traditions in oral literature and narratives and, in some cases, written records that were kept in Arabic or in a European language. Some Portuguese ethnographers of Guinea have compiled and translated some of the traditional African literary sources. The most important example of modern literature by a Guinean of African origin is found in the works of poetry by António Batica Ferreira. See: BADIUS; BATUCO; CRIOULO; FERREIRA, A.; FUNANA.

LIVESTOCK. In both Guinea-Bissau and Cape Verde, the Portuguese paid only marginal attention to systematic livestock raising. The post-colonial governments have also not made significant attempts to develop animal husbandry for commercial purposes, although Guinea-Bissau has exported a small number of animal hides. Livestock raising is practiced extensively throughout the countryside in Guinea-Bissau for the purposes of domestic consumption and village market trading. National livestock totals in the early 1980s show approximately 220,000 cattle, 125,000 pigs, 140,000 goats, 60,000 sheep, 420,000 chickens, and 12,000 ducks. These figures have been typical for at least the last twenty years, although higher numbers of cattle have been known. While cattle may be found on at least a small scale virtually everywhere in the country, most of the cattle herding, and all of the large scale herding, is monopolized by the Fula groups in the north and east and some of the Beafada and Mandinga peoples. Among all groups, men are largely responsible for tending the cattle, while women usually raise the other livestock. See: AGRICULTURE.

- M -

MAC. See: MOVIMENTO ANTI-COLONIALISTA.

MAIO (15°10'N, 23°10'W). Sixth largest island (103.8 sq. mi.) in the Sotavento (leeward, southern) group of the Cape Verde archipelago. This relatively low (maximum altitude, 1,430 feet), sandy island lies just to the east of São Tiago. Maio has the two main towns of Vila do Maio and Santo António, but the population is small. The island was not effectively settled until the early 16th century, and its small economy was based on livestock and slave trading on the Guinea coast. As early as 1643, slave ships from New England (U.S.) traded at Maio. Trade in salt was also an important feature of the Maio economy until about 1850; salt was traded on the coast for slaves and to passing ships in exchange for manufactured goods.

MALFANTE, ANTONIO. Genoese merchant who visited Timbuktu in 1447 in pursuit of early Portuguese efforts to contact the Empire of Mali and establish commercial and diplomatic relations. See: CADAMOSTA; MALI.

MALI. Following the collapse of the Empire of Ghana, the
Empire of Mali entered its formative phase in the late
11th century. Mali's early capital was at Kangaba on
the Upper Niger River. Mali's economy was based on
trade, especially of slaves, and subsistence agriculture
of the Sudanic crops. The gold traded in Mali was
mainly from the Bambuk goldfields south of Niani and
out of Mali's military control and Islamic influence. Likewise, the source of ivory was mainly south of the Sahel,
but trade in ivory, gold and slaves was what built the
Sudanic states. The most important group of Mande
traders upon whom Mali depended were the Soninke-
derived Dyulas (sometimes known as Wangarawa), who
were instrumental in the Islamization of Mali. Islamic
conversion of the Malian ruling class and large numbers
of the farming people took place between the 11th and
13th centuries. Perhaps the first member of the Malian
ruling class to be converted was Barmandana Keita in
1050. Mali was very hierarchical in socio-political structure, which included nobility, soldiers, traders, artisan
castes and slaves.
        Mali is formally dated from 1230, when Sundiata
(Sundjata) and his general Maridiata defeated the Susu
leader Sumaguru at the battle of Kirina, thus ending
the Susu resurgence. Sundiata was the son of Nare
Famaghan, of the Keita dynasty of Mali (at Kangaba).
Earlier, Famaghan had been defeated by Sumagura in
the effort to reestablish the Empire of Ghana. Sundiata
ruled Mali from 1230 to 1255 and made Islam the state religion. Sundiata's son Mansa Uli (1255-1270) extended
the rule of Mali to the trade center at Gao. Under
Mansa Sakura (d. 1300) Tekrur was conquered in 1285.
According to the Arab historian Umari, Mansa Musa related to the Governor of Cairo that seafaring Malians
had actually ventured to the New World before 1312.
Under the rule of Mansa Muhammad (son of Qu) 200
ships carrying men and 200 carrying gold, water and supplies were sent. One of the ships returned, to be followed by another 1,000 filled with men and 1,000 with
supplies. These interesting reports have not been fully
substantiated.
        It was during the reign of Mansa Kankan Musa
(1312-1337) that Mali reached its greatest influence. In
1324-25 for example, Mansa Musa is reported to have
made a flamboyant pilgrimage to Mecca via Egypt with

an entourage of thousands of followers carrying gold
gifts of astonishing abundance. In the year of his return his soldiers occupied Dar Tichitt, Wallata and other
key trading centers. The following year Gao, the capital city of Songhai, and Timbuktu also came under the
armies of Mansa Musa. By 1375 Mali was noted on European maps even though Europeans had still not traveled
along the West African coast. At its peak, Mali included
the Mandingo kingdom of Gabu, in an area between the
upper Corubal and upper Cacheu Rivers, to the Gambia
River, then all the way to the Atlantic coast through
Wolof, Serer and Tukulor areas, northward up the coast
until just beyond the mouth of the Senegal River. At
this time Mali controlled Futa Jallon through the Dialonke
tributary chiefs and a lesser degree of control was exerted
in subduing rebellions in Tekrur.

The empire thrived through the late 14th and early
15th centuries by supplying as much as one sixteenth of
the entire world supply of gold. Arab travelers and
early historians visited Mali in 1352-53 and brought back
reports about its glories to northern Africa and Europe.
However, by the 15th century the fortunes of Mali had
gradually begun to decline. Tekrur and the Wolof provinces rebelled and regained their independence in the
early 15th century, and by 1433 Timbuktu had seceded.

The Portuguese, who were on the scene in the late
15th century and noted the state of hostility between
Mali and its neighbors, only wanted African products
and slaves and gave no aid to Mali. In 1473 Jenne was
lost to the empire, which prompted Mansa Mahmoud I of
Mali to send a message to King João II of Portugal re-
questing military aid against Fula and Songhai enemies.
The Portuguese still did not respond. By the 16th
century Mali's power had eroded even further, although
it is interesting to note that it continued to produce
more gold than the New World gold mines of the time.
In 1534 another request for aid was directed to Portugal's King João III, and ambassadors from Mali actually
traveled to Portugal. Needing slaves and war captives
and not wanting to back a loser, Portugal again declined
to provide any aid to Mali. This trend reached its cli-
max in 1546, when Songhai invaders sacked Niani, the
Malian capital, thereby bringing to an end this major
West African empire. See: BAMBARA; FUTA JALLON;
FUTA TORO; GABU; SONGHAI; SUSUS; TEKRUR.

MANDINGO (Manding, Mandinga, Malinke, Mali, Mande).
The Mandingo and related peoples of Guinea-Bissau are
representatives of the Nuclear Mande or Manding language family of the Niger-Congo linguistic stock. Manding is a principal language of Africa and is spoken in
one form or another in about nine West African countries
with as many as ten million speakers. As with many
West African languages, it is tonal with no uniformly
accepted written form.
   The Mandingo began to arrive in their present
distribution in the mid-13th century with the expansion
of the Empire of Mali, to which they are all related to
various degrees. However, even though Mali fell in
1546, the Mandingo kingdom of Gabu in Guinea-Bissau
continued until 1867. Before the consolidation and expansion of Gabu, many Senegambians such as the Papeis,
Manjacos and Brames were found in eastern Guinea-Bissau.
These groups assimilated a moderately hierarchical system of political administration from the intrusive Malians.
Other Senegambians such as the Balantes, Banhuns and
Beafadas were either driven west toward the coast or
were simply stranded as small groups within expanding
Gabu. Various Fula peoples became interspersed in
Gabu as cattle herders until the time when the Fula
themselves took over full control of Gabu in 1867.
   When the Portuguese arrived they called the language of the Mande peoples Mandunca, from which the
term "Mandingo" is derived. Throughout the centuries
of slaving, the Mandingos of Gabu had important trade
centers at Farim on the Cacheu River headwaters, at
Cacheu at the River's mouth, at Ziguinchor on the Casamance, and at Geba on the Geba River. These posts
permitted contact with Europeans (e.g., Portuguese,
French and English) and access to firearms in exchange
for war captives or slaves. The local Fula herdsmen
provided livestock, while the Mandingo farmers grew
the basic staples of the Sudanic food complex. In the
mid-19th century the Fula, or Futa Jallon, expanded
and brought an end to Mandingo dominance. By the
end of the century, after the Berlin Congress, Portuguese incursions to the interior were laying the groundwork for later colonial wars against the Mandingo. In
1900 the Mandingo formally submitted to Portuguese rule,
but the Oio branch showed continued resistance to Portuguese "pacification" in the campaigns of 1897, 1902,

and 1913. From 1913 to 1915 Portuguese Captain Teixeira
Pinto, known for his brutality and widespread destruction, was able to use Mandingo auxiliaries equipped with
modern weapons in "pacification" programs elsewhere in
Guinea-Bissau.

    Today the Mandingo people are still concentrated
around Gabu in the north and central areas, but there
are various clusters throughout the eastern and interior
regions. The Mandingo represent about 14 percent of
the total population of Guinea-Bissau. See: GABU;
MALI; PINTO.

MANJACO (Mandyako). Ethnic group of the Senegambian
    cultural stock, Atlantic subfamily of the Niger-Congo or
    Nigritic language group. The Manjacos show some very
    slight Islamization and some hierarchical organization
    which they may have acquired through contact with the
    Mandingos. The Manjacos are related to the Brame,
    Mancanha and Papei peoples. Their economy is based
    on shifting agriculture and rice cultivation. They are
    mainly concentrated in the area south of the Cacheu
    River and north of the Mansoa River. The Manjacos
    provided stiff and early resistance to Portuguese settle-
    ment between 1878-90 when they were among the first
    to try to halt the Portuguese penetration of the interior.
    They also fought between 1913-15 during the "pacifica-
    tion" campaigns of Teixeira Pinto. The 1950 population
    census identified 71,700 Manjacos (14.2 percent of the
    population); in 1960 their population was put at an esti-
    mated 80,000.

MANSOA, RIO (Mansoa River). The fourth longest river of
    Guinea-Bissau, the Mansoa courses about 120 miles from
    the coast and is navigable for at least two thirds of the
    way. Its route follows that of the Farim-Cacheu, which
    flows roughly parallel to and north of the Mansoa. The
    headwaters of the Mansoa are found to the east of Man-
    saba in the Farim concelho. The Mansoa was used as a
    corridor through the coastal swamps for trade to the
    interior.

MENDES, FRANCISCO (Chico Té) (1939-1978). Prime Minister
    of Guinea-Bissau. Mendes did not complete his formal
    education because he joined the PAIGC in 1960 at the
    age of 21. He was born in southern Guinea-Bissau in

the village of Enxude. From 1960 to 1962 Mendes was
the political commissioner at the PAIGC training program
in Conakry. From 1962 to 1963 he was assigned to under-
ground organizational work in the eastern town of Bafatá,
and from 1963 to 1964 he served as the political commissioner in the North Front. At the time of the first
PAIGC Congress in 1964, Mendes became a member of
the Political Bureau and in 1965 was appointed to the
War Council in the capacity of political commissioner.
From 1970 to 1971 his War Council responsibility was
military logistics. In 1972 Mendes was appointed to the
CEL, and following the independence of Guinea-Bissau
he became the Prime Minister of the Permanent Secretariat of the nation. Mendes was killed in an automo-
bile accident in Bafatá in July 1978. See: CEL; PAIGC.

MESTIÇOS. People of a "mixed" racial heritage and often
incorporated into middle-level administrative and economic
strata in the Portuguese colonial system. Crioulos of
Cape Verde are sometimes considered to be mestiços,
and those Cape Verdeans in Guinea-Bissau are likewise
in an ambiguous position since they may have connections to the slave and colonial systems but were born
and raised in Guinea. Such complex relations result in
continuing tension between those Guineans of African
heritage and those of mestiço or Crioulo origin. See:
LADINOS; LANÇADOS; TANGOMAUS.

MILLET. See: AGRICULTURE.

MINERALS. In March 1958 the Portuguese gave the American oil company ESSO (now Exxon) exclusive oil-
prospecting rights in Guinea-Bissau at an annual cost
of U.S. $250,000. The Portuguese received an addi-
tional $14 to $60 for each square kilometer where prospecting actually took place as well as a 12.5 percent tax
on production and a 50 percent tax on profits. In 1966
and in 1973 the contract between the Portuguese colonial
government and Esso Exploration was renewed and expanded to include other minerals. The revenue generated by this contract gave the Portuguese badly needed
financial support during the period of nationalist insurgency.
    In 1980, the IDA (World Bank) financed a loan of
$6.8 million for a 3,900-mile seismic survey along Guinea-

Bissau's coast, which was carried out by Digicon (U.S.)
in 1981. In 1983, ten data packages were purchased by
a consortium of Western oil companies for $4 million, and
a second series of offshore seismic studies was carried
out by Digicon with an additional $13.1 million IDA loan.
The state-run oil company, Petrominas, signed its first
exploration agreement with foreign oil companies (Canada,
England, and West Germany) in 1984.
    Petrominas also regulates mining and prospecting
in Guinea-Bissau. Total bauxite deposits are now said
to be 200 million tons (42-48 percent alumnia); phosphate
deposits were discovered in Cacheu and Oio Provinces in
1981, and gold has also been found. However, the
enormous investments needed to construct ports, rail-
road and other transport linkages for the mining and
processing of these minerals have thus far been considered too expensive. As a consequence, these mineral
resources remain virtually untapped.

MORANCA. Extended family grouping within villages in
    Guinea-Bissau, especially among the Balantes.

MOUVEMENT DE LIBERATION DE LA GUINEE "PORTUGAISE"
    ET DES ÎLES DU CAP VERT (MLGCV). This united
    front organization was based in Dakar and was consti-
    tuted primarily by the UPG of Henri Labery. The other
    two member organizations, the UDG and the UDCV,
    were of far less significance. The MLGCV joined with
    the UPA (União das Populações de Angola) in 1962 to
    form a front called the FACCP (Frente Africana Contra
    O Colonialismo Português). While little is known of the
    MLGCV, it is established that the UPA was receiving
    funds from the American Central Intelligence Agency
    (CIA) at the time and that the FACCP was set up to
    rival the more militant FRAIN, founded two years ear-
    lier. The MLGCV was a temporary affiliate of the
    PAIGC in 1960, and some reports suggest that Amílcar
    Cabral sought to establish unity with the MLGCV in
    1958 but soon realized it would be impossible to find a
    common program.

MOUVEMENT DE LIBERATION DES ÎLES DU CAP VERT
    (MLICV). The MLICV was formed in 1960 and immedi-
    ately joined the FLGC in the same year. Its role was
    very minor and represented little more than a paper

organization. The MLICV was based in Dakar and was
led by Mello e Castro. At times the MLICV called for
the liberation of the Cape Verde Islands by armed struggle, but this tactic and goal was only enunciated, not
practiced by the MLICV in the islands.

MOVIMENTO ANTI-COLONIALISTA (MAC). The MAC was
formed in Lisbon in 1957 by revolutionary intellectuals
from Portuguese African colonies. Thus the MAC was
the precursor of FRAIN, which started in 1960, and the
CONCP, which began in 1961. In effect, the unity
spawned in the MAC has persisted in the programs of
the PAIGC, FRELIMO, and the MPLA until the present
time.

MOVIMENTO DE LIBERTAÇÃO DA GUINE (MLG). The MLG
was headed by François Mendy Kankoila, who based
much of the organization on the Manjaco ethnic group
partly residing in Senegal. The MLG joined the RDAG
in 1961 to form the FLG, which joined FLING in 1962.
Mendy feared any loss of autonomy within FLING, to
which he gave only hesitating support, just as he had
to its predecessor, the FLGC. Neither the MLG nor
FLING had programs relating to the independence of
the Cape Verde Islands.
    In July 1961, while Amílcar Cabral was trying to
develop the FUL, Mendy launched attacks at Suzanna
and at a Varela hotel. These isolated acts confirm that
the MLG was the most militant member group of FLING.
As a result of the military efforts of the MLG in 1961,
the Portuguese staged a swift counterattack which resulted in the breaking of diplomatic relations between
Senegal and Portugal. Despite this event, the government of Senegal was lukewarm at best to the PAIGC and
preferred to support the MLG and, more broadly, the
FLING, which had some base of support with Senegalese
Manjacos and was anti-PAIGC. The MLG also sought to
divide Cape Verdean supporters from the PAIGC, and it
is alleged that it bribed PAIGC members to desert. The
MLG was dissolved in 1964.

MOVIMENTO DE LIBERTAÇÃO DA GUINE PORTUGUESA
(MLGP). The MLGP was one of the three component
groups which merged in 1960 to form the FLG, later
leading to FLING. See: FLING.

MOVIMENTO PARA INDEPENDÊNCIA NACIONAL DA GUINE
PORTUGUESA (MING). MING was founded in 1954 but
soon proved to be ineffective. However, MING was the
direct forerunner of the PAIGC, which was formed in
1956. MING was organized by Amílcar Cabral (who later
helped found the PAIGC) and by Henri Labery (who became a founder of the MPG). MING was formed clandestinely in Bissau by commercial workers and civil servants.
There was no reference to the Cape Verde Islands in its
initial program.

MUSA MOLO (?-1931). Musa Molo was the son of Alfa Molo
and the last effective king of the Fula state in Guinea-
Bissau. The son of Musa Molo, Cherno Bande (d.
1950s), acted as a Fula king afterward but with no real
power. When Alfa Molo died in 1881, he was succeeded
by his brother, Bakari Demba, but through continuous
intrigues and conspiracies Musa Molo became the king in
1893. During his reign Musa Molo sought to consolidate
and expand his rule to the northwest into the territory
of the south bank of the Gambia then controlled by Fode
Kaba, a Muslim soldier-cleric. Because Alfa Molo had
killed the father of Fode Kaba, the conflict was inherited
by both sons. Fode Kaba proved very intractable to
French and British attempts to curb the slave trade, and
in 1901, through a joint understanding and effort between
Musa Molo and the two European powers, Fode Kaba was
killed. In attempting to unify and expand Fula control,
Musa Molo suppressed a revolt by his brother Dikori,
and he frequently eliminated other contenders by assassination. As a result his rule generally was considered
ruthless. In the early 1900s he settled in Gambia, where
he was awarded a 500-pound annual stipend by the British. In 1919 he was exiled to Sierra Leone but returned
in 1923 to Gambia, where he died in 1931. After the
death of Musa Molo, the British appointed Cherno Bande
as the head of the Fula. Bande's real function was to
encourage local peanut production as an agent for the
British United Africa Company. See: ALFA MOLO;
FUTA JALLON; GABU.

- N -

NALUS (BAGAS). The Nalus are a Senegambian people who

are socio-politically characterized by petty chiefdoms which they developed as a result of notable Mandingo contact. They appeared on the coast in the 15th century and are mainly concentrated in the Susu area near the town of Catio. These rice cultivators are most closely related to the Bissago people. See: BISSAGOS; SUSU.

NHÔ LOBO. The lazy wolf of Cape Verdean folklore. A large part of the Crioulo oral tradition, Nhô Lobo stories have been passed down through the generations. At informal gatherings, a storyteller would repeat the Nhô Lobo stories, particularly for the children who would delight in their telling. Typically, the adventures of Nhô Lobo contain a lesson about life to be learned by the young listeners.

NIGER-CONGO LANGUAGES. This large family of African languages is also known by the term Nigritic or Congo-Kordofanian languages; the classification is subject to various interpretations and types of linguistic categories. In any case, the Niger-Congo languages include the West Atlantic and Senegambian stocks as well as the Mande languages which are spoken in Guinea-Bissau. Even the Fula languages, which also have Berber derivation, are essentially originated from the West Atlantic group of the Niger-Congo family. Aspects of contemporary Guinean culture which are rooted in the heritage of the Niger-Congo language family include the language of Crioulo, the badius of São Tiago and expressions specific to the production and exchange of pano textiles. See: BADIU; PANO; APPENDIX C.

NORTH ATLANTIC TREATY ORGANIZATION (NATO). At the conclusion of World War II, the United States proposed the creation of a military alliance of the capitalist nations of the North Atlantic. The pact came into effect on March 18, 1949, the same year in which Portugal joined. While areas to the south of the equator were officially out of NATO's jurisdiction, Portugal's membership permitted NATO to contribute significant military and economic aid to Portugal, thus directly assisting the Portuguese to carry out counterinsurgency wars in the Luso-African colonies.

Before 1958 Portugal spent 3-4 percent of GNP on

the military, a proportion similar to that spent by other
Western European nations on their armed forces; by 1964
Portugal's "defense" requirements had reached 8 percent
of its GNP.   In 1965 more than half of state revenues
went to the military.   Portugal was supported mainly by
West Germany and the United States through loans and
grants and by purchases of colonial products.

U.S. aid to Portugal through NATO measured in
the hundreds of millions of dollars.   Between 1949 and
1968 United States military aid to Portugal officially
reached $349 million, but this does not include other
bilateral agreements which aided Portugal's own hard-
pressed economy.   In 1972 alone, the United States
arranged financial assistance to Portugal of well over
$400 million.   The vast portion of Portuguese forces
committed to NATO were actually in Africa, while NATO
equipment, especially heavy artillery, armored vehicles
and aircraft, not to mention U.S.-trained counterinsurgency specialists, all figured importantly in Portugal's
prosecution of its wars in Africa from 1961 to 1974.

NOVA LAMEGO.   Town in eastern Guinea-Bissau formerly
known as Gabu before the advent of colonial rule.   Nova
Lamego is located in the Gabu circunscrição at 12°17'N,
14°13'W.   See: GABU; MANDE.

- O -

OIL PALM.   Oil-bearing palm fruits produce large amounts of
oil for use as a foodstuff and body lotion.   The oil-bearing
palm (Elaeis guineensis) is a major contributor to fats in
the diet of West Africans.   In addition, palm oil is an
important export commodity with various food and commercial purposes.   To a large degree the decline of the
slave trade relates to the rise in the "legitimate" trade
in palm oil for industrial and cosmetic uses.   The oil
palm is native to West Africa and is found especially in
the tropics.   In areas of less rainfall closer to the savanna regions, the oil palm is replaced by the shea-butter
tree (Butyrospermum parkii), also known as karite.

ORGANIZATION OF AFRICAN UNITY (OAU).   This first
modern Pan-African organization was formed on May 25,
1963, by the then independent African nations.   The

African Liberation Committee of the OAU sought to co-
ordinate political and military support for liberation
movements such as the PAIGC. From 1963 to 1967 the
OAU sought to unite FLING with the PAIGC to build a
broader and more moderate coalition. After 1967 it only
gave recognition to the PAIGC as the sole legitimate political expression of the peoples of Guinea-Bissau and
Cape Verde. The Republic of Guinea-Bissau became the
42nd member nation of the OAU when it joined in November 1973; the Republic of Cape Verde joined the OAU on
July 18, 1975.

OURI. Ancient African "store-and-capture" game derived
from Egypt in dynastic times. Ouri is considered to be
the evolutionary forerunner of backgammon. This game
is known by a wide variety of names and is now played
throughout the Middle East, everywhere on the African
continent, in the Caribbean, and by some Afro-American
populations. The game is more complex than checkers
but less complicated than chess and can be played with
two, three or four players. The object is to defensively
store your own markers (made of seeds, pebbles or buttons) while seizing the markers of your opponents in an
offensive "seeding" play. Ouri is played widely in Cape
Verde and Cape Verdean immigrant enclaves. A prized
possession is the family's hand-carved wooden ouri board.

- P -

PANO. A unique form of untailored textile which has been
produced for centuries. These panos are woven on a
narrow loom from cotton fiber grown on the Cape Verde
Islands and in various parts of Guinea-Bissau. The
particular colors and patterns employed vary according
to local and ethnic customs and available dyes. Six
strips (about six to seven inches each) are sewn together to make a wider cloth; this weaving technique is
of Mande origin and has become an integrated part of
cloth production through West Africa. In Cape Verde
panos are only blue and white, but African weavers
usually use more than two colors.

Panos are worn exclusively by women as a shawl
or waist sash as part of the traditional costume and for
folk dancing. Mothers also use panos to carry their
infants on their hips in a typically African manner.

Facing a relative scarcity of iron bars to exchange
in the slave trade, the panos came to be a measure of
value by the 16th century, when they were used widely
in barter exchange as elsewhere in Africa, such as the
rafia cloths of the Congo. By 1680 two high quality
panos were standardized in value as equal to one standard iron bar. In 1721 the Portuguese declared that
the trade in panos was illegal, carrying severe penalties,
in an effort to reassert the crown monopoly in trade and
to curb Guineans and Cape Verdeans from dealing in this
trade. Today, pano trade is widespread throughout
Guinea-Bissau, and Guinean pano traders commonly migrate temporarily to Senegal, Gambia, Guinea-Conakry
and elsewhere in order to exchange their goods and to
obtain needed materials. See: BATUCO; INDIGO.

PAICV (African Party for the Independence of Cape Verde).
This is the successor political party which rules in the
Republic of Cape Verde. Essentially the structure and
personnel are the same as that of the Cape Verdean
branch of the PAIGC, which preceded the PAICV. The
PAICV was formed in January 1981 following the November 1980 Bissau coup which toppled Luís Cabral as
President of Guinea-Bissau. Aristides Pereira, who had
been Secretary General of the PAIGC since Amílcar Cabral's death in 1973, became head of the PAICV and
President of Cape Verde. With the breach in party
policy and decision-making following the coup, the
PAICV in Cape Verde was renamed to symbolize its
separate path despite the years of effort to unify the
two nations, peoples, and parties under the single nationalist banner. Despite some initial mutual hostility,
both countries today maintain friendly, diplomatic relations. See: PAIGC.

PAIGC (African Party for the Independence of Guinea-Bissau
and Cape Verde). The PAIGC is the victorious nationalist organization formerly based in Guinea-Bissau and
Cape Verde which was founded clandestinely in Bissau
on September 19, 1956. The PAIGC was the organizational descendant of the MING, founded in 1954 by Henri
Labery and Amílcar Cabral. Labery later went on to
form FLING, a small but persistent rival to the PAIGC,
while Amílcar Cabral and his associates founded and remained with the PAIGC. The main difference between
the MING and the PAIGC arose over whether to include

independence for the Cape Verde Islands, which was
favored by the PAIGC but not the MING. Also, there
were more craftsmen and manual workers in the PAIGC
than in the MING. As the PAIGC began to grow it attracted some port and transport workers who later helped
to organize the National Union of Guinea Workers (UNTG)
in 1961. In 1958, with a membership of only about fifty
people, the PAIGC and these workers helped to organize
a wave of nationalist strikes.

The independence of Guinea-Conakry in 1958 helped
stimulate an effort by the PAIGC to hold a nationalist-
oriented strike of the Pijiguiti dockworkers in Bissau on
August 3, 1959. To counter nationalist demands and
labor militance, Portuguese soldiers and armed settlers
reacted with twenty minutes of gunfire, killing fifty pro-
testors and wounding about a hundred strikers. Subsequently, 21 people were convicted of subversion by the
colonial authorities. In September 1959 the PAIGC General Secretariat was moved to Conakry, and in the following year the Portuguese began a more serious effort
at arrests and repression of the PAIGC. From December
1960 to September 1961 the PAIGC responded with an
agitational program calling for a peaceful end to colonial
rule. PAIGC members distributed some 14,000 tracts and
wrote two open letters to the Portuguese people as well
as sending various documentation to the United Nations
with the same appeal. April 1961 saw the creation of the
CONCP in Casablanca, with the PAIGC playing a leading
role in this organization which linked the struggle in
Guinea and Cape Verde to those initiated in Angola and
Mozambique. Toward the end of 1961, the PAIGC determined that a course based on direct armed action
would be the only realistic approach to bring national
independence. In order to block this move, the Portuguese secret police arrested Rafael Barbosa in March
1962, the same month in which the PAIGC staged an
abortive attack on Praia in the Cape Verde Islands. In
June and July the PAIGC responded again with acts of
sabotage inside Guinea-Bissau. This escalation soon put
Bissau under martial law, with as many as 2,000 suspected activists arrested while Portuguese military strength
reached about 10,000 soldiers.

The years from 1959 to 1963 had been devoted to
carefully building a hierarchical party structure of groups
and sections united into 13 zones and six regions so that

all activities could be closely coordinated. In January
1963 the movement entered a new phase of protracted
armed struggle when it launched a series of attacks in
the southern regions of the country. By July 1963 the
PAIGC had opened a second front of military activity in
northern Guinea-Bissau. In November of that year,
Portugal made a feeble effort to disguise the colonial
status of Guinea-Bissau with a special decree from Lisbon stating that Guinea-Bissau had become an "overseas
province," hence an integral part of Portugal. This was
a case of too little too late, and the PAIGC continued to
consolidate its gains to such a degree that on February
13-17, 1964, the first Party Congress was held in the
liberated zones in the southern front at Cassaca. Some
of the notable actions taken at this Congress included
(1) an enlargement of the Central Committee from 30 to
65 members; (2) the establishment of seven departments:
armed forces, foreign affairs, cadre control, training
and information, security, economy and finance, and mass
organizations; and (3) the formation of the Peoples Revolutionary Armed Forces (FARP) as well as Peoples' Stores,
and a decision to expand medical and educational services.

     In April 1964 the PAIGC engaged the Portuguese
in an intensive military confrontation on the large south
coastal island of Como. This 65-day offensive forced the
Portuguese to withdraw 3,000 troops after losing hundreds.
By 1965 approximately half of the countryside was under
PAIGC control even though the Portuguese soldiers now
numbered about 25,000. From 1965 to 1966 there was
something of a military standoff until, in the later part
of 1966, the PAIGC reintensified its efforts to gain the
initiative, particularly in the newly opened eastern front
which included parts of the former northern and southern
regions. The December 1966 reorganization of FARP
helped to restore momentum to the struggle. Military
headway accounted for political gains at the OAU, which
now gave its full support to the PAIGC in 1967, thus
abandoning efforts to reconcile FLING with the PAIGC.
Other accomplishments of the PAIGC in that year included
the start of the Party's Rádio Libertação and the restructuring of the original seven departments of the Central
Committee by reducing them to five: control, security,
foreign relations, national reconstruction, and internal
organization and orientation. In 1968 the main thrust
was consolidation of the political organization and

strengthening of the infrastructure in the liberated
zones. On February 19, 1968, the PAIGC military
forces stunned the Portuguese occupation forces by attacking the Bissalanca International Airport at Bissau.
By February 1969 the Portuguese were forced out of
Medina Boé in the south, thus giving the FARP units
of the PAIGC a much broader area of entry. Throughout 1969 and 1970 more notable military and political
reverses were suffered by the Portuguese despite their
claims of 614 PAIGC dead in 1969 and 895 killed in 1970.

    In Rome on July 1, 1970, Amílcar Cabral and
leaders of FRELIMO from Mozambique and the MPLA from
Angola were given an audience with the Pope. As Portugal is a strongly Catholic nation, the Portuguese ruling class was enraged at this diplomatic victory for the
liberation forces. In a futile and frustrated gesture on
November 22, 1970, a Portuguese raiding party from
Bissau invaded the neighboring capital city of Conakry
with the intention of overthrowing the government of
Sekou Touré and killing the leading members of the
PAIGC who then had offices based in that city. The
abortive invasion failed after bloody fighting but served
to underscore the frantic efforts by the Portuguese to
halt the spread of PAIGC control and influence. The
Portuguese made another effort in the early 1970s to
halt the PAIGC with the introduction of General Spínola's
"Better Guinea" program, which proclaimed certain mini-
mal reforms. The PAIGC responded in 1971 by carrying
out even bolder attacks by rocket and light artillery
against the towns of Farim, Bafatá, and Bissau. The
Portuguese claimed 1,257 PAIGC dead in 1971, the highest such statistic for the war, which served to indicate
the heightened intensity of the fighting. Formal revisions of the Portuguese Constitution in 1971 and the
Overseas Organic Law of 1972 gave still more formal
autonomy to the "overseas provinces" of Guinea and
Cape Verde, but the pace set by the PAIGC was now
running out of the grasp of the Lisbon authorities.

    New anti-aircraft guns and small but effective
surface-to-air missiles from the Soviet Union permitted
the PAIGC to open competition for the air space over
Guinea-Bissau, which had formerly been the exclusive
domain of Portuguese helicopter gunships and deadly
napalm and white phosphorus dropped by fighter-
bombers. The PAIGC began to bring down two or three

enemy aircraft each month. In April 1972 a unique mission of the United Nations visited the liberated zones, and the 848th session of the U.N. Decolonization Committee recognized the PAIGC as the only effective movement operating inside Guinea-Bissau. The observations and recognition of the Special Mission were endorsed by the 27th session of the United Nations General Assembly later in the same year, representing a major diplomatic triumph for the PAIGC's long effort to isolate and discredit Portuguese colonial rule. In August 1972 another first occurred with elections in the liberated zones for 273 regional commissioners and 99 representatives to the PAIGC's Peoples' National Assembly, which met in late 1973. In an address delivered in the United States, Amílcar Cabral announced that the PAIGC would soon declare national independence for Guinea-Bissau, but on January 20, 1973, this towering African nationalist and revolutionary philosopher was assassinated in Conakry in an intricate plot to take over the PAIGC and protect certain strategic interests of the Portuguese. The conspiracy, which had been well organized, used PAIGC dissident elements, FLING partisans, and logistic and intelligence support from the Portuguese. While the loss was sharply felt, the organization that Amílcar Cabral had carefully built went on to greater achievements. In May 1973 "Operation Amílcar Cabral" resulted in the seizure of Guiledge, a large fortified base near the southern frontier. This was possible, in part, because of the introduction of the new anti-aircraft weapons, but especially because of the collective resolve of the PAIGC military organization to redress the loss of its Secretary General.

From July 18-22, 1973, the PAIGC held its second Party Congress at Boé which elected Aristides Pereira as the new Secretary General; made certain revisions in the proposed Constitution; enlarged the Supreme Committee of the Struggle (CSL) from 81 to 85 members; and created a Permanent Commission of the Executive Committee. This new formation was headed by A. Pereira, with the Deputy Secretary General being Luís Cabral, and the two other members consisting of Francisco Mendes and João Vieira. The July Congress applied the last official touches to the preparations for the September 23-24, 1973, historic meeting of the First Peoples' National Assembly, which formally proclaimed the Declaration of

State, adopted the constitution, and elected the executive organs of the state including Luís Cabral as the president of the 15-member Council of State, eight state commissioners (Ministers), and eight sub-commissioners of state (Deputy Ministers). Immediately scores of nations around the world recognized the new republic, and by early October 1973 diplomatic recognition had been extended by 61 nations even though Portuguese troops still occupied the major towns.

Elsewhere in Africa, especially in Mozambique, liberation movements were showing comparable gains, and it was increasingly clear that the end was near for Portuguese colonialism. On April 25, 1974, the Portuguese Armed Forces Movement (MFA) overthrew the colonial, fascist regime of Prime Minister Caetano and made General Spínola, recently returned from Guinea-Bissau, the new President of Portugal. The leader of the Portuguese Socialist Party, Mario Soares, met with Aristides Pereira on May 15, 1974, and negotiations for full independence were initiated. By July 27, Portugal officially stated that it was prepared to grant independence, and the final details were determined in accords reached in meetings held in Algiers in August. On September 4, the first representatives of the Executive Committee of the Struggle (CEL) entered Bissau and on September 10, Portugal gave de jure recognition to the new Republic of Guinea-Bissau. Luís Cabral and Aristides Pereira officially entered Bissau on October 19, 1974.

Meanwhile, in Cape Verde, matters were more complicated, as the PAIGC had had a different history and had not engaged in any sustained armed struggle but had concentrated on clandestine political organizing. A number of rival Cape Verdean groups emerged, and a climate of uneasiness prevailed through late September and into October until it was made clear in discussions, negotiations, demonstrations and a general strike that the PAIGC was to be the sovereign political party in the islands. On December 18, 1974, a transitional government was formed from members of the PAIGC and the MFA. In early 1975 relations between Portugal and Guinea-Bissau became strained over financial matters, and the PAIGC nationalized the Portuguese Overseas National Bank. In this context of instability, the moribund FLING movement was prompted to make another attempt at bringing down the PAIGC in a poorly planned

coup d'état on March 21. The apparatus of the new
state became more fully engaged with the April 28-May 6
Popular National Assembly, held for the first time in
Bissau, and with the first meeting of the PNA since the
Declaration of State in the southern forests a year earlier. On June 30, 1975, there was an election for representatives to the Cape Verdean Peoples' National Assembly, and with this act the islands became the independent
Republic of Cape Verde on July 5, 1975. However,
since the PAIGC program called for unity between the
sister republics there were already many agreements
which united the two lands in commerce, transport, education, and communication. Most importantly, the PAIGC
was the ruling party in both countries although there
were two separate national assemblies.

Notable events in 1976 as a result of PAIGC policy
included the creation of the Guinean peso to replace the
Portuguese escudo on February 28 and the Second Session of the Popular National Assembly from April 22 to
May 3 as well as visits to Bissau from President Samora
Machel of Mozambique and President Agostino Neto of
Angola. Both Machel and Neto have since died. On November 15-20, 1977, the PAIGC held its Third Party Con-
gress. After some delays and about a year of meticulous
and widespread preparation, the central themes of this
major event were unity between Guinea-Bissau and Cape
Verde, economic development and political consolidation.
The former Permanent Secretariat of four members was
enlarged to eight; the CSL was increased to 90 members;
and the new CEL was expanded from 24 to 26 members.
The four new members of the Permanent Secretariat were
Pedro Pires, Umaro Djalo, Constantino Teixeira, and
Abilio Duarte. The new thrust of the PAIGC was to
form a vanguard political party which would organize,
dynamize, and mobilize the peoples of Guinea-Bissau and
Cape Verde.

Thus, after independence, the PAIGC successfully
consolidated power in Bissau and devoted itself to building the new post-colonial state. But by concentrating so
intensely on state construction in Bissau, the party began to neglect its links to the countryside, and the con-
nection between the PAIGC leadership and its peasant
supporters became increasingly tenuous. At the same
time, despite a genuine and largely successful effort to
balance party cadres from Guinea-Bissau and Cape Verde,

it was clear that Cape Verdeans predominated in the
upper levels of the party and state apparatuses while
Guineans filled out the middle and lower ranks. Between
1979 and 1980, sensing rising dissension among Guinean
party cadres and soldiers, President Cabral (who is of
Cape Verdean extraction) appointed key party and army
leadership posts to Cape Verdeans he knew to be loyal
to him. This move further served to frustrate Guinean
soldiers and cadres. In addition, the drought of 1977-
1980 had resulted in rice shortages throughout the country which could not be relieved by the economically
handicapped government and which thereby intensified
popular dissatisfaction with Cabral's rule. When in November 1980 Cabral attempted to modify the Constitution
in order to enhance his legal powers over the party and
armed forces, the final straw had been drawn, and all
these factors coalesced in the shape of a decisive and
successful army coup. The coup was carried out on
November 14, 1980, by the armed forces of Guinea-
Bissau, overthrowing the regime of President Luís Cabral, who was arrested and later exiled. After the coup,
many Cape Verdeans were ousted from the highest party
and government posts, and the new party and military
leadership was all Guinean.

The coup was virtually bloodless; only two deaths
occurred, both of Cabral supporters who resisted capture
by the army. A nine-member Revolutionary Council,
which included Commander João Nino Vieira as President,
eight military men, and one civilian, was formed to take
charge of the country, serving as its highest decision-
making organ and replacing the civilian-dominated Council of State. During the 1981 Extraordinary Party Congress, the PAIGC's Supreme Council of the Struggle
(CSL) was replaced by a newly formed sixteen-member
Politburo, and a 51-member Central Committee replaced
the former Executive Council of the Struggle (CEL). In
1984 the military-dominated Revolutionary Council was itself replaced by a reconstituted 15-member Council of
State, evenly divided between army officers and state
officials and presided over by President Vieira; it has
served as the nation's most powerful political organ since
that time.

Since the 1980 coup, the republics of Guinea-Bissau
and Cape Verde have been separated. The PAIGC is no
longer considered the ruling party of the Cape Verde

Islands, and the high level of unity which existed in the
immediate post-independence period has been sharply
limited. Both the PAIGC of Guinea-Bissau and the
PAICV of Cape Verde claim the political and ideological
legacy of Amílcar Cabral as their own, and they both
assert that they adhere to his basic political principles.
See: CABRAL, A.; CABRAL, L.; CEL; CSL; FLING;
MING; PAICV; POPULAR NATIONAL ASSEMBLY; SPINOLA,
A.; VIEIRA, J.

PEANUTS. See: AGRICULTURE.

PEOPLES' STORES. See: ARMAZENS DO POVO.

PEREIRA, ARISTIDES MARIA (1924-). A founder of the
PAIGC, Pereira is President of the Republic of Cape
Verde. Born on Boa Vista island in the Cape Verde
archipelago, he attended liceu before receiving specialized training as a radio-telegraph technician. Pereira
was one of the organizers of the Pijiguiti strike in 1959,
and he worked in Bissau as the Chief of Telecommunica-
tions until 1960, when he left for security reasons to
join Amílcar Cabral in Conakry. As a member of the Political Bureau of the Central Committee, he organized in
Bissau and other urban areas. In 1964 Pereira was the
joint Secretary General of the PAIGC and a member of
the War Council after 1965. Following organizational
restructuring in 1970, Pereira became a member of the
Permanent Commission of the Executive Committee for
the Struggle (CEL) with Luís Cabral and Amílcar Cabral.
In this position his chief responsibilities were security
and control, and foreign affairs. Before the death of
Amílcar Cabral, Pereira was the Deputy Secretary General of the PAIGC, but after Cabral's death, Pereira became the top political officer of the PAIGC. Subsequent
to the independence of Cape Verde on July 5, 1975,
Pereira also became President of the Republic of Cape
Verde. In this position he has maintained his commit-
ment to socialism and nonalignment and has often been a
mediator among the nonaligned nations. Following the
1980 coup in Bissau, Pereira helped to form the new
PAICV, of which he became its top officer, and he has
retained his post as President of Cape Verde. See:
PAICV; PAIGC.

PEREIRA, CARMEN (1937-). Born in Guinea-Bissau as a
lawyer's daughter, she joined the PAIGC in 1962. Her
husband Umaru Djallo was a party activist, and when he
fled to avoid arrest she stayed in Bissau to work as a
dressmaker and to care for her children. In 1964 she
also left Guinea-Bissau to engage in fulltime party assignments. In 1965 Pereira headed a nurses' training
delegation to the Soviet Union. As the liberation war
progressed, she became the Political Commissioner for
the entire south front. She was the only woman in the
24-member Executive Committee of the Struggle (CEL)
and was the head of the Women's Commission. Pereira
is the Second Vice-President of the Peoples National
Assembly and one of the 15 members of the Council of
State. See: WOMEN.

PEREIRA, DUARTE PACHECO. Portuguese explorer who
accompanied Azambuja in the founding of El Mina in 1482.
He was at El Mina when Cão sailed south from that fort.
He was rescued by Bartolomeu Dias on returning from
the Cape of Good Hope. Pereira later sailed to India.
Between 1505 and 1508 he wrote Esmeraldo de Sita Orbis,
a book of sea routes, in which he described details of
the West African coast. He also provided an account of
coastal trade and environment. In 1506 he wrote about
active trade in gold, ivory and slaves at Arguim at a
period when Lisbon eagerly backed slavery. See:
AZAMBUJA; CÃO; DIAS.

PERMANENT SECRETARIAT. Within the CEL and the War
Council was found the Permanent Secretariat of the
PAIGC. Until 1973 the Permanent Secretariat was composed of Amílcar Cabral, the PAIGC Secretary General
in charge of political and military affairs; Aristides
Pereira, Vice Secretary General responsible for economy
and security; and Luís Cabral, responsible for national
reconstruction, health and education. After the 1973
death of Amílcar Cabral and the subsequent Second Party
Congress, the secretariat changed its name to the Permanent Commission and was expanded by one member to
include João Bernardo Vieira and Francisco Mendes as
Secretaries of the Commission. Since independence the
commission has been expanded again to eight members.
The commission handles the day-to-day decisions of the
government. See: CABRAL, A.; CABRAL, L.; CEL;
CSL; MENDES, F.; PAIGC; PEREIRA, A.; VIEIRA, J.

PETROFINA and SOCIEDADE ANONIMA DE REFINAÇÃO DE
    PETROLEOS (SACOR). These two oil companies have
    been the main suppliers of petrochemical products in
    Guinea-Bissau and Cape Verde. Both Petrofina and
    SACOR are affiliated with the Portuguese Overseas Na-
    tional Bank (BNU) and thus are linked to CUF through
    political alliances and interlocking directorates. See:
    BNU; CUF.

PIJIGUITI. Site of the dockyards in Bissau at the broad
    estuary of the Geba River. In one of the first tests of
    strength of the PAIGC, a dockworkers' strike was or-
    ganized to express labor grievances and nationalist senti-
    ments. On August 3, 1959, the colonial government re-
    sponded with gunfire, killing 50 and wounding 180. The
    Pijiguiti Massacre, as it came to be known, was the turn-
    ing point for the PAIGC, which then determined that a
    course of armed struggle would be the only way to
    achieve independence.

PINTO, MAJOR TEIXEIRA (1876-1917). Pinto is best known
    for a series of four brutal "pacification" campaigns car-
    ried out in Guinea-Bissau between 1913 and 1915 during
    which he used field action, sea coverage, foreign mer-
    cenaries, collaboration with Fula chiefs, and modern
    arms to destroy villages of the Bissagos, Papeis, Balan-
    tas, Felupes, Manjacos, and Oincas. His military force
    was commanded by six European officers and about 400
    Africans, especially Fulas and Mandingos who had long
    made war on the coastal peoples. Before the campaigns,
    Pinto traveled in the Oio River area disguised as a
    French trader to spy on some Mandingo groups. He
    was aided in this intelligence work and the campaigns
    themselves by the Senegalese chief and adventurer Abdul
    Indjai. At the conclusion of the campaigns, the town of
    Canchungo was named Teixeira Pinto, but the former
    name was restored after independence in 1974. In 1915
    a public outcry in Lisbon against the excesses of Pinto
    forced an inquiry into his brutal administration. In
    World War I Pinto was stationed in Mozambique, where
    he was killed in combat.

PIONEERS OF THE PARTY (PP). The youth organ of the
    PAIGC during the period of armed struggle and after-
    ward seeks to educate children under the leadership of
    the party. Especially after 1972, the PP acted as the

political branch of the education policy in the liberated
areas and at the Pilot School. Children aged 10-15
were eligible to join and participate under the slogan of
"Study, Work, Struggle." While the PP was relatively
small in the beginning, it was very active at PAIGC
boarding schools (semi-internatos) and carefully cultivated youth leadership qualities within Guinea and through
participation at international youth forums and festivals.
"Blufo," the PP newsletter, was published more or less
quarterly and featured educational, cultural, and political articles and puzzles.

Since September 12, 1974, the main work of youth
organizing is channeled through Juventude Africana
Amílcar Cabral (JAAC), which has chapters in most
schools or neighborhoods. JAAC has concentrated its
efforts on national reconstruction projects such as drug
eradication, literacy campaigns, and general youth improvement. It is particularly targeted for work among
urban youth who had not been integrated into the structures of the liberated zones during the war. In the
early to mid-1980s, however, JAAC expanded the focus
of its activities to include political organizing in the
rural areas and mobilization for agricultural production.
The Pioneers remains the principal party organization
for very young children and is now mainly concerned
with cultural activities.

PIRES, GENERAL PEDRO VERONA RODRIGUES. During the
war (1963-1974) Pires was the Commander of the southern
frontier region and member of the War Council. Pires is
also a leading member of the Executive Committee of the
Struggle (CEL). After the independence of Cape Verde,
Pires became the first PAIGC Prime Minister. He is currently the Chairman of the Cape Verdean National Committee of the PAICV.

POLICIA INTERNACIONAL E DE DEFESA DO ESTADO (PIDE).
The major Portuguese fascist secret police organization.
As early as 1957 PIDE arrived in Guinea-Bissau to assist
in intelligence, counterinsurgency operations, and widespread arrests of suspected nationalists. In 1961 an additional organ, the Polícia de Segurança Pública (PSP)
was introduced to curb the anti-fascist and anti-colonial
movements in Portugal and the African colonies. In the
early 1970s PIDE had received such notoriety that it

changed its name to the Direção Geral de Segurança
(DGS). In 1971 a contingent of 105 PIDE agents arrived in Cape Verde to infiltrate and break up under-
ground operatives of the PAIGC. PIDE/DGS was disbanded after the Portuguese revolution of 1974. See:
TARRAFAL.

POPULAR NATIONAL ASSEMBLY. The Popular National
Assembly was first constituted in the liberated territories in August-October 1972, one year before the end
of the independence struggle. Voters chose 273 regional
councillors who in turn elected 91 of their peers to
serve as National Assembly deputies. Voting procedures
consisted of yes/no balloting for a single candidate who
had been selected previously by the party in the course
of discussions with the local populace. The 91 elected
deputies combined with 21 deputies appointed by the
party, five representatives of the national worker's
union, and three representatives of the party youth
group to form a Popular National Assembly of 120 delegates. The second national elections were held after
independence, in December 1976, using the same electoral procedures as the 1972 voting. However, membership for this second National Assembly was expanded to
147, with two thirds being elected from among the regional councillors and one third selected by the party.
This assembly was disbanded immediately following the
1980 coup d'état, but a third National Assembly, with
150 members, was formed through elections held in
March-April 1984.
    The Popular National Assembly is officially the
highest political body in Guinea-Bissau, but in fact,
from 1972 to 1979 and since 1984, it convened and continues to meet only once a year for several days. The
assembly does not wield substantial political power,
most of which lies with the top-level party and state
structures. See: PAIGC.

POPULATION. See: DEMOGRAPHY.

PORTUGAL. In 1143 Portugal broke from the Spanish monarchy and established its own king under Dom Henriques.
From 1384 to 1910 the House of Aviz (Knights of Calatra-
va) was the royal ruling lineage. Between 1420 and 1470
Portugal was absolute master of the great oceans, and

Prince Henry's significant navigational achievements and
exploration of Africa took place under the influence of
João II. The coast of Guinea was reached in the 1440s
and the Cape Verde Islands in the 1460s. In West Africa, Portugal's dominance declined rather quickly in de-
ference to the French, English, and Dutch through the
following centuries, but Portugal continued to be a major
supplier of slaves to the New World, especially to Brazil
until the late 19th century. From 1580 to 1640 Portugal
was returned to the Spanish crown, but this had relatively little effect on those African territories with links
to Portugal.

In 1656 private Cape Verdean tax collection was
eliminated, and a direct officer of the Portuguese crown
was appointed to strengthen Portugal's hold on the islands and along the African coast. Throughout the 17th
and 18th centuries, Guinea-Bissau and Cape Verde continued to supply slaves to the New World through services of Luso-African traders (lançados) on the coast.
In 1836 Portugal officially ended the slave trade, which
nevertheless continued for several more decades. In
1868 England yielded its claims on Bolama to Portugal,
and following the 1884-85 Berlin Congress, Portugal and
France agreed on the southern and northern borders of
Guinea-Bissau. Portugal was virtually bankrupt at the
close of the 19th century, and the monarchy sought dic-
tatorial powers to make certain reforms. Following the
assassination of the king and crown prince in 1907 and
a popular revolt in 1910, the monarchy was abolished
and the House of Bragança was banished. The Republican government prevailed from 1911 until May 28, 1926,
when a military putsch overthrew the democratic republic
and installed a fascist government. A case of resistance
to the fascist government is recorded in Guinea-Bissau
in 1931 with a month-long revolt of deported politicians
taking place in Bolama and Bissau.

From 1886 to the 1930s, the Portuguese conducted
military expeditions of "pacification" against most of the
coastal peoples of Guinea-Bissau. In 1963 the nationalist
movement in Guinea, led by the PAIGC, began a protracted armed struggle which paralleled those in Angola
and Mozambique. As a result of these wars and economic
and political contradictions inside Portugal, the Armed
Forces Movement (MFA) ended Portuguese fascism and
colonialism on April 25, 1974, and restored a multiparty

democracy. The change in power in Lisbon was largely
a consequence of the wars in Africa, and thus it led
directly to the independence of Guinea-Bissau on September 24, 1974, and of Cape Verde on July 5, 1975.
See: CAETANO; FOREIGN AFFAIRS; PAIGC; SALAZAR;
SPINOLA.

PORTUGUESE. See: LANGUAGES.

- R -

RASSEMBLEMENT DEMOCRATIQUE AFRICAIN DE LA GUINEE
(RDAG). This Malinke-oriented, Senegalese-based organization led to the formation of the FLG when it
merged with the MLG in 1961. In 1962 the FLG joined
with FLING.

REGULO. Paramount African chief, often incorporated into
the system of colonial administration (regimen do indíge-
nato). To a limited extent regulos inherited their positions, but usually they were appointed by the colonial
administration as civil servants, soldiers, police of inter-
preters and were paid token salaries. They carried out
the highly unpopular tasks of tax collection and labor
recruitment and were assisted by brutal armed police.

RELIGION. An estimated 60 to 65 percent of the population
are animists, including Balante, Papei, Mandjaco, Diola,
Bijagos, Nalus, Brames, and others. Most of the remainder are Muslim or have syncretic versions of Islam
and African traditional religions, including the Fula,
Mandingo, Beafada, Susu, and several smaller groups.
The Islamized sector is mostly located in the cattle-
growing interior, while the animist groups are found
more along the coastal regions and in certain parts of
the interior. The Fula jihads were important in the introduction of Islam into Guinea-Bissau, especially after
the fall of Gabu.
     There are a small number of Protestants and Catho-
lics, but these are largely urban residents who had
been exposed to Portuguese and Italian missionaries
during the colonial period. Those Guineans of Cape
Verdean extraction are almost all Catholics, as are most
Cape Verdeans.

The government is particularly tolerant of religious diversity in Guinea and takes care to allocate time on the national radio and in the national newspaper to a broad sector of religious offerings and regular programs. For example, on Sunday morning Catholic church services are often broadcast live on the radio, and one frequently finds large sections of the newspapers devoted to cultural or historical presentation of animist or Islamic traditions and practices. Unlike its largely Islamic neighbors to the north (Senegal, Mali, and Mauritania) or a number of Catholic, Protestant, or animist dominated West African nations to the south, no single religious group possesses special political or social power, so that all religions are treated in a balanced manner. Social or educational programs that are independent of the government, such as Islamic schools, animist ceremonies, Protestant or Catholic churches, and missionary societies, are generally allowed to operate freely and without interference from the state. See: FULA; JEWS.

RESISTANCE. In terms of Luso-African relations, the first known example of resistance to European encroachment in Guinea-Bissau took place in 1447 in the Bissagos Islands with the death of Nuno Tristão and several of his crew. Since the Portuguese had already begun slaving further up the western coast, we may assume that slave trading may have been part of Tristão's intended mission. One may therefore date the African resistance to this first arrival of hostile European forces. The second period of resistance was directed against the slave system, which was already well developed by the late 1600s. Slavery instigated competition between regions and peoples who desired to obtain firearms, economic goods and power, a competition which benefited European mercantile and industrial interests as well as African traders and some chiefs. This was a period of intense resistance against the slave wars between African peoples that had been inspired by the lançados and the Portuguese. Previous forms of African slavery in the region lacked both the scale and numbers of the European plantation and chattel slave systems.

After slavery ended slowly in the course of the 19th century, attempts at territorial conquest were launched by the Portuguese and their local allies, who had no regular control of the interior before this period. Some

of the first serious challenges to this incursion were the
1825 and 1826 mutinies at Cacheu. In 1843 the Portuguese initiated a program of writing coercive treaties
with the people of Guinea-Bissau because slavery and
slave wars had become obsolete and increasing amounts
of labor were required for palm oil, coconut oil, rice,
and peanut production. Treaties were signed with the
Mandingo at Badora, the Banhun and Cobianas. From
1844 to 1845 numerous local uprisings took place as
Portuguese encroachment increased and resulted in
treaties with other Banhun sections and some of the
peoples in the vicinity of Cacheu. Relative peace prevailed until the Bissau mutiny and the Geba trader revolt of 1853. In 1860 risings against the Portuguese
were reported throughout the country, while some
neighboring Dyulas and Balantas submitted to French
rule. However, the heroic and protracted guerrilla
war of Samori Touré from 1860 to 1870 in Guinea-Conakry
presented the neighboring French with extremely effective opposition to their authority. Some Bissagos leaders relented to colonial authority in 1861, and the state
of Gabu fell in 1867 to the Fula, who were not opposed
by the Portuguese since Portugal's authority did not yet
reach the interior. When the Fulas had finally destroyed
the Mandingo state of Gabu, it was only a matter of time
before they were brought under colonial rule.

In January 1871 the Portuguese governor of Guinea-
Bissau was assassinated by an African grumetta, and an
uprising in the following month had to be vigorously
suppressed. The year of 1874 saw the offensive of the
Mandingo--Foday Kabba in the Casamance region--and
provoked considerable anxiety in colonial ruling circles.
From 1878 to 1880, the Portuguese organized a series of
attacks against the Felupes and Manjacos, and from 1880
to 1882 military expeditions were waged against the
Beafadas and some Fula sections. The campaigns were
followed by two years (1883-5) of war against the Balantas and against the Papeis in 1884, and in 1886 attacks
were made against both Papeis and Beafadas. These
events reflect the intensification of warfare against African peoples just before and, especially, after the infamous Berlin Congress of 1884-5 which arranged for the
Eruopean powers to partition the entire African continent
for open colonial rule. European claims were accepted
on the basis of whether the colonial power could demonstrate

effective control of the territories which it claimed as its own. Thus the "scramble" for Africa was an episode of frenetic military activity and oppression. Some of the acephalous Balantas fell under a Portuguese military campaign in 1891, and from that date until 1894 there were virtually continuous revolts of Papeis, who blocked the Cacheu river. In November of 1894 a rising in Bissau shook the colonial government, and from 1891 to 1910 rebellions of other Papeis, Balantas and Malinkes were quite frequent. At the close of the century in 1897, colonial troops were dispatched against the Oincas section of the Mandingo stock.

A number of Fula chiefs formally submitted to colonial rule in 1900, but two reinforced Portuguese columns were needed to put down a Fula insurgency in 1907-8. After this period the cephalous Fula remained effectively controlled as the Portuguese placed the Fula chiefs on colonial retainers. At the turn of the century, expeditions in the interior were again waged against the Mandingos and Beafadas while fierce resistance continued among coastal peoples, especially on Canhabaque Island and in the Bissagos archipelago. In 1901 and 1903 forces returned to the Felupes and in 1902 against the Oincas. The Cacheu Papeis resumed their river blockade in 1904, which instigated several Portuguese counterattacks. In 1906 the Bissagos people on Formosa Island revolted and were put down. The Beafada chief Infali Sonco revolted in the Geba region in 1907, thus cutting off Bafata and Gabu, in the interior, from coastal Bissau. This year also witnessed strong Fula revolts and a rising in the Cuor region. The unending nature of these revolts and resistance provoked the brutal military "pacification" campaigns of 1912-15 led by Major Teixeira Pinto and met by the fierce opposition of the Balantas, Oincas, the Papeis of the Bissau region, the Manjacos of Xuro-Caixo and again on the Bissagos Islands. Supposed submission of the Balantas of Mansoa was achieved in 1914 and of the Bissau Papeis in 1916. Other Balanta, Felupe, and Papei groups were also attacked in 1915. By the end of that year the colonial government underwent reorganization, and Major Pinto's crimes were investigated and exposed by a colonial commission which admitted his excesses.

Another form of colonial oppression that provoked resistance came in the form of a myriad of taxes such as those for houses, burials, palm trees, livestock, censuses, and a host of fines for various infractions of colonial law. Consequently, tax revolts broke out among the Bissagos and Papeis in 1917; while they were declared defeated in 1918, they organized other tax revolts in 1924 and 1925. Another wave of widespread tax resistance re-emerged in the 1930s, especially with the 1936 revolt of the Papeis.

In short, the earliest hostility shown to Guineans by Tristão in 1447 ended with his death at the hands of the Bissagos people. Throughout the intervening centuries between "discovery" and the Berlin Congress, African resistance consisted of fighting the slave-raiders, either African or European, and from 1825 to 1936 a decade did not go by without revolts, uprisings, mutinies, or other acts of resistance. In 1956 the multi-ethnic and tightly disciplined PAIGC nationalist movement was organized and continued the heritage of opposition to colonial rule. The 1959 workers' strike at the Pijiguiti docks in Bissau was reminiscent of the Papeis revolts in that region, and the savage repression of the strike recalled the campaigns of Major Pinto. Subsequently, the PAIGC leadership determined that a well-organized, protracted, armed guerrilla struggle would be the only course which would lead to national independence. During the war (1963-1974) most of the various ethnic groups were unified by basic goals and were not susceptible to the divide-and-rule tactics of the colonial military force. Much still needs to be researched and written about African resistance movements, but these events attest to a long history of opposition. See: BISSAU; CACHEU; GABU; PAIGC, PIJIGUITI; PINTO, T.; SLAVERY; TRISTÃO; REBELADOS; and specific ethnic groups.

RICE (Arroz, Mancarra). Rice (Oryza, Sp.) has long been an important staple in the Sudanic regions, along with millet and sorghum. Both wild and cultivated forms may be found. Oryza breviligulata is considered to be the wild ancestor of Oryza glaberrima, which is cultivated on the Middle Niger by Mande peoples and by the coastal Senegambians. O. glaberrima may have been cultivated as early as 1500 BC. Oryza sativa is a much later Asiatic species which is widely cultivated today. Although regions as far north as Tekrur grew rice in the Middle Ages, it is grown more extensively as one moves

south and toward the coastal wetlands inhabited by
Mandingos, Balantas or Susus. In these wetter areas
rice is the only suitable starch crop. Approximately 30
percent of the total cultivated acreage in Guinea-Bissau
is devoted to rice farming. Rice is generally not grown
in Cape Verde because of inadequate water and inappro-
priate soils.

Before the war, the colonial economy exported over
100,000 tons of rice annually. In the mid 1960s rice production fell to about 30,000 tons per year, and by 1967
production reached only 19,000 tons. As the liberated
zones expanded, the Portuguese were finally forced to
begin to import rice. Just before independence in 1974,
the colonial imports to Guinea-Bissau reached 35,000 tons.
By 1976 a small rice surplus was already being generated
and imports had been substantially reduced, but the
1977-1980 drought devastated rice production, forcing
the government to rely increasingly on rice imports,
which amounted to 13,000 tons in 1977, 30,000 tons in
1978, and 82,000 tons for 1981. Normal rainfall in 1982
and 1983 lessened rice imports in those years, but
drought in 1983 forced the government to import 42,000
tons.

This tall grass is grown as a grain crop in flooded
paddies with extensive irrigation canals throughout much
of coastal Guinea-Bissau. In some wet delta areas, rice
may grow wild and other species of upland rice will
grow on dry land like other grains. Rice is commonly
served with chicken or fish and with a palm oil sauce.
Rice is known as malu in Balanta, malo in the Mande
languages, maro in Fula, and as umane in Manjaco or
Brame. See: AGRICULTURE; ARMAZENS DO POVO;
ECONOMICS (TRADE); MILLET; SORGHUM.

- S -

SACOR. See: PETROFINA.

SALAZAR, DR. ANTONIO DE OLIVEIRA (1889-July 27, 1970).
Prime Minister of Portugal from 1932 to 1968, when he
was incapacitated by a stroke. Following the overthrow
of the Portuguese crown and instability of the Republican
government, Salazar became Prime Minister in 1932. In
1933 Salazar and Dr. Marcelo Caetano were the chief

architects of the absolutist Portuguese constitution and
of the "Estado Novo" policy which maintained fascist
control of industry, labor, and the press in Portugal
and its African colonies. See: CAETANO; PORTUGAL.

SALUM (SALOUM). See: FUTA TORO; GABU.

SAMA KOLI (Kelemankoto Baa Saane). The first king of the
Mandingo state of Gabu, Sama Koli was either the son or
grandson of Tiramakhan Traore, a general of Sundiata of
Mali. Sama Koli married Nyaaling of Bonje and continued
the matrilineal line of Gabu kings with his son Saarafa
Nyaaling Jeenung, grandson Kuntinka Sira Bula Jeenung
and great-grandson Saamanka Dala Jeenung.

SÃO TIAGO. (15°5'N, 23°38'W). The largest island (328.5
sq. mi.) of the Cape Verdean archipelago. This island
is rocky and mountainous with some permanent sources
of fresh water. The present capital is Praia (25,000
population) on a beach from which it draws its name.
The former capital was at Ribeira Grande, now known
as the ruined city and fort of Cidade Velha.
  São Tiago was first noted by the Portuguese in
May 1460 by the ships of António de Noli and Diogo
Gomes. Within a few years the first permanent settlers
from the Algarve went to São Tiago and founded Ribeira
Grande as the first capital. A commerce in slaves grew
to develop the island and to become an important export
from the islands. By 1466 settlers and lançados traded
freely in African slaves and products, soon resulting in
the Crioulo population characteristic of the islands. As
a consequence of this long history, São Tiago is considered to have the most African population of the
archipelago. As an example of the scale of the trade,
between 1514 and 1516 almost 3,000 slaves were landed
at Ribeira Grande. The relative prosperity and autonomy of the captaincies on São Tiago resulted, in 1564,
in the rule reverting back to the Portuguese crown for
fuller monopolization of island and coastal trade. This
oscillation and competition between island autonomy and
colonial monopolies remained a central theme through
most of Cape Verdean history.
  Ribeira Grande reached a permanent population of
1,500 by 1572 although the interior town of Santa Cata-
rina was already larger by this time. The slave plantation

system was deeply entrenched, with a few dozen "whites" and "mestiços" in full authority using a small group of "free Africans" as overseers who regulated some 90 percent of the population of African slaves.

Aside from the central role of slavery in the economy, São Tiago was also a common stopping place for fresh water for ships going to South America or down the West African coast. Local production of livestock and plant dyes (urzella and indigo) was sometimes important, and São Tiago horses were much prized for riding and in slave exchange. It is ironic in this regard that Matthew Perry's anti-slavery "African Squadron" was based in São Tiago in the 1850s and 1850s.

SÃO TOME. Discovered in 1471, the "Cacão Islands" of São Tomé and Príncipe in the Gulf of Guinea were administered as one colony by the Portuguese. who set up a plantation economy on the two islands using laborers contracted primarily from Angola and the Cape Verde Islands. Conditions on these coffee- and cacao-producing islands were so poor and the means of recruitment so coercive that the labor migrations to São Tomé and Príncipe did not differ much from the system of slavery which preceded it. With the official emancipation of slavery in 1869, the contract labor system emerged and continued well into the 1950s. Forced emigration to "the south," as the Crioulos termed it, was a desperate and despised alternative to the threat of famine. The laborers worked exhausting hours, routinely suffering the abuses of torture, beatings, and chains. Disease was also rampant. This form of recruitment was prohibited in the Barlavento islands so that the bulk of the workers came from the badius of São Tiago and from Fogo. See: BADIUS; BIKER.

SARACOTES (Saracole). This very small group of the Soninke branch of the Mande stock may be found in small clusters between Gabu (Nova Lamego) and Bafata.

SENEGAL. See: FOREIGN AFFAIRS.

SENEGAMBIANS. This large cluster of the coastal Atlantic stock of the Niger-Congo (or Nigritic) peoples includes virtually all of those people of Guinea-Bissau who are of neither Fula nor Manding (Mande) stocks. The Sene-

gambians include the Balantas, Banyuns, Biafadas,
Bijagos, Diolas, Nalus, Papeis, Brams, Manjacos, Serer,
Wolof and Mankanyas. Senegambian peoples were found
as far north as Mauritania until the 11th-century expansion of the Berbers, when they were pushed back southward. They extended eastward through most of present
Guinea-Bissau until they were pushed westward toward
the coast by the creation of Gabu and the secondary
Mande kingdoms. The southward spread of the Senegambians was similarly checked by the consolidation of
power in the Guinea highlands at Futa Jallon and with
the expansion of the Susu kingdom. At an early date
the Senegambians incorporated the Sundanic food complex and added rice farming as a local specialty. The
numerous small Senegambian groups represent the shat-
tering effect from the pressure on all sides by more
powerful centralized hierarchies. The Senegambians are
either acephalous or only slightly centralized and are
mostly animist except for more recent Islamization among
some. Sometimes Senegambians are known as "Semi-
Bantu" peoples of the Guinea Littoral.

SERER. This Senegambian group is mainly located in southeastern Senegal but is related to the Diola of Guinea-
Bissau and to the small, stratified Sine and Salum kingdoms which were tributary states of Mali between the
13th and 15th centuries. See: TEKRUR; MALI (Mande).

SILLA, ERNESTINA (?-1973). This exemplary woman militant
and CSL member of the PAIGC was born in the Tombali
region of Guinea-Bissau. As a teenager in 1962, she
contacted the Party and then left home to dedicate herself to the nationalist struggle. Her main assignment
was public health work in the liberated zones of the
northern region. Her active work did not prevent her
from marrying and raising children. On January 31,
1973, she was killed in combat on the Farim River on
the way to the funeral for Amílcar Cabral in neighboring
Guinea-Conakry. In March 1977 the "Titina" Silla Juice
Factory was opened in Bolama in her memory. See:
WOMEN.

SIN (Sine). See: FUTA TORO; GABU.

SINTRA, PEDRO DA. Portuguese navigator who sailed off
the coast of Guinea-Bissau in 1460 to reach Sierra Leone.

SLAVERY. The Portuguese first captured African slaves in the early 1440s on the Moroccan coast. Until the discovery of the New World, slaves were used as domestic servants in Europe and on sugar plantations in the various Atlantic islands. Slavery in Cape Verde was at its height between 1475 and 1575. Guinea-Bissau did not use the slave plantation system to any degree but was chiefly an exporter. During the 15th century the export of slaves from Africa did not exceed 1,000 annually and was a uniquely Portuguese enterprise that occurred only on the upper reaches of the West African coast. The slave trade in the 16th century was still monopolized by Portugal, but Spanish and English slavers began to erode the monopoly in the late 16th century. Cape Verdeans and lançados (coastal middlemen) were directly involved in the trade along the coast, which depended upon slave wars waged in the interior. Cape Verdean panos (textiles), horses and salt were brought from the islands to trade along the coast, while the majority of African slaves were brought from Guinea and Senegambia. The pace of slaving increased through the century, reaching a height of some 5,000 slaves annually by the 1570s. Most of these slaves went to the New World, especially to the Caribbean and to Brazil, although a small trickle still went to the Cape Verde Islands and to Europe.

Through the 17th century the Portuguese slave trade in Senegambia and Guinea-Bissau declined in both absolute and relative terms. More European powers were involved and Portuguese slavers became more active in Angola and Mozambique. In the first half of the 17th century the portion of slaves from Guinea and Senegambia fell to about 6 percent of the total number of slaves from Africa, where it had been as much as 75 percent in the century before. Likewise, the number of slaves fell from previous highs of about 5,000 per year to an average of 650 per year. The earlier figures related to the various wars of the autonomous state of Gabu in Guinea-Bissau which generated large numbers of slaves for trade and export. In the 17th century Gabu became less dynamic and more stable, thus slowing the production of slave captives.

The early 17th century saw renewed efforts by other European powers to engage in West African slavery; the real heyday of competitive and aggressive slaving had

begun. The English Royal African Company averaged
some 10,000 slaves each year in the area between Senegal and Sierra Leone in the late 17th century, but this
large figure represented only 12 percent of their total
slave trade from Africa at the time. At about the same
period two Cape Verdean companies were established as
slave trade monopolies at Cacheu in Guinea-Bissau. With
a marked growth in the New World plantation system, the
demand was high and insecurity prevailed among peoples
of the coast and the interior as all of the major Sudanic
states in the West African savanna had come to an end.
The portion of slaving done by Portuguese vessels or
with Portuguese traders continued to fall. Indeed, the
coastal lançados and Dyula traders had almost free reign
on trading because of virtual anarchy of slave commerce
at this time. Slaves were being drawn from peoples located further within the interior as the various Fula
wars generated a high degree of insecurity in the 18th
century. In 1753 a Brazilian slave trade company was
given monopoly rights at Bissau to acquire slaves for
the Brazilian states of Maranhão and Grão Pará. This
accounted for a resurgence of slaving in Guinea-Bissau,
as slave exports rose to average some 700 per year in
the late 18th century. Many of these slaves were generated from the incessant wars between the Mandingo state
of Gabu and the Fula people of Labé Province of Futa
Jallon.
      The early 19th century saw the start of European
abolition of slavery when it was realized that a cash
economy (rather than slave barter) and industrial exports on a massive scale would be served better by
"free labor," workers who could purchase European
goods and enter a system of colonial taxation in which
unpaid slaves could not "participate." The wage-slave
system began to cut away at the older system of chattel
slavery. As a poor European nation, Portugal was slow
to make this transition, and slavery lingered on into the
19th century. To a limited extent there was even some
slight increase in the slave trade at this time in Guinea-
Bissau as the abolition and anti-slavery patrols created
a relative scarcity of the slave supply, thus temporarily
forcing an increased demand. At this point the decentralized coastal peoples were again raided, but as the
century wore on there were larger numbers of slaves
from the Mandingo-related peoples when the Fulas

continued to press their attacks on Gabu in eastern
Guinea-Bissau. The Brazilian slave company still kept
its monopoly in Bissau, from which they took the vast
portion of their slaves, but the annual numbers had
fallen to only a few hundred per year. Despite the
rather rapid spread of the abolition movement, Portugal
was more often in violation of restrictions and agreements
to limit the trade.

The independence of Brazil from Portugal in 1822
and the Emancipation Proclamation in the United States
in 1863 provided a formal basis for the sharp decline
and ultimate extinction of the trade in Guinea-Bissau by
the third quarter of the 19th century. At the close of
the 19th century and into most of the 20th century of
open Portuguese colonialism, a system of contract labor
replaced slavery, although the life of a "contratado" was
only a slight improvement, as wages were pitifully low
and the conditions of employment were most oppressive.
The contract labor system was particularly important to
the economy of Cape Verde, which has long had great
difficulty in supporting its own population by island
agriculture because of prolonged droughts, gross colonial mismanagement, and backward systems of land
ownership. Some Africans enjoyed short-term, personal
benefits from the slave trade, but the protracted brutality associated with this commerce in human beings
certainly stands as one of the most exploitative and in-
human epochs in human history. Indeed, few Europeans
in Europe or in the New World benefitted from slavery
either; not only was there chronic insecurity and anxiety
under the slave system, but only the small European
class of slave owners and traders were the true "bene-
ficiaries" of this launching of the great African diaspora.
See: AFRICA SQUADRON; BISSAU; CACHEU; GOMES,
D.; GONÇALVES, A.; HAWKINS, J.; LANÇADOS; PANOS;
SÃO TIAGO; SÃO TOME; TRISTÃO, N.

SOCIEDADE ANONIMA DE REFINAÇÃO DE PETROLEOS. See:
PETROFINA.

SONGHAI. Songhai was a major Sudanic state and became
dominant on the Middle Niger after the slow disintegra-
tion of Mali, although Songhai had been first established
as a small Niger River state in 1504. Sonni Ali Ber (b.
1443?-d. 1492) is considered to be the founder of the

Empire of Songhai as a result of his military campaigns
in the 1460s which led to the capture of Timbuktu in
1469. Timbuktu had already fallen away from Mali in
1433 when it was seized by Tuareg invaders. Jenne also
fell to Songhai after a long siege in 1473. The reign of
Songhai was punctuated by military conflict with the Fula,
who put up strong resistance. In 1492 Sunni Ali was
replaced by his Soninke general, Askia Muhammad, who
had a colorful reign until 1528. In 1496-8 Askia Muhammad undertook a celebrated pilgrimage <u>haji</u> to Mecca, and
in 1512 he carried out military expeditions against Coli
Tenguella (I). Niani, a capital town of Mali, fell to
Songhai in 1546, but in 1591 the Askia dynasty of
Songhai came to an end with the conquest by Moroccan
troops. The influence of Songhai was not as directly
felt in Guinea-Bissau as in Mali, but it did have the effect of pushing various ethnic groups toward the coast
and disrupting those already living along the coastal
areas. <u>See</u>: MALI; TEKRUR; TENGUELLA.

SONINKE. The Soninke are members of the Nuclear Mande
    stock of the Niger-Congo language family, but they
    speak a distinct Manding language. While the Soninke
    are found in eastern Senegal and Western Mali, they are
    related to the Susu and Dyula of Guinea-Bissau. The
    most notable achievement of the Soninke people is their
    founding of the Sudanic empire of Ghana (literally, in
    Soninke, "war chief"). The Soninke include a mixture
    from the Malinke, Fulani, Bambara and especially the
    Berber people. The Soninke, who received Islam from
    the neighboring Tukulor, have both class stratification
    and traditional hierarchies of nobility. In 990 AD the
    Empire of Ghana seized Awdoghast and established its
    maximum control of trans-Saharan trade. By 1054 the
    Almoravids captured Awdoghast from Ghana, and in 1076
    the sometime capital of Ghana at Kumbi Saleh also fell to
    the Almoravids. The Dyula branch of the Soninke was
    central in the trade and Islamization of the Upper and
    Middle Niger, which led to the formation of the state of
    Mali. During the rule of Askia Mohammad (1493-1529)
    in the Empire of Songhai, the Soninke scholar, Moham-
    mad Kati, lived in Timbuktu and wrote the important
    <u>Tarikh al-Fettash</u>. <u>See</u>: DYULA; MALI; SUSUS;
    TEKRUR.

SPINOLA, GENERAL ANTONIO SEBASTIÃO RIBEIRO DE
(April 11, 1910-). Born in Estremoz, Portugal,
Spînola received a strict military education and was a
noted horseman. As his family was close to the ruling
circles of the Portuguese government and the powerful
Champalimand banking group, he was long a prominent
military officer. In the Second World War, Spînola was
invited by Hitler to inspect conquered areas of the
Soviet Union and is reported to have visited the German
Sixth Army during its unsuccessful attempt to seize
Stalingrad. Spînola was the commander of the Portuguese army in Guinea-Bissau during the nationalist war
of the PAIGC. In his book, Portugal E O Futuro, he
outlined a plan whereby Portugal could maintain its relationship with its African colonies.

SUSUS (Sossos, Sosos). This Mande derived group is found
in the extreme south of Guinea-Bissau's coastal areas
and in adjacent Guinea-Conakry. In Guinea-Bissau they
are concentrated around Catio and Cacine. The Susus
are related to the Dyulas and Soninke, who were the
chief founders of the Empire of Ghana. With the fall of
Kumbi Saleh (the capital of Ghana near Walata) in 1076,
the Susu branch of the Soninke fled to the south, away
from the Almoravids. In the flight to the south, the
Susus spread the main crops of the Sudanic agricultural
complex to new areas. Later, on the coast and in the
coastal interior of today's Guinea-Conakry, the Islamized
paramount chiefs blocked further southward expansion of
the Senegambians. In about 1200 one Susu state called
Kaniaga emerged and was also to gain enough strength
to reconquer Kumbi Saleh in 1203, thus ruling southern
Soninke groups and northern Malinkes. The head of
this Susu state was Sumaguru (Soumaora, Sumawuru),
Kante (Konteh) of a Tekrur dynasty. Sumanguru's rule
at Kumbi Saleh was considered harsh and oppressive and
helped to precipitate the final decline of ancient Ghana.
In 1230 Sumaguru extended his empire with the conquest
of Kangaba, near the important Wangara gold mines which
he ruled along with Diara as Susu states. During his
rule he killed eleven of the local Mandingo kings, spar-
ing the life of only one, a cripple named Sundiata Keita,
who was later to become the powerful founder of the
major state of Mali. Even before the actual defeat of
Sumaguru, the growing trade at Walata had already
eclipsed that of Kumbi Saleh.

Further expansion of the Susu states was halted
by the growth of Mali under Sundiata. At the battle of
Kirina in 1235, Sundiata's forces defeated the army of
Sumuguru. By 1240 Sundiata occupied the remaining
remnants of Ghana and founded the Keita dynasty of
Mali. The Susus moved back south to Futa Jallon where
they stayed until the period of the Fula jihads in the
late 18th century, which reduced them to slaves or drove
them to the coast of Guinea-Conakry and southern Guinea-
Bissau. On the coast the Susus acquired local customs
and, to a certain extent, brought the Islam they had ob-
tained from Futa Jallon. Today the coastal Susu play an
important role in commerce. See: FUTA JALLON; MALI.

- T -

TABANCA COMMITTEES. These committees, formed by the
PAIGC in villages throughout the liberated zones during
the nationalist struggle, served to link the party with
the peasantry. Since independence, an estimated 3,600
tabanca committees have been established throughout most
of the countryside as well as in urban neighborhoods.
They are theoretically each composed of three men and
two women who are elected by the local population, and
their official responsibilities include tax collection, helping to implement health programs, monitoring outsiders,
and arranging meetings between party officials and villagers. In practice the committees vary greatly, but
very few include women members, many consist of just
one or two village leaders, and difficulties in communication and transport between the countryside and the
Bissau-based PAIGC have prevented the committees from
carrying out their duties in many cases.
In Cape Verde, the term "tabanca" refers to aspects of the musical and folklife of the badius.

TANDAS. This tiny concentration of Senegambian people is
found to the northeast of Gadamael near the southern
frontier with Guinea-Conakry.

TANGOMAUS. Meaning "tattooed men," they were African
slavers who were middlemen for the Portuguese and
acculturated to the lançado lifestyle. See: LANÇADOS.

TARRAFAL. A notorious political prison located on the

northern end of São Tiago in the Cape Verde archipelago.
This prison camp was established during the Portuguese
fascist era in 1936 to house Communist Party members
and their sympathizers opposed to the rule of Salazar.
As the nationalist wars began, the camp was filled with
Africans as well. Tarrafal had a particularly nasty
reputation for torture, brutality, and death. Its extremely isolated location made escape virtually impossible.
In 1971 more than 100 PIDE agents arrived in Cape Verde
to infiltrate and arrest the PAIGC membership. Nationa-
alists were confined at the Tarrafal <u>concelho</u> prison or
the work camp of Chão Bom. Although politically important, the prison staff consisted of about a dozen guards
and administrators. <u>See</u>: POLICIA INTERNACIONAL.

TEKRUR. One of the earliest Islamized states of the western
Sudan from which the Fulus of Guinea-Bissau have originated. Tekrur appeared at or about the time of ancient
Ghana, as early as the 3rd century A.D. and certainly
no later than the 6th century. The Tukulor peoples of
Tekrur (Senegal) actively competed with Ghana for control of trans-Saharan trade. The Tukulor and the Fula,
to whom they are related, are members of the Atlantic
subfamily of the Niger-Congo language stock. Tekrur
was based on a trading and bureaucratic superstructure
built from traditional settled village political systems and
subsistence agriculture. In the 8th and 9th centuries
Tekrur experienced significant growth, and until the
end of the 10th century Tekrur was a fully autonomous
state on the middle Senegal River valley and was about
the equal of Ghana. However, in 990 A.D. Ghana conquered the Berber trade center at Awdoghast and then
forced Tekrur into a tributary status.

   Between the late 10th century and the mid-11th
century Islamized Berber traders entered Tekrur, where
they settled, married local women, and acquired slaves.
The admixture of Berber and Tukulor elements resulted
in the emergence of the Fula peoples, who spread throughout most of the sub-Saharan Sahel and savanna regions.
The sedentary farmers and traders of Tukulor stock became devout Muslims, while the cattle-herding Fula resulting from the Berber-Tukulor merger were somewhat
less Islamized, although they had a more North African
appearance. When the Almoravids sought to restore
their control of the trade lost to Ghana and avenge

their loss of Awdoghast, the leaders of Tekrur allied
with them to aid in the defeat of Ghana in 1076, thus
permitting Tekrur to return to its independent status
until the late 13th century, when it became a tributary
state of expanding Mali. The Islamic traveler and historian Al-Idrisi visited Tekrur in 1153-54 and described
it as a place of active trade. During its height, Tekrur
was linked to Marrakesh by an overland trade route
about 200 miles inland from the Atlantic coast.

Although the first Moslems of Tekrur were traders
and their slaves, the 11th century saw the incorporation
of Islam as the court religion of the Tekrur ruling class.
Many neighboring and subordinated peoples remained
animists and even anti-Islamic, including some of the
early cattle-herding Fulas. The formative empire of
Mali was first converted to Islam at a later period than
Tekrur; this is generally considered to have occurred
in 1050, when Barmandana of Mali accepted this faith
and established the Keita dynasty. In fact, Islam was
spread to and through Mali by Dyula peoples (a Soninke
group) who conducted east-west trade from Tekrur under the Denianke dynastic line. This east-west trade
became especially important in the 12th and 13th centuries, when the Empire of Mali (1230-1546) experienced
its greatest growth. A new Soninke ruling class came
to power in Tekrur in about 1250, briefly permitting
Tekrur to control Senegal until 1285, when it was brought
under the authority of the Malian ruler Sakura. Tekrur
was only under the direct control of Mali until 1350, when
the Malian representatives were deposed by the Wolof,
thus taking this state beyond the frontiers of Mali once
again. Tekrur, or more properly, Futa Toro, regained
independent status in 1520 at the time of Coli Tenguella
(II); the line he established endured until 1893, when
Tekrur was subjugated by the French. See: DIALONKE;
DYULAS, FULA; FULA TORO; FUTA JALLON; MALI;
SENEGAMBIANS; TENGUELLA, COLI.

TENGUELLA, COLI or KOOLI (Teengala, Tengela, Temala).
Fula leaders of the same name who led the Fula occupation of Futa Toro and Futa Jallon in the late 15th and
early portions of the 16th centuries. Apparently the
senior Coli Tenguella came from Termes, Mauritania, at
the end of an early period of Fula migration. In the
1490s he defeated most Senegalese Wolof and portions of

western Mali, thereby establishing the Denianke (Denaanke)
dynasty (1490s-1775) in the Futa Toro plateau of Senegal.
Once he and his followers occupied the fertile flood plain
of the Senegal River, he was proclaimed as the Sitatigui
(leader of the way) of the Futa Toro Denianke. The
existence of Futa Toro cut the western trade and communication links of the Empire of Mali, which had become important to the Portuguese as a source of gold
and slaves.

The visit of a Portuguese emissary of King João II
in about 1494 prompted Mali's Mansa (Emperor) Mamudi I
to complain about the attacks of Tenguella. Conflict was
inevitable over such a strategic piece of territory, and
Coli Tenguella was finally forced out of Futa Toro and
retreated to the southern plateau region of Futa Jallon
in Guinea-Conakry, which was also part of a generally
declining Malian Empire. Futa Jallon had been occupied
by Dialonke, Susa, and various Manding peoples as well
as by some Fula before Coli Tenguella arrived, but it
was he who merged these various peoples into a new
state which was opposed to the rule of Mali. Although
one of his several wives was from the Malian ruling class,
Tenguella organized local resistance to Mali in the late
15th century and in 1510 he and his followers returned
to Futa Toro. In 1511 Coli Tenguella was killed in a
battle at Amar by a general of Askia Muhammad of Songhai. The Fula warrior bands had acculturated and assimilated sufficient Manding (Malinke) peoples, including
some from Guinea-Bissau, that the Denianke dynasty
continued until 1775.

Tenguella's son, Coli Tenguella (II), led the army
after his father's death and continued to re-establish and
expand Futa Toro rule at the expense of the neighboring
Soninke and Wolof of Senegal, although an effort to expand in Guinea-Bissau was successfully resisted by the
Beafadas. An attempt to take over the Bambuk goldfields failed in 1534, and three years later Tenguella (II)
was killed. The Denianke followers, however, proceeded
to enlarge their control in an area between the Sahel and
Futa Jallon. The lineage of Coli Tenguella has not yet
been fully unraveled by historians, who offer varied interpretations of this man and his successors. There may
have been a Coli Tenguella (III), who in alliance with
Manding fragments overthrew the Soninke chiefs of Futa
Toro in 1559 to perpetuate the Denianke line. In any

...RAL DOS ESTUDIANTES DA AFRICA NEGRA
...N). The UGEAN was formed in Europe for mili-
...tionalist students by the PAIGC and the MPLA in
...

...AL DOS TRABALHADORES DA GUINE-BISSAU
...B). The UGTGB emerged in 1963 in association
...ING and was a rival of the PAIGC's workers'
..., the UNTG, which had been formed in 1959.

...IONAL DOS TRABALHADORES DA GUINE (UNTG).
... in 1959 and affiliated with the PAIGC as a party
...tion. In 1961 its first statutes were drafted with
...oral acting as the Secretary General. The UNTG
...o organize the working class of Guinea and dur-
...war sought to organize the working class of
...rde. On May 1, 1976 (May Day), the Comissão
...dora dos Sindicatos Caboverdeanos (COSC, the
...ng Commission of Cape Verdean Unionists) was
...s the complement and parallel body of the UNTG
...ape Verde Islands.

...LAR PARA LIBERTAÇÃO DA GUINE (UPLG).
...G was formed in 1961 and then merged with
...1962.

...ESSORTISSANTS DE LA GUINEE PORTUGAISE
... The URGP was formed in 1963 and became
...th FLING in 1964.

...ONS. On December 14, 1960, the 1,514th
... the General Assembly passed a resolution on
...olonization which gave great support to anti-
...d nationalist movements in Africa. In 1961 the
...mitted documentation to the United Nations re-
...e effects of Portuguese colonialism, and on
...1972, a special United Nations team entered
...sau as a guest of the PAIGC. As the intended
...e of this trip, the Special Committee on De-
...announced on April 13, 1972, that the PAIGC
...y and authentic representative" of the people
...Subsequent resolutions in the U.N. General
...nd the U.N. Security Council reaffirmed the
...lf-determination and independence" in Novem-
...hus weakening Portugal's position and
...y strengthening the PAIGC. After the

case this early Denianke period saw the emergence of sedentary Fula who began to dominate those Fula who remained as pastoralists.

During the Tenguella periods the Fula followers often crossed over portions of eastern Guinea-Bissau and brought in new Fula people. Under the influence of the Tenguellas, the Fulas were stimulated to build more permanent settlements. As a result of these movements of the Fula, a population of Fulacundas, or non-Muslim, semi-sedentary cattle herders, was generated from Fula and Manding peoples already living in the Gabu kingdom of Guinea-Bissau. In the 18th and 19th centuries the Fulacunda population of Guinea-Bissau increased consid-erably. See: DIALONKES; FULA; FUTA JALLON; FUTA TORO; GABU; MALI; SONGHAI.

TIMENES. This very small Senegambian group is located south of Gabu and was isolated from other Senegambians after Mandingo expansion.

TIRAMAKHAN (TIRAMANG), TRAORE. A general of Sundiata Keita (d. 1255 A.D.) of Mali. Tiramakhan entered the Senegambian region to crush the revolt of a Wolof king against Sundiata and to strengthen the control of Mali after it defeated the Susu people under Sumanguru in 1235. Thus, at some time in the mid-13th century, Tiramakhan's control was consolidated and he married Nyaaling, who was perhaps a Mandingo of the local area before the arrival of Tiramakhan's forces. His presence laid the foundation for the Mandingo state of Gabu (ca. 1250-1867). Sources are unclear as to the exact genea-logical relationship between Tiramakhan and the first Gabu king, Sama Koli (Kelemankoto Baa Saane), but it appears that he was either the son or grandson of Tiramakhan in a royal line of matrilineal descent. See: GABU; MALI; MANDING.

TOMAS. This very small Senegambian group is located just east of Gabu. See: SENEGAMBIANS.

TRADE. See: ECONOMICS.

TRISTÃO, NUNO. Portuguese navigator and captain of an armed caravel who, along with Antão Gonçalves, cap-tured a dozen Africans (Moors) at Cape Blanc (north coast of Mauritania) in 1441 and returned to Portugal with them and a cargo of gold dust. One of the captives was of noble birth. Tristão personally engaged in slave capturing and the killing of those who resisted. In 1443-44 Tristão reached Arguim, seizing 29 men and women. Merchants soon grasped the idea of large and easy profits. In 1444 Tristão decided to outfit a major raiding expedition of six ships under Lançarote and Gil Eannes, thus initiating one of the earliest European-inspired slave raids on the African coast. In the same year Tristão became the first European to venture beyond the Mauritanian desert, as he reached the mouths of the Senegal, Gambia, and Salum rivers, thinking they were branches of the Nile. In 1446 Tristão reached the area of Bissau and Bolama, but in the following year his aggressive exploits came to an end when he was killed in the Bissagos Islands while trying to claim them for Portugal.

- U -

UNIÃO CABOVERDEANA PARA A INDEPENDÊNCIA E DEMOCRACIA (UCID). Founded in 1981 in Cape Verdean emigrant communities, the UCID is a right-wing opposition group based in Lisbon. It has opposed PAICV foreign and domestic policies such as agrarian and land reform and relations with the socialist nations.

UNIÃO DAS POPULAÇÕES DAS ILHAS DE CABO VERDE (UPICV). The UPICV was led by José Leitão da Graça and his wife Maria Querido, who was named its secretary general. The UPICV sought to preserve the Cape Verdean "personality" in its program of limited social transformation. Apparently the UPICV was first formed in 1959 in the United States. Following the Lisbon coup the UPICV supported the UDCV position of a referendum on unity with Guinea-Bissau, charging that the PAIGC would make Cape Verde "a Soviet military base." In the mid-1970s the UPICV spouted certain Maoist terminology and on May 23, 1975, renamed itself the Peoples Liberation Front of Cape Verde. Following the independence of Cape Verde on July 5, 1975, the central leaders of the UPICV were exiled to Portugal although the UPICV claimed responsibility for a small anti-PAIGC disturbance in São Vicente in August 1975. See: UDCV.

UNIÃO DEMOCRATICA DA GUI emerged in the late 1950s and the UPG to form the N was from such groups as in 1962. See: FLING.

UNIÃO DEMOCRATICA DAS M Verde), UDEMU. UDEMU to officially represent the within the anti-colonial f WOMEN.

UNIÃO DEMOCRATICA DE C The UDCV emerged in t UDG and the UPG in 19 ultimately led to the for Through most of the 19 not exist. In 1974, fo former UDCV members for a referendum on t] Bissau and the possib Cape Verde and feder prevent PAIGC contro inent leaders of the U a leading Cape Verde Jorge Fonseca, who ests in the islands. ganize some anti-PAI Both were exiled aft American supporters the Juridicial Congr Verdean lawyer whc Roy Teixeira and h ton on behalf of th deans declared the called for the over

UNIÃO DOS NATURAI Sought independe Benjamin Pinto Bu negotiations whicl FLING one year ; Bull's brother, J UNGP and was n BULL, B.; BUL]

UNIÃO GE (UGEA tant n Angola

UNIÃO GE (UGTG with Fl affiliate

UNIÃO NAC Founde organiza Luís Ca serves ing the Cape Ve Organiza Organizi formed in the C

UNIÃO POPU The UPL FLING in

UNION DES (URGP). aligned w

UNITED NATI meeting of global dec colonial ar PAIGC su garding th April 2-8, Guinea-Bis consequenc colonizatio "is the only of Guinea. Assembly a "right of s ber 1972, t substantiall

PAIGC declared the independence of Guinea in September 1973, the U.N. General Assembly adopted a resolution on October 22, 1973, condemning Portugal's continuing occupation. On November 2, 1973, the General Assembly recognized the new Republic of Guinea-Bissau, which was admitted to the United Nations as a full member on September 17, 1974, following the April coup in Lisbon. These events preceded the negotiated independence for Cape Verde. Just prior to independence, the U.N. Special Committee on Decolonization undertook a fact-finding mission in Cape Verde to determine its health, financial, educational and developmental needs. The Republic of Cape Verde officially joined the U.N. on September 17, 1975.

UNITED STATES. See: FOREIGN AFFAIRS.

URZELLA. See: INDIGO, PANOS.

- V -

VIEIRA, JOÃO BERNARDO "NINO" (1939-   ). President of the country's highest political organs since the 1980 coup d'état, including the Council of State (formerly the Revolutionary Council) and the PAIGC Politburo, as well as commander-in-chief of the armed forces and secretary general of the PAIGC. Born in Bissau and an electrician by trade, Vieira joined the PAIGC in 1960 and in the following year attended the party school in Conakry led by Amílcar Cabral. From 1961 to 1964 Vieira was political commissioner in the Catio region in southern Guinea-Bissau. Having received advanced military training in Nanking, China, Vieira was made military head of the entire southern front in 1964 and became a member of the PAIGC Political Bureau as a result of the First Party Congress in that year. In 1965 he became the vice-president of the War Council and continued his work as military head of the southern front. From 1967 to 1970 he was the ranking member of the Political Bureau assigned to the southern front, and after 1970 he held full national responsibility for military operations of the War Council. In 1971 he became a member of the CEL and subsequently was the secretary for the PAIGC Permanent Secretariat.

Following independence, Vieira became the commander-in-chief of the armed forces as well as pre-

siding over the Peoples National Assembly. In August
1978, he was appointed Prime Minister of Guinea-Bissau
following the death of Francisco Mendes in July of that
year. In November 1980 Vieira overthrew President Luís
Cabral in a coup to become the president of the republic
and chairman of the Revolutionary Council. Following the
1984 elections and the adoption of a new constitution,
Vieira became the chairman of the Council of State.
Vieira increasingly consolidated his rule between 1981
and 1986, and he was promoted to the rank of brigadier
general in 1983. See: PAICV; PAIGC; CABRAL, L.

VILLAGE COMMITTEES. See: TABANCA COMMITTEES.

- W -

WEST AFRICAN CROPS. See: AGRICULTURE.

WOMEN. The PAIGC has, from its inception through to the
present time, put forth the full liberation of women as
one of its central goals. A number of women were incorporated into leadership positions within the PAIGC's
fighting forces during the nationalist armed struggle,
and the party insisted that at least two of the members
of tabanca committees be women. Also, the Democratic
Union of Guinean and Cape Verdean Women (UDEMU)
was formed by the PAIGC in the mid-1960s and remains
active today in promoting women's issues. However, the
party has not yet succeeded in placing more than a tiny
handful of women into leadership posts in the party and
government. Also, while educational opportunities for
women have been expanded since independence, the male-
dominated nature of the social and familial structure has
not been seriously challenged, and very few women are
able to pursue economic independence.
    There are no restrictions for women being in the
PAIGC, except that neither a woman nor a man in a
polygynous union is permitted, as the institution of
plural marriages is not favored by the PAIGC. During
the growth of the PAIGC's liberated zones, divorce was
made easier for women, especially Muslim women, who
had rather limited rights to divorce. Marriages are only
permitted by joint consent, and forced marriage or child
marriage is opposed. The institution of bridewealth is
also curbed. In general the position of women has been
improved given the predominant traditions which were

widely based on male supremacy. Now the rights of
women are legally protected. For example, children born
out of wedlock must be supported by their fathers, and
the status of "illegitimacy" has been legally abolished.
The numbers of women in industry are increasing even
though the overall numbers of industrial jobs are few.
Since independence, International Women's Day, March 8,
is now observed.

Within the PAIGC about 12 percent of the regular
members are women, and there is one woman member in
the Politburo and many women members of the Central
Committee and the Popular National Assembly. Women
are commonly found in the health and educational services, where such possibilities were limited during colonial rule. During the armed struggle UDEMU was
created to assist in the mobilization of women for the
war effort. UDEMU was replaced by the Comissão
Feminina (Women's Commission) toward the close of the
war, but the preoccupation with military affairs and resistance to change by male chauvinists ultimately resulted
in the failure of the Comissão Feminina under the leadership of Carmen Pereira. Since independence, efforts
to organize women have resumed under COM (Comissão
da Organização das Mulheres) to address special needs of
women and to incorporate them more fully into national
reconstruction. Articles 13, 16, and 25 of the Constitution of the Republic of Guinea-Bissau provide for the
legal, social, and electoral equality of men and women.

A number of women made distinguished contribu-
tions during the nationalist war: among them are Dr.
Maria Boal, Director of the Pilot School and Friendship
Institute; Carmen Pereira, the highest ranking woman in
the PAIGC; and Ernestina Silla, exemplary heroine.
See: PEREIRA, C.; SILLA, E.; UDEMU.

- Y-Z -

YOUTH. See: PIONEERS OF THE PARTY.

ZURARA, GOMES EANES DA. A well-known 15th century
chronicler for Prince Henry. He wrote of the 1415 Cueta
campaign in the "Key to the Mediterranean." In 1453 he
wrote "Cronica de Guiné," which described some of the
earliest kidnapping of Africans and of their resistance to
the predations of the early slavers. See: HENRY.

BIBLIOGRAPHY

Introduction

The purpose of this bibliography is to provide a substantive listing of some of the principal works about Guinea-
Bissau, thereby laying the groundwork for further research
and reading. By no means do we claim to be all-inclusive:
our focus is on the more significant and accessible publications. In this vein, we made a particular effort to include
English-language entries, as these are likely to be the most
useful to the majority of readers. While this means that
numerous sources in foreign languages have been omitted,
we did include many foreign language references to aid the
multilingual researcher in a more thorough search of the literature, and because a number of significant aspects of
Guinea-Bissau have only been discussed or referred to in
those languages (usually Portuguese or French). The relative lack of English language studies on the history of
Guinea-Bissau is in part a consequence of the purposeful
effort of the Portuguese to restrict non-lusophone contact
with their colonies, except regarding slavery and certain
aspects of foreign trade in which relations with the non-
lusophone world were selectively encouraged. The successful nationalist war for independence and the internationally
acclaimed writings and speeches of Amílcar Cabral, the leader of the independence struggle, generated a much greater
volume of English language publications. Today the majority
of works about Guinea-Bissau continue to be published in
Portuguese and French, but there is an expanding literature
in English reflecting widening academic, journalistic, diplomatic, economic and cultural exchanges between Guineans
and anglophones.

We would like to point out that the bibliographies by
McCarthy (1977) and Lopes (1985) provide excellent comple-

ments to the present work, and that the bibliography by
Patrick Chabal on pages 241-269 of his book, Amílcar Cabral;
Revolutionary Leadership and People's War, constitutes the
single most comprehensive collection of works written by or
concerning Cabral.

The organization of the bibliography is as follows:

1. Bibliographies

2. Periodicals Relating to Guinea-Bissau

3. General References: Statistical

4. General References: Historical/Legal/Political

5. History of Guinea-Bissau

6. Physical Features, Geography, Flora and Fauna

7. Anthropology and Ethnology

8. Language, Literature, and Crioulo Culture

9. Health and Education

10. Agriculture, Economics, and Development

11. By and About Amílcar Cabral

12. On National Liberation

13. Post-Independence Politics

1. BIBLIOGRAPHIES

Bell, Aubrey F.G. Portuguese Bibliography. New York, 1922.

Berman, Sanford. "African Liberation Movements: A Preliminary Bibliography." Ufahamu, III, 1 (Spring), 1972.

Bibliografia científica da Junta de Investigações do Ultramar. Lisbon, 1980.

Boletim de bibliografia portuguesa. Lisbon: Biblioteca Nacional.

Cahen, Michel. "Bibliographie" [of relations between Portugal and luso-African countries], Afrique contemporaine, 137 (January-February-March 1986): 45-55.

Chabal, Patrick. "Bibliography" [of works by or concerning Amílcar Cabral] in his Amílcar Cabral: Revolutionary leadership and people's war. Cambridge: Cambridge University Press, 241-269.

Chilcote, Ronald H. "Amílcar Cabral: A Bio-Bibliography of His Life and Thought, 1925-1973." Africana Journal, V. 4 (1974): 289-307.

_____. Emerging Nationalism in Portuguese Africa: A Bibliography of Documentary Ephemera Through 1965. Stanford, CA: Hoover Institution, 1969.

Duignan, Peter (ed.) Guide to Research and Reference Works on Sub-Saharan Africa. Stanford: Hoover Institution Press, 1972.

_____, and Gann, L.H. Colonialism in Africa 1870-1960, vol. 5: A bibliographical guide to colonialism in sub-Saharan Africa. London: Cambridge University Press, 1973.

Figueiredo, Jaime de. "Bibliografia caboverdeana: subsídios para uma ordenação sistematica." Cabo Verde: Boletim de Propaganda e Informação. V (49)31; (50)31; (54)31; (56)37; 1953-4.

Flores, Michel. "A Bibliographic Contribution to the Study of Portuguese Africa (1965-1972)." Current Bibliography on African Affairs, VII, 2 (1974): 116-37.

138

Gibson, Mary Jane. Portuguese Africa: A Guide to Official Publications. Washington, D.C.: Library of Congress, Reference Department, 1967.

Gonçalves, José Júlio. "Bibliografia antropológica do ultramar português." Boletim Geral das Colonias, (1961): 281-90, 335-41, 431-71, 483-501.

Kornegay, Francis A., Jr. "A Bibliographic Memorial to Amílcar Cabral: Selected Survey of Resources on the Struggle in Guinea-Bissau." Ufahamu, III, 3 (Winter 1973): 152-59.

Lopes, Carlos. 1100 Referências para a Pesquisa em Ciências Sociais na Guiné-Bissau, 2e edição. Geneva: Centre de Documentation, Institut Universitaire d'Etudes du Développement, 1985.

McCarthy, Joseph M. Guinea-Bissau and Cape Verde Islands: A Comprehensive Bibliography. New York: Garland, 1977.

Matthews, Daniel G. "African Bibliography Today: Selected and Current Bibliographical Tools for African Studies, 1967-1968." Current Bibliography on African Affairs (November 1968).

Rogers, Francis Millet and David T. Haberly. Brazil, Portugal and Other Portuguese-Speaking Lands: A List of Books Primarily in English. Cambridge, MA: Harvard University Press, 1968.

Ryder, A.F.C. Materials for West African History in Portuguese Archives. London: Athlone Press, 1965.

Rydings, H.A. The Bibliographies of West Africa. Ibadan: Ibadan University Press, 1961.

Tenreiro, Francisco. "Bibliografia geográfica da Guiné." Garcia de Orta, II, 1 (1954): 97-134.

U.S. Library of Congress. A List of References on the Portuguese Colonies in Africa (Angola, Cape Verde Islands, Mozambique, Portuguese Guinea, São Tomé and Príncipe). Washington, D.C., 1942.

2. PERIODICALS RELATING TO GUINEA-BISSAU

Acta (Conselho do governo). Bissau.

Africa. Lisbon.

Africa Confidential. London.

Africa. Literatura--Arte e Cultura. Triannual review focusing on the luso-African countries. Lisbon.

Africa News. A twice-weekly service for broadcast and print. Durham, N.C.

Africa Report. Rutgers University: New Brunswick, New Jersey.

Afrique Asie. Paris.

Bantaba. Journal of the secondary school, Kwame N'Krumah. Bissau.

Blufo. Mimeographed journal for the liberated areas. Conakry: PAIGC.

Boletim Arquivo Histórico Colonial. Lisbon.

Boletim Cultural da Guiné Portuguesa. Organ of the Centro de Estudos da Guiné Portuguesa. 1946+. Lisbon.

Boletim da Sociedade de Geografia de Lisbôa. Lisbon.

Boletim de Informação Sindical. União Nacional de Trabalhadores da Guiné. Bissau.

Boletim Geral das Colónias. Lisbon.

Boletim oficial da Guiné Portuguesa. Weekly, 1880+. Bolama & Bissau.

Boletim trissemanal da Agência Noticiosa da Guiné-Bissau (A.N.G.).

Cabo Verde; Boletim de propaganda e informação. Monthly, 1949-1964. Praia.

Diario de noticias. Lisbon.

Ecos da Guiné: Boletim de informação e de estatística. Bissau, 1951+.

Facts and Reports. Press cuttings on Angola, Mozambique, Guinea-Bissau, Portugal, and Southern Africa, edited by the Angola Comité. Amsterdam.

Garcia de Orta. Lisbon.

Le Soleil. Senegal.

Libertação. Mimeographed journal for the liberated areas. Conakry: PAIGC.

O Militante. Publication of the Secretariat of the Central Committee
    of the PAIGC. Bissau.

Mundo Português. Lisbon.

Nô Pintcha. Official PAIGC publication in Guinea-Bissau since
    independence. Three times weekly.

Nôs Luta. Orgão de informação da Radio Voz de S. Vincente.

Objective: Justice. Quarterly magazine covering United Nations
    activity against apartheid, racial discrimination and colonialism.
    New York: United Nations Office of Public Information.

PAIGC (Partido Africano da Independência da Guiné e Cabo Verde).
    Edição dos Servicos Cultarais do Conselho Superior da Luta.

PAIGC Actualidades. Boletim Informativo do CC do PAIGC.
    Monthly.

PAIGC Actualités. Bulletin d'Information édité par la Commission
    d'Information et Propagande du Comité Central du PAIGC.
    Monthly, 1969-1974. Conakry.

PAIGC Actualités. LSM Information Center, Richmond, B.C.,
    Canada; quarterly English edition.

PAIGC Actualités: La vie et la lutte en Guinée et Cap-Vert.
    Monthly; nos. 21-36, 38 (17 numbers in all); September, 1970-
    February, 1972. Conakry.

Portugal. Anglo-Portuguese Publications.

Portugal em Africa. Lisbon.

Portuguese and Colonial Bulletin. Anti-colonial bulletin published
    by K. Shingler, London (during the colonial wars).

Présence Africaine. Paris.

Revista Militar. Lisbon.

Revista Portugal em Africa. Lisbon.

Soronda. Review of Guinean Students. Published by the National
    Institute of Studies and Research (INEP) as of April 1986.
    Bissau.

Southern Africa. New York.

Terceiro Mundo. Lisbon.

Tricontinental Bulletin. Published in Spanish, English and French by the Executive Secretariat of the Organization of Solidarity of the Peoples of Africa, Asia and Latin America. Habana, Cuba.

Ufahamu. Berkeley, California.

West Africa. London.

3. GENERAL REFERENCES: STATISTICAL

Agência Geral do Ultramar. Portugal Overseas Provinces: Facts and Figures. Lisbon, 1965.

_____. Províncias ultramarinas portuguesas: dados informativos. Lisbon, 1962-66.

Anuário da Guiné Portuguesa. Lisbon: Sociedade Industrial de Tipografia, 1946+.

Anuário estatístico. Annuaire statistique. Lisbon: Tipografia Portuguesa, 1947+.

Anuário estatístico. II. Províncias ultramarinas, 1969. Lisbon: Instituto Nacional de Estatística, 1971.

Brito, Eduíno. "Guiné Portuguesa--Censo da população não civilizada de 1950." Boletim Cultural da Guiné Portuguesa, VII, 28 (October 1952): 725-56.

Colvin, Lucie Gallistel. The Uprooted of the Sahel: Migrants' Quest for Cash in the Senegambia. New York: Praeger, 1981.

Curtin, Philip D. The Atlantic Slave Trade: A Census. Madison, Wis.: University of Wisconsin Press, 1969.

Heisel, Donald Francis. "The Demography of the Portuguese Territories: Angola, Mozambique and Portuguese Guinea." In W.I. Brass et al. (eds.), The Demography of Tropical Africa. Princeton, NJ: Princeton University Press, 1968, pp. 440-465.

Lima, José Joaquim Lopes de. Prospecto estatístico-econômico da Província de Cabo Verde. Lisbon, 1875.

_____. "Sobre a statística das ilhas de Cabo Verde e suas dependências na Guiné Portuguesa." In José Lima (ed.), Ensaios sobre a statística das possessões portuguesas, vol. 1. Lisbon, 1844.

PAIGC. "La République de Guinée-Bissau en chiffres." Conakry: Commissariat d'Etat à l'Economie et aux Finances, 1974.

PAIGC. "Sur la création de l'Assemblée Nationale Populaire en Guinée (Bissau). Résultats et bases des élections générales réalisés dans les regions libérées en 1972." Conakry, 1973.

Província da Guiné--Censo da população de 1950, 2 vols. Bissau: Imprensa Nacional, 1951.

Recenseamento Geral da População e da Habitação. 16 de Abril de 1979. Bissau: Ministério da Coordenação Econômica e Plano, August 1981.

Resumo Estatístico Aduaneiro--Província da Guiné no Ano de 1914. Lisbon: Ministério das Colônias, Imprensa Nacional, 1916.

Resumo Estatístico Aduaneiro--Província da Guiné no Ano de 1917. Lisbon: Ministério das Colônias, Imprensa Nacional, 1918.

Vieira, Ruy Alvaro. "Alguns aspectos demográficos dos Bijagós da Guiné." Boletim Cultural da Guiné Portuguesa, X(1955): 23-34.

4. GENERAL REFERENCES: HISTORICAL/LEGAL/POLITICAL

Abshire, David M. and Michael A. Samuels (eds.). Portuguese Africa: A Handbook. New York: Praeger, 1969.

Agência Geral do Ultramar. Guiné. Lisbon, 1967.

_____. Guiné: pequena monografia. Lisbon, 1961.

Almeida, Pedro Ramos de. História do Colonialismo Português em Africa (Cronologia, do sec. XV a XX). Lisbon: Editorial Estampa, 1979.

Angola Comité. Portugal and NATO, 3rd edition. Amsterdam, 1972.

Axelson, Eric. Congo to Cape: Early Portuguese Explorers. New York: Barnes and Noble, 1973.

_____. Portugal and the Scramble for Africa, 1875-1891. Johannesburg: Witwatersrand University Press, 1967.

Barbosa, Honório José. O processo criminal e civil no Julgado Instructor e no Tribunal Privativo dos Indígenas. Bissau: Imprensa Nacional, 1947.

Beazley, Charles Raymond. Prince Henry the Navigator (1394-1460). New York: G.P. Putnam, 1895.

Biker, Joaquim Pedro Vieira Judice. "Relatório Sobre a pacificação da Guiné." Province of Guine, October 1903.

Blake, J.W. (ed.). Europeans in West Africa 1460-1560, 2 vols. 1942.

Boxer, Charles R. Four Centuries of Portuguese Expansion, 1415-1825. Berkeley and Los Angeles: University of California Press, 1972.

————. Portuguese Society in the Tropics. Madison and Milwaukee: University of Wisconsin Press, 1965.

————. Race Relations in the Portuguese Colonial Empire 1415-1825. Oxford, 1963.

Caetano, Marcello. Colonizing Traditions, Principles and Methods of the Portuguese. Lisbon: Agência Geral do Ultramar, 1951.

————. Portugal's Reasons for Remaining in the Overseas Provinces. Lisbon. 1970.

Caroço, Jorge F. Velez. Relatório anual do governador da Guiné, 1921-1922. Coimbra, 1923.

Carreira, António. Guiné Portuguesa, 2 vols. Lisbon, 1954.

Carson, Patricia. Materials for West African History in the Archives of Belgium and Holland. London: Athlone Press, 1962.

Castro, Armando. O Sistema Colonial Português em Africa (meados do século XX). Lisbon: Editorial Caminho, 1979.

Chilcote, Ronald H. Emerging Nationalism in Portuguese Africa: Documents. Stanford, CA: Hoover Institution, 1972.

————. Portuguese Africa. Englewood Cliffs, NJ: Prentice-Hall, 1967.

Church, R.J. Harrison. West Africa. A Study of the Environment and of Man's Use of it. New York: John Wiley, 1961.

Cipolla, C.M. Guns and Sails in the Early Phase of European Expansion (1400-1700). London, 1965.

Conselho de Inspecção de Produtos de Exportação. Regulamento. Aprovado por Portaria numero 139, de 23 de dezembro de 1935. Bolama: Imprensa Nacional, 1936.

Conselho do Govêrno da Guiné Portuguesa. Acta. Bissau, 1919+.

Conselho Legislativo. Actas do sessões. Bissau, 1925+.

Corpo de Polícia de Segurança Pública. Regulamento, 1956 maio 12. Praia: Imprensa Nacional, 1956.

Corrêa, António A. Mendes. Ultramar Português. II. Ilhas de Cabo Verde. Lisbon: Agência Geral do Ultramar, 1954.

Cortesão, Jaime. Os portugueses em Africa. Lisbon: Portugália Editora, 1968.

Cultru, P. Premier voyage du sieur de La Courbe fait à la coste d'Afrique en 1685. Paris: Champion & Larose, reprinted 1973.

Duarte, Fausto Castilho. Anuário da Guiné Portugesa, 1946-1948. Lisbon: Agência Geral das Colonias, 1948.

_____. "A libertação de Guiné Portuguesa pela carta de lei de 1879." Boletim Cultural da Guiné Portuguesa, VII, 28 (October 1952): 789-832.

Duffy, James. Portugal in Africa. Baltimore: Penguin Books, 1962.

_____. Portuguese Africa. Cambridge, Mass., 1961.

Dumont, René and Marie France Mottin. L'Afrique Etranglée. Paris: Seuil, 1982.

Duncan, T. Bentley. Atlantic Islands: Madeira, the Azores, and the Cape Verdes in Seventeenth-Century Commerce and Navigation. Chicago: University of Chicago, 1972.

Dunn, John. West African States: Failure and Promise. Cambridge: Cambridge University Press, 1978.

Durieux, A. "Essai sur le statut des indigènes portugais de la Guinée, de l'Angola et du Mozambique." Mémoires de l'Académie royale des Sciences coloniales - 8, V, 3 (1955).

Ellis, Alfred Burdon. West African Islands. London: Chapman and Hall, 1885.

Estatuto da Província da Guiné. Lisbon: Agência Geral do Ultramar, 1955.

Estatuto dos indígenas portugueses das províncias da Guiné, Angola e Mozambique. Lisbon, 1954.

Estatuto político-administrativa da Guiné. Lisbon: Agência Geral do Ultramar, 1963.

Estatuto político-administrativa da Guiné. Lisbon: Agência Geral do Ultramar, 1964.

Estatuto político-administrativa da Guiné. Ultramar, II, (1973): 120-38.

Estatuto político-administrativa da Província da Guiné, 542/72. Lisbon: December 22, 1972.

Fage, J.D. "Slavery and the Slave Trade in the Context of West African History." Journal of African History, 3(1969).

Fargues, G. "Guinée-Bissao et archipels portugais." In Année Africaine, 1968. Paris: A. Pédone, 1970, pp. 259-60.

Ferreira, Eduarto de Sousa. Portuguese Colonialism from South Africa to Europe. Germany: Druckerei Horst Ahlbrecht, 1972.

_____. Portuguese Colonialism in Africa: The End of an Era. Paris: Unesco Press, 1974.

First, Ruth. Portugal's Wars in Africa. London: Christian Action Publications Ltd., 1972.

Galli, Rosemary and Jocelyn Jones. Guinea-Bissau: Politics, Economics and Society. Boulder, Colorado: Lynne Rienner Publs., 1987.

Gibson, Richard. African Liberation Movements. Contemporary Struggles Against White Minority Rule, London: Oxford University Press, 1972.

_____. Portuguese Guinea. London: His Majesty's Stationery Office, 1920.

Gouveia, Pedro Ignacio. "Relatório do Governador da Província da Guiné Portuguesa." 1882.

Hakluyt, Richard. Voyages and Discoveries. Baltimore: Penguin Books, 1972 (first published in 1589.)

Hammond, Richard J. Portugal and Africa, 1815-1910: A Study in Uneconomic Imperialism. Stanford, CA: Stanford University Press, 1966.

_____. "Race Attitudes and Policies in Portuguese Africa in the Nineteenth and Twentieth Centuries." Race. January 1968.

Humbaraci, Arslan and Nicole Muchnik. Portugal's African Wars. New York: Third World Press, 1973.

Lança, Joaquim da Graça Correia. Relatório da Provincia da Guiné Portuguesa referido no anno económica de 1888-1889. Lisbon: Imprensa Nacional, 1890.

Lavradio, Marques do. Portugal em Africa depois de 1851. Lisbon: Agência Geral das Colonias, 1936.

Lawrence, A.W. Trade Castles and Forts of West Africa. 1963.

Liberation Struggle in Portuguese Colonies. New Delhi: Peoples Publishing House, 1970.

Livermore, Harold. A New History of Portugal. Cambridge, 1966.

Luttrel, A. "Slavery and Slaving in the Portuguese Atlantic to about 1500." In The Trans-Atlantic Slave Trade from West Africa. Edinburgh: Centre of African Studies, University of Edinburgh, 1965.

Markov, P. "West African History in German Archives." Journal of the Historical Society of Nigeria. December 1963.

Marques, A.H. de Oliveira. History of Portugal, 2 vols. New York: 1972-3.

Martins, Alfredo Cardoso de Soveral. "Relatório do Governador da Guiné." Bolama: 1903.

Mello, Guedes Brandão de. Relatório do Governor Geral da Província de Cabo Verde, 1890. Lisbon: Imprensa Nacional, 1891.

Minter, William. Portuguese Africa and the West. Baltimore: Penguin Books, 1972.

Moore, Francis. Travels into the Inland Parts of Africa. London: Edward Cave, 1738.

Moreira, Adriano. Portugal's Stand in Africa. New York: University Publishers, 1962.

Mota, Avelino Teixeira da. Guiné Portuguesa, 2 vols. Lisbon: Agência Geral do Ultramar, 1954.

Nielson, Waldemar A. African Battleline: American Policy Choices in Southern Africa. New York: Harper and Row, 1965.

Nogueira, Franco. The United Nations and Portugal. A Study of Anti-Colonialism. London: Tandem, 1964.

Park, Mungo. Travels in the Interior Districts of Africa. London: G. & W. Nicol, 1799.

"Portugal's African Wars." Conflict Studies 34 (March 1973).

Prestage, E. The Portuguese Pioneers. New York: Barnes and Noble, 1967.

Reade, Winwood. The African Sketch Book, 2 vols. London: Smith, 1873.

Roberts, George. The Four Voyages of Captain George Roberts; Being a Series of Uncommon Events, Which Befell Him in a Voyage to the Islands of the Canaries, Cape de Verde, and Barbadoes, from which He Was Bound to the Coast of Guiney. London: A. Bettenworth, 1726.

Rodney, Walter. A History of the Upper Guinea Coast, 1545-1800. New York: Oxford University Press, 1970.

Rodrigues, M.M. Sarmento. No governo da Guiné. Lisbon: 1954.

Salazar, António de Oliveira. H.E. Professor Oliveira Salazar, Prime Minister of Portugal, Broadcast on 12 August, 1963, Declaration on Overseas Policy. Lisbon: Secretariado Nacional da Informação, 1960.

_____. "Policy in Africa." Vital Speeches, XXXIV (March 15, 1968): 325-28.

Saunders, A.C. de C.M., A Social History of Black Slaves and Freemen in Portugal 1441-1555. Cambridge: Cambridge University Press, 1982.

Serrão, Joaquim V. História breve da historiografia portuguesa. Lisbon: 1962.

Serrão, Joel (ed.). Dicionário de História de Portugal, 4 vols. Lisbon: 1963-70.

Silva, Francisco Teixeira de. "Relatório do Governo da Província da Guiné Portuguesa com referência a 1887-1888." Lisbon: 1889.

Spínola, António de. Portugal e o futuro. Lisbon: Arcadia, 1974.

Steeber, Horst. "The European Slave Trade and the Feudal Mode of Production on the West African Slave Coast." Ethnographische-Archaeologische Zeitschrift, #4, 1969.

Teixeira da Mota, A. Guiné Portuguesa, 2 vols. Lisbon: 1954.

União Nacional de Guiné. Guiné--Ano XVI da revolução nacional. Bissau: 1943.

United States. Department of State. Portuguese Guinea. Washington, D.C.: 1966.

Valdearan, Marcos. "De los antigos reinos al domínio português." Revista Africa Hoy (Madrid), 4 (1980).

Vasconcelos, Ernesto Júlio de Carvalho e. As colónias portuguesas, 2d edition. Lisbon: 1904.

_____. Guiné portuguesa. Lisbon: Tipografia da Cooperativa Militar, 1917.

Venter, Al J. Africa at War. Old Greenwich, CT: The Devin-Adair Company, 1974.

War on Three Fronts: The Fight Against Portuguese Colonialism. Committee for Freedom in Mozambique, Angola and Guinea, 1971.

Whitaker, Paul M. "The Revolutions of 'Portuguese' Africa." Journal of Modern African Studies, VIII, 1 (April 1970): 15-35.

5. HISTORY OF GUINEA-BISSAU

Alexis de Saint-Lô. Relation du voyage au Cap Verd. Paris: 1637.

Almada, André Alvares de. Relação ou descripção de Guinée. Lisbon: 1733.

Almeida, Francisco de. "O Antigo Testamento e a Guiné Portuguesa (Alguns confrontos ergalogicsos)." Dissertation, Biblioteca do Instituto Técnica, Lisbon, 1971.

Almeida, J.B.P. Exploração da Senegambia Portuguesa. Lisbon: 1878.

Alves, Frederico. Romance da conquista da Guiné. Lisbon: 1944.

Andrade, António Alberto de. "História breve da Guiné Portugesa." Ultramar, VII, 4 (April-June 1968): 7-56.

Andrade, Elisa. The Cape Verde Islands from Slavery to Modern Times. Dakar: U.N. African Institute for Economic Development and Planning, May 1973.

Azurara, Gomes Eannes. Discovery and Conquest of Guine, 2 vols. Ed. and trans. E. Porestage and C.R. Beazley. London: 1896-99.

Barcellos, Christiano José de Senna. Subsídios para a história de Cabo Verde e Guiné, 7 vols. Lisbon: 1899-1913.

Barreto, Honório Pereira. Memória sobre o estado actual de Sene-gâmbia Portugueza, causas de sua decadencia, e meios de a fazer prosperar. Lisbon, 1843. Reprint ed., Bissau, 1947.

Barreto, João. História da Guiné, 1418-1918. Lisbon: 1938.

Barros, João de. Chronicles of the Voyages of Cadamosto. Lisbon: 1937.

Barros, Simão. Origens da Colónia de Cabo Verde. Lisbon: n.d.

Beaver, P. African memoranda. Relative to an attempt to estab-lish a British settlement on the island of Bulama. 1805. New York: Humanities Press, 1968.

Bénézet, A. Relation de la côte de la Guinée, 4th ed. London: 1788.

_____. Some Historical Accounts of Guinea. Philadelphia: 1771.

Brazao, Arnaldo. "A vida administrativa da Colônia da Guiné." Separata do Boletim Cultural da Guiné Portuguesa, 7 (July 1947): 751-782.

Brooks, Geroge E. "Bolama as a Prospective Site for American Colonization in the 1820s and 1830s." Boletim Cultural da Guiné Portuguesa, XXVIII (January 1973): 5-22.

Brosselard, le Capitaine H. "Voyage dans la Senegambie et la Guiné Portuguaise.: Le Tour du Monde--Nouveau Journal des Voyages (Paris), LVII (1889): 97-144.

Campos, Valentim da Fonseca. "Guiné à saque--Documentos e factos para a história." Lisbon: 1912.

Carreira, António Augusto Peixoto. "Alguns aspectos da adminis-tração publica em Cabo Verde no século XVIII." Boletim Cultural da Guiné Portuguesa, XXVII, 105 (January 1972): 123-204.

_____. "Aspectos históricos da evolução do Islamismo na Guiné Portuguesa." Boletim Cultural da Guiné Portuguesa, XXI (1966): 405-56.

_____. As Companhias Pombalinas de Navagação. Lisbon: 1969.

_____. Documentos Para a História das Ilhas de Cabo Verde e "Rios de Guiné". Lisbon: 1983.

_____. Os Portugueses nos rios de Guiné (1500-1900). Lisbon: 1984.

Castro, Armando Augusto Gonçalves de Moraes. Memória da Província da Guiné. Bolama: 1925.

Chagas, C.I.R. das. Escoberta e ocupação da Guiné só pelos
portuguesas. Lisbon: 1840.

Congresso Comemorativo do Quinto Centanário do Descobrimento da
Guiné, 2 vols. Lisbon: 1946.

Corbeil, R., R. Mauny and J. Charbonnier. "Préhistoire et proto-
histoire de la presqu'ile du Cap-Vert et de l'extrême Ouest
Africain." Bulletin. Institut Français d'Afrique Noire, X(1948):
378-460.

Cortesão, Armando Zuzarte. "Subsídios para a história do descobrimento da Guiné e Cabo Verde." Boletim Geral das Colónias.
LXXVI, 1(1931): 2-39.

Costa, Abel Fontoura da. Cartas das ilhas de Cabo Verde de
Valentim Fernandes, 1506-1508. Lisbon: Agência Geral do
Ultramar, 1939.

Cunha, Amadeu. Quinto centenário da descoberta da Guiné, 1446-
1946. Bissau: 1946.

Dinis, Antonio J. Dias. O V centenário do descobrimento da Guiné
Portuguesa à luz da crítica histórica, 1446-1946. Braga: 1946.

Duarte, Fausto Castilho. "Os caboverdeanos na colonização da
Guiné." Cabo Verde: Boletim de Propaganda e Informação.
I, 2(1949-50): 13.

_____. "O descobrimento da Guiné--Aires Tinoco--Um héroi
ignorado." Boletim Cultural da Guiné Portuguesa, VII, 27 (July
1952): 645-56.

_____. "Guiné Portuguesa. A influência política, social e
económica dos regimentos na formação da Colonia." Boletim
Cultural da Guiné Portuguesa, V, 18 (April 1950): 225-56.

_____. "A influência de Cabo Verde na colonização da Guiné."
Boletim da Sociedade de Geografia de Lisbôa, (1943): 57-64.

Faro, Jorge. "Duas expedições enviades a Guiné anteriormente a
1474 e custeadas pela fazenda de D. Afonso V," Boletim Cultural
da Guiné Portugesa, XII, 45 (January 1957): 47-104.

_____. "O movimento comercial do porto de Bissau de 1788 a
1794." Boletim Cultural da Guiné Portuguesa, XIV, 54 (April
1959): 231-60.

Bibliography 152

_____. "A organização administrativa da Guiné de 1615 a 1676." Boletim Cultural da Guiné Portugesa, XIV, 53 (January 1959): 97-122.

_____. "Os problemas de Bissau, Cacheu e suas dependencias visitos em 1831 por Manuel António Martins." Boletim Cultural da Guiné Portuguesa, XIII, 50 (April 1958): 203-18.

Fonseca, Alfredo Loureiro da. Guiné. Alguns aspectos ineditos da actual situação da Colônia. Lisbon: Sociedade de Geografia de Lisboa, 1915.

Gomes, Diogo. De la première découverte de la Guinée. Centro de Estudos da Guiné Portuguesa, publication 21. Bissau: 1959.

_____. "As relações do descobrimento da Guiné e das ilhas dos Acores, Madeira e Cabo Verde." Boletim da Sociedade de Geografia de Lisbõa, XIV, 5(1898-9): 267-93.

Hawkins, John. A True Declaration of the Troublesome Voyage to the Parts of Guinea and the West Indies in 1567 and 1568. London: 1569.

Hawkins, Joye Bowman. "Conflict, Interaction, and Change in Guinea-Bissau: Fulbe Expansion and Its Impact, 1850-1900." Ph.D. Diss., UCLA, Los Angeles, 1980.

Ilha de Canhabaque. Relatório das operações militares em 1935-36 pelo Governador Major de Cavalaria, Luiz António de Carvalho Viegas. Bolama: Imprensa Nacional, 1937.

Innes, Gordon. Kaabu and Fuladu; Historical Narratives of the Gambian Mandinka. London: School of Oriental and African Studies, University of London, 1976.

Keymis, Lawrence. A Relation of the Second Voyage to Guinea, Performed and Written in the Year 1596. London: 1596.

Leite, Duarte. Acerca da "Crónica dos feitos de Guiné." Lisbon: Bertrand, 1941.

_____. "O Cinco centenário do descobrimento da Guiné Portuguesa à luz da crítica histórica." Seara Nova (October 26, 1946): 122-30.

_____. "Um crítico da crónica da Guiné." Revista de Universidade de Coimbra, XIV (1942).

_____. "Do livro inédito: 'Acerca da crónica da Guiné.'" O Diabo, III, 142(March 14, 1937).

Lereno, Alvaro de paiva de Almeida. Subsídios para a história da moeda em Cabo Verde, 1460-1940. Lisbon: Agência Geral das Colonias, 1942.

Lobato, Alexandre. "A expansão ultramarina portuguesa nos séculos XVI e XVII." Ultramar, #29 (1967).

_____. "As fontes e as formas da reorganização ultramarina portuguesa no século XIX." Ultramar, #30 (1967).

_____. "A política ultramarina portuguesa no seculo XVIII." Ultramar, #30 (1967).

Lopes, Edmundo Armenio Correia. A escravatura: Subsídios para a sua história. Lisbon: 1944.

Lyall, Archibald. Black and White make Brown. London: Heinemann, 1936. A study of Portuguese Guinea and Cape Verde.

Manding Studies Conference. London: School of Oriental and African Studies, 1972.

Marinho, Joaquim Pereira. Primera Parte do Relatório de Alguns Accontecimentos Notaveis em Cabo Verde, reposta a Differentes Acusações Feitas Contra O Brigadeiro. Lisbon: 1838. 78 pps.

Mauny, Raymond. "Navigations et découvertes portugaises sur les côtes ouest-africaines." Boletim Cultural da Guiné Portuguesa, VII, 27(July 1952): 515-24.

Mauro, Frédéric. Le Portugal et l'Atlantique au XVIIeme siècle, 1570-1670. Etude économique. Paris: Ecole Pratique des Hautes Etudes, 1960.

Mees, Jules. "Les manuscrits de la 'Chronica do descobrimento e conquista de Guiné' par Gomes Eannes de Azurara et les sources de João de Barros." Revista portuguesa colonial e maritima, IX, 50(1901): 50-62.

Monod, T., Avelino Teixeira da Mota and R. Mauny. Description de la côte occidentale d'Afrique par Valentim Fernandes (1506-1510). 1951.

Monteiro, Júlio, Jr. "Achegas para a história de Cabo Verde." Cabo Verde: Boletim de Propaganda e Informção, I, 12(1949-50): 23.

Moreira, Adriano. "As 'elites' das provincias portuguesas de indigenato (Guiné, Angola, Mocambique)." Garcia de Orta 4, 2 (1956): 159-189.

Mota, Avelino Teixeira da. As viagens do Bispo D. Frei Vitoriano Portuense a Guiné e a cristianização dos Reis de Bissau. Lisbon: Centro de Estudos de Cartografia Antiga, 1974.

_____. "O centenário da morte de Honório Barreto." Boletim Cultural da Guiné Portuguesa, XIII, 50(April 1958): 195-202.

_____. "Chronologia e âmbito das viagens portuguesas de descoberta da Africa Occidental, de 1445 a 1462." Boletim Cultural da Guiné Portuguesa, II, 6(April 1947): 315-41.

_____. "A descoberta da Guiné." Boletim Cultural da Guiné Portuguesa, I, 1(January 1946): 11-68; 2(April 1946): 273-326; 3(July 1946): 457-509.

_____. "Descoberta de bronzes antigos na Guiné Portuguesa." Boletim Cultural da Guiné Portuguesa, XV, 59 (July 1960): 625-34.

_____. "Notas sobre a historiografia da expansão portuguesa e as modernas correntes da investigação africana." Anais do Clube Militar e Naval, LXXIX, 7-9(July-September 1949): 229-94.

Nazareth, Ilido Marinho Falcao de Castro. Projecto de ocupação da Província da Guiné e sua organização militar. Lisbon: Imprensa Nacional, 1911.

Oliveira, José Marques de. "Honório Barreto e os interesses portugueses em Africa." Cabo Verde: Boletim de Propaganda e Informação, XI, 123(1959-60): 13.

PAIGC. História da Guiné e ilhas de Cabo Verde. Porto: 1974.

Pereira, Pachecho. Esmeraldu de Situ Orbis. 1937.

Pimpão, Alvaro Júlio da Costa. "A 'Cronica da Guiné' de Gomes Eanes da Zurara." Biblos, XVII (1926): 374-89, 595-607, 674-87.

Pinto, João Teixeira da. A ocupação militar da Guiné. Lisbon: Agência Geral das Colonias, 1936.

Quinn, Charlotte A. Mandingo Kingdoms of the Senegambia. Evanston, IL: Northwestern University Press, 1972.

_____. "A 19th Century Fulbe State." Journal of African History, XII (1971): 427-40.

Ravenstein, E.G. "The Voyages of Diogo Cão and Bartolomeu Dias, 1482-88." Geographical Journal, (1900): 625-55.

Rema, Henrique Pinto. "As primeiras missões da costa da Guiné (1533-1640)." Separata do Boletim Cultural da Guiné Portuguesa, 22, 87/88 (1967): 225-268.

Rocha, Carlos Ayala Vieira da. João Teixeira Pinto. Uma vida dedicava ao ultramar. 1971.

Schoenmakers, Hans. "The Establishment of the Colonial Economy in Guinea Bissau." Les Cahiers du CEDAF, Brussels, 2-3-4 (June-July 1986): 3-29.

Sidibe, Bakar. "The Traditional Story of Kabu." (Paper presented at the University of London, School of Oriental and African Studies, Manding Conference), 1972.

Silva, Joaquim Duarte. Honório Pereira Barreto. Lisbon, 1939.

Silva, Maria da Graça Garcia Nolasco da. "Subsídios para o estudo dos 'lançados' na Guiné." Boletim Cultural da Guiné Portuguesa, Bissau, vol. 25, nos. 97-100 (1970).

Silva, Viriato Lopes Ramos da. "Subsídios para a história militar da ocupação da Província da Guiné." Boletim da Sociedade de Geografia de Lisboa, XXXIII, 9-10 (September-October 1915): 33-50.

Smith, William. A New Voyage to Guinea. London: John Nourse, 1744.

Snelgrave, William. Nouvelle relation de quelques endroits de Guinée et du commerce d'esclaves qu'on y fait. Amsterdam: 1735.

"Sur le Rio Cacheo--L'esclavage en Guinée Portuguesa--Moussa Molo." Bulletin de la Société de Geographie de Lille, Lille (France), vol. 19, no. 6 (1893).

Teague, Michael. "Bulama in the Eighteenth Century." Boletim Cultural da Guiné Portuguesa, XIII, 50(April 1958): 175-94.

Teixeira, Cândido da Silva. "Companhia de Cacheu, Rios e Comércio da Guiné (Documentos para a sua história)." Boletim do Arquivo Histórico Colonial I(1950): 85-521.

Trigo, António B. Morais. "A morte de Nuno Tristão." Boletim Cultural da Guiné Portuguesa, II, 5(January 1947): 189-92.

Viegas, Carvalho. "História militar da Guiné na sua história geral." Revista militar (1946).

Walter, Jaime (ed.) Honório Pereira Barreto: biografia, documentes.

Bissau: Centro de Estudos da Guiné Portuguesa, publication 5,
1947.

Wren, Walter.   The Voyage of Mr. George Fenner to Guine, and the
Islands of Cape Verde, in the Year of 1566.   London: J.M.
Dent, 1927.

Zurara, Gomes Eanes da.   The Chronicle of the Discovery and Conquest of Guinea, 2 vols.   London: Hakluyt Society, 1896-9.
First published in 1452.

_____.   Crónica dos feitos de Guiné, 2 vols.   Lisbon: 1949.

6. PHYSICAL FEATURES, GEOGRAPHY,
FLORA AND FAUNA

Brito, Raquel Soeiro de.   "Guiné, Cabo Verde e São Tomé e
Principe, Alguns aspectos da terra e dos homens."   Lisbon:
1966.

Cabral, Rego and J.M. Seguro.   "Pequeno estudo sobre os
pavimentos terreos da Guiné e o endurecimento das ruas de
Bissau."   Boletim Cultural da Guiné Portuguesa, IV, 14 (April
1949):   265-72.

Carvalho, Jose A.T. and Fernando J.S. de F.P. Nunes.   Contribuição para o estudo do problema florestal da Guiné Portuguesa.
Lisbon: Junta de Investigações do Ultramar, 1956.

Castel-Branco, Armando J.F.   "Entomofauna da Guiné Portuguesa e
S. Tomé e Príncipe: Hemípteros e Himenópteros."   Boletim Cultural da Guiné Portuguesa, XI, 44 (October 1956):   67-86.

Costa, João Carrington S. da.   Fisiografia e geologia da Província
da Guiné.   Porto: Imprensa Moderna, 1946.

Crespo, Manuel Pereira.   Trabalhos da Missão Geo-Hidrográfica da
Guiné, 1948-55.   Bissau: Centro de Estudos da Guiné Portuguesa, publication 18, 1955.

Ferreira, Fernando Simoes da Cruz.   "A Guiné--Suas características
e alguns problemas."   Boletim Geral das Colónias, XXVI, 306
(December 1950):   9-27.

Galvão, Henrique.   Outras terras, outras gentes, vol. 1.   Lisbon:
1944.

Guerra, Manuel dos Santos.   Terras da Guiné e Cabo Verde,
Lisbon: 1956.

Guimarães, C. "As chuvas na Guiné Portuguesa." Boletim Cultural da Guiné Portuguesa, XII, 47(July 1957): 315-32.

_____. "O clima da Guiné Portuguesa." Boletim Cultural da Guiné Portuguesa, XIV, 55(July 1959): 295-358.

Henriques, Fernando Pinto de Almeida. "'Secas' e 'crises' no Arquipélago de Cabo Verde." Cabo Verde: Boletim de Propaganda e Informação, XII, 143(1960-61): 35.

Mota, Avelino Teixeira da. Toponimos de origem portuguesa na costa ocidental de Africa desde o Cabo Bojador ao Cabo de Santa Caterina. Bissau: Centro de Estudos da Guiné Portuguesa, publication 14, 1947.

Stallibrass, Edward. "The Bijonga or Bissagos Islands." Proceedings of the Royal Geographical Society, XI(1889): 595-601.

Teixeira, A.J. da Silva. Os Solos da Guiné Portuguesa. Lisbon: 1962.

U.S. Department of the Interior. Army Map Service. Geographic Names Division. Portuguese Guinea: Official Standard Names Approved by the U.S. Board on Geographic Names. Washington, D.C.: U.S. Government Printing Office, 1968.

Vasconcelos, Ernesto Julio de Carvalho e. Colónias portuguesas: Estudo elementar de geografia física, económica e política. Guiné Portuguesa. Lisbon: 1917.

Viegas, Luis António de Carvalho. Guiné Portuguesa, 3 vols. Lisbon: Sociedade de Geografia de Lisbõa, 1936-40.

7. ANTHROPOLOGY AND ETHNOLOGY

Ameida, António de. "Das etnonomias da Guiné Portuguesa, do Arquipélago de Cabo Verde e das ilhas de São Tomé e Príncipe." Boletim Geral das Colónias, LIV, 109-48 (1938).

_____. "Sobre e etno-economia da Guiné Portuguesa." Boletim Geral das Colónias, LV, 166-67(1939): 22-32.

Barbosa, Octávio C. Gomes. "Breve notícia dos caracteres étnicos dos indígenas da tribo Beafada." Boletim Cultural da Guiné Portuguesa, I, 2(April 1946): 205-71.

_____. "Contribuição para o estudo dos Biafadas." Disertação, Instituto Superior de Ciências e Política Ultramarina, Universidade Técnica, Lisbon, n.d. [c. 1968].

Bibliography 158

Barros, Augusto de. "A invasão Fula da Circunscrição de Bafata.
Queda dos Beafadas e Mandingas. Tribos 'Gabu ngabé.'"
Boletim Cultural da Guiné Portuguesa, II, 7(July 1947): 737-43.

Barros, Luis Frederico de. Senegambia Portuguesa ou notícia
descriptiva das diferentes tribus que habitam a Senegambia
Meridional. Lisbon: Matos Moreira, 1878.

Bérenger-Féraud, L.J.B. Les peuplades de la Sénégambie.
Paris: 1879.

Bernatzik, H.A. Aethiopien des Westens, 2 vols. Vienna: 1933.

Brito, Eduíno. "Aspectos demográficos dos Balantas e Brâmes do
Território de Bula." Boletim Cultural da Guiné Portuguesa,
VIII, 31(July 1953): 417-70.

_____. "O direito costumeiro e o conceito especial de personali-
dad." Boletim Cultural da Guiné Portuguesa, XX, 79(July 1968):
213-34.

_____. "Festas religiosas do islamismo Fula." Boletim Cultural
da Guiné Portuguesa, XI, 41(January 1956): 91-106.

_____. "Notas sobre a vida familiar e jurídica da tribo Fula.
Instituições civis. I. A família." Boletim Cultural da Guiné
Portuguesa, XII, 47(July 1957): 301-14.

_____. "Notas sobre a vida familiar e jurídica da tribo Fula.
Instituições civis. II. O casamento." Boletim Cultural da
Guiné Portuguesa, XIII, 49(January 1958): 7-24.

_____. "Notas sobre a vida religiosa dos Fulas e Mandingas."
Boletim Cultural da Guiné Portuguesa, XII, 46(April 1957): 149-
90.

_____. "Onomástica Fula e os graus de parentesco." Boletim
Cultural da Guiné Portuguesa, X(1955): 599-616.

_____. "A poligamia e a natalidade entre os grupos étnicos
Manjaco, Balanta e Brâme." Boletim Cultural da Guiné
Portuguesa, VII, 25(January 1952); 161-79.

Bull, Jaime Pinto. "Balantas de Mansoa." Inquerito Ethnografico
(Bissau), (1947).

_____. "Subsídios para o estudo da circumcisão entre os
Balantas." Boletim Cultural da Guiné Portuguesa, VI, 24
(October 1951): 947-54.

Cardoso, Carlos. Mythos, Religion und Philosophisches Denken
in Guinea-Bissau. Cuba: CEAMO.

Caroço, Jorge F.V.   Monjur; o Gabu e a sua história.   Bissau:
Centro de Estudos da Guiné Portuguesa, publication 8, 1948.

Carreira, António Augusto Peixoto.   "Alguns aspectos do regime
jurídico da propriedade imobiliária dos Manjacos."   Boletim
Cultural da Guiné Portuguesa, I, 4(October 1946):   707-12.

_____.   "Aspectos da influência da cultura portuguesa na area
compreendide entre o rio Senegal e o norte da Serra Leõa
(Subsídio para o seo estudo)."   Boletim Cultural da Guiné
Portuguesa, XIX (1964):   373-416.

_____.   "Aspectos históricos da evolução do Islamismo na Guiné
Portuguesa."   Boletim Cultural da Guiné Portuguesa, Separata
do No. 84 (1946):   405-437.

_____.   "A etnonímia dos povos de entre o Gâmbia e o estuario
do Geba."   Boletim Cultural da Guiné Portuguesa, XIX (1964):
233-76.

_____.   Fulas do Gabú.   Bissau: Centro de Estudos da Guiné
Portuguesa, 1948.

_____.   Mandingas da Guiné Portuguesa.   Bissau: 1947.

_____.   "Manjacos-Brames e Balantas."   Boletim Cultural da
Guiné Portuguesa, 22, 85/86 (1967):   41-62.

_____.   Mutilações corporais e pinturas cutaneas rituais dos
negros da Guiné Portuguesa, 51 pp.   Bissau: Centro de
Estudos da Guiné Portuguesa, publication 12, 1950.

_____.   O fundamento dos etnónimos na Guiné Portuguesa.
Bissau: Centro de Estudos da Guiné Portuguesa, 1962.

_____.   "O levirato no grupo étnico Manjaco."   Boletim Cultural
da Guiné Portuguesa, VIII, 29(January 1953):   107-12.

_____.   "Organização social e economica dos povos da Guiné
Portuguesa."   Boletim Cultural da Guiné Portuguesa, XVI, 64
(October 1961):   641-736.

_____.   Panaria Cabo Verde-Guineense Aspectos históricos e
socio-econômicos.   Lisbon: Museu de Etnologia do Ultramar,
1968.

_____.   "A poligamia entre os grupos étnicos da Guiné Portu-
guesa."   Boletim Cultural da Guiné Portuguesa, VI 24(October
1951):   924-25.

_____.   "As primeiras referências escritas à excisão clitoridiana no Ocidente Africano." Boletim Cultural da Guiné Portuguesa, XX (1965): 147-50.

_____. "Região dos Manjacos e dos Brâmes." Boletim Cultural da Guiné Portuguesa, XV, 60(October 1960): 735-84.

_____. "Social and Economic Organization of the People of Portuguese Guinea." Translations on Africa (October 5, 1962): 1-99.

_____. Vida, religião e morte dos Mandingos. Lisbon: 1938.

_____. Vida Social dos Manjacos. Bissau: 1947.

_____ and A. Martins de Meireles. "Notas sobre os movimentos migratórios da população natural da Guiné Portuguesa." Boletim Cultural da Guiné Portuguesa, XIV, 53(January 1959):

Carroco, J. Vellez. Monjur. Bissau: 1948.

Carvalho, Joaquim Pereira Garcia. "Nota sobre a distribuição e história das populações do Posto de Bedanda." Boletim Cultural da Guiné Portuguesa, IV(April 1949): 307-18.

Castro, Armando Augusto Gonçalves de Morais e. "Etnografia da Colónia da Guiné." Mensario administrativo, VII, (April 1948): 27-30.

Cesar, Amandio. Em 'Chao papel' na terra da Guine. Lisbon: 1967.

Cisse, Nouha. "La Fin du Kaabu et les Débuts du Royaume du Fuladu." Mémoire de Maîtrise, Université de Dakar, 1977-78.

Conduto, João Eleuterio. Influência do islamismo na vida económica dos fulas. Lisbon: 1965.

Corrêa, António A. Mendes. "Etudes anthropologiques sur les populations de l'archipel de Cap Vert et de la Guinée Portugaise," vol. 2. Dakar: Institut Français d'Afrique Noire, 1950-51.

_____. Uma jornada científica na Guiné Portuguesa. Lisbon: Agência Geral das Colonias, 1947.

_____. "Movimentos de populações na Guiné Portuguesa." Actas y Memorias. Sociedad Española de Anthropologia, Etnografia y Prehistoria, XXII, 1/4 (1947): 179-96.

_____. Raças do Império. Lisbon: 1943.

_____ and Alfredo Ataíde. "Contribution à l'anthropologie de la
Guinée Portugaise." In Quinzième Congrès International
d'Anthropologie et d'Archéologie Préhistorique. Porto: 1930.

Correia, Carlos Bento. Oamendoim na Guiné Portuguesa. Lisbon:
1965.

Coutouly, Gustave de. "Les populations de l'archipel des Bissagos."
Revue d'Ethnographie et des Traditions Populaires, I (1921):
22-25.

Cunha Taborde, A. de. "Apontamentos etnográficos sobre as
Felupes de Suzana." Boletim Cultural da Guiné Portuguesa,
5 (1950): 187-223.

Diagne, Ahmadou Mapaté. "Contribution à l'étude des Balantes de
Sédhiou." Outre-Mer, V, 1(March 1933): 16-42.

Dias, José Manuel de Braga. "Mudança socio-cultural na Guiné
Portuguesa." Disertação, Instituto Superior de Ciências Sociais
e Política Ultramarino, Universidade de Lisbôa, Lisbon, 1974.

Dinis, António Joaquim Dias. "As tribos da Guiné Portuguesa na
história." Portugal em Africa, 2 ser., III, 16(July-August
1946): 206-15.

_____. "As tribos da Guiné Portuguesa na história (Algumas
notas)." Congresso Comemorativo do Quinto Centenário do
Descobrimento da Guiné, vol. 1, Lisbon (1946): pp. 241-71.

Ethnological Studies on Portuguese Guinea. Translations on Africa,
137(December 3, 1964): 1-55.

Fiel, Conde de Castillo. "Geografia humana de la Guinea Portuguesa:
impresiones de un viage de estudos à travers del Africa
occidental." Archivos del Instituto de Estudios Africanos, II,
4(June 1948).

Fonseca, A.H. Vasconcelos da. "Questionário de inquérito sobre as
raças da Guiné e seus caracteres étnicos." Boletim Oficial da
Colónia da Guiné, suplemento ao 17 Abril, 1927.

Gomes, Barbosa O.C. "Breve notícia dos caracteres étnicos dos
indígenas da tribo Biafada." Boletim Cultural da Guiné
Portuguesa, 1 (1946): 205-274.

Gonçalves. José Júlio. "A cultura dos Bijagós." Cabo Verde:
Boletim de Propaganda e Informação, X, 117(1958-9): 13.

_____. "O islamismo na Guiné Portuguesa." Boletim Cultural
da Guiné Portuguesa, XIII, 52(October 1958): 397-470.

Handem, Diana L. "Nature et fonctionnement de pouvoir chez les Balanta-Brassa." Ph.D. dissertation, School of Higher Studies of the Social Sciences, Paris, 1985.

Hawkins, Joye Bowman. "Conflict, Interaction, and Change in Guinea-Bissau: Fulbe Expansion and Its Impact, 1850-1900." Ph.D. Dissertation, UCLA, Los Angeles, 1980.

Lampreia, Jose D. "Catalogo-universitário da secção de etnografia do Museu da Guiné Portuguesa." Lisbon: 1962.

_____. "Etno-história dos Bahuns da Guiné Portuguesa." Garcia de Orta, #4 (1966).

Leprince, M. "Notes sur les Mancagnes ou Brames." Anthropologie 16(1905): 57-65.

Lima, Augusto J.S. Organização económica e social dos Bijagós. Bissau: Centro de Estudo da Guiné Portuguesa, publication 2, 1947.

Lima, J.A. Peres de and Constâncio Mascarenhas. "Populações indígenas da Guiné Portuguesa." Arquivo de Anatomia e Antropologia, XIII, 4(1929-30): 595-618.

Lopes, Carlos. Etnia, Estado e Relações de Poder na Guiné-Bissau. Lisbon: Edições 70, 1983.

Lopes, Edmundo Armenio Correia. "Antecedentes da aculturação dos povos da Guiné Portuguesa." Mundo Português, XI, 124 (April 1944): 135.

McCullough, Charles Ross. "The State of Prehistoric Archaeology in Morocco, Spanish Sahara, Mauritania, Mali, Gambia, Portuguese Guinea and Senegal." Unpublished master's thesis, University of Pennsylvania, 1969.

Mané, Mamadou. Contribution à l'histoire du Kaabu, des origines au XIXe siècle. Dakar: IFAN, 1979.

Marques, José Eduardo A. da Silva. "A gerontocracia na organização social dos Bijagós." Boletim Cultural da Guiné Portuguesa, X (1955): 293-300.

Mascarenhas, Constâncio and J.A. Pires de Lima. "Populações indígenas da Guiné Portuguesa." Arquivo de Anatomia e Antropologia, XIII (1929-30).

Mateus, Amílcar de Magalhaes. "Acerca da pre-história da Guiné." Boletim Cultural da Guiné Portuguesa, IX, 35(July 1954): 457-72.

_____. "Estudo da população da Guiné Portuguesa. Relato preliminar da primeira campanha da Missão Etnológica e Antropologica da Guiné." Anais. Junta de Missões Geograficas e de Investigações do Ultramar, I (1946): 243-60.

Meireles, Artur Martins de. "Baiu (Gentes de Kaiu). I. Generalidades." Boletim Cultural da Guiné Portuguesa, III, 11(July 1948): 607-38.

_____. Mutilações etnicas dos Manjacos. Bissau: Centro de Estudos da Guiné Portuguesa, publication 22, 1960.

Moreira, José Mendes. "Breve ensaio etnográfico acerca dos Bijagós." Boletim Cultural da Guiné Portuguesa, I, 1(January 1946): 69-115.

_____. Fulas do Gabu. Bissau: Centro de Estudos da Guiné Portuguesa, publication 6, 1948.

_____. "Da ergologia dos Fulas da Guiné Portuguesa." Boletim Cultural da Guiné Portuguesa, XXVI, 101-102(January-April 1971).

_____. "Os Fulas da Guiné Portuguesa na panoramica geral do mundo fula." Boletim Cultural da Guiné Portuguesa, 19, 75, 76 (1964): 289-432.

Mota, Avelino Teixeira da. "A agricultura de Brâmes e Balantas vista através da fotografia aéra." Boletim Cultural da Guiné Portuguesa, V, 18(April 1950): 131-72.

_____. "Etnográfica." Boletim Cultural da Guiné Portuguesa, I, 1(January 1946): 183-90.

_____. Inquérito etnográfico organizado pelo Governo da Colónia no ano de 1946. Bissau: Publicação Comemorativa do Quinto Centenário da Descoberta da Guiné, 1947.

_____. "Notas sobre o povoamento e a agricultura indígena na Guiné Portuguesa." Boletim Cultural da Guiné Portuguesa, VI, 23(July 1951): 657-80.

_____. "A Secunda Conferência Internacional dos Africanistas Ocidentais." Boletim Cultural da Guiné Portuguesa, III, 9(January 1948): 13-74.

_____ and Mario G. Ventim Neves. A Habitação Indígena na Guiné Portuguesa. Bissau: Centro de Estudos da Guiné Portuguesa, publication 7, 1948.

Murdock, George Peter. Africa: Its People and Their Culture and History. New York: McGraw-Hill Book Co., 1959.

Nogueira, Amadeu I.P. "Monografia sobre a tribo Banhum."
Boletim Cultural da Guiné Portuguesa, II, 8(October 1947):
973-1008.

Oliveira, Armindo Estrela de. "Estudo geográfico da Guiné: O
povo balanta." Disertação, Lisbon, 1970.

Pereira, A. Gomes. "Contos Fulas." Boletim Cultural da Guiné
Portuguesa, III, 10(April 1948): 445-52.

Pereira, F. Alves. "Utensílios da época da pedra na Guiné
Portuguesa." O Archéologo Portugueses, XIII (1918).

Quintino, Gernando R. Rogado. "Os povos da Guiné." Boletim
Cultural da Guiné Portuguesa, XXII, 85-86(January-April 1967).

_____. "No segredo das crencas. Das instituições religiosas na
Guiné Portuguesa." Boletim Cultural da Guiné Portuguesa, IV,
15(July 1949): 419-88; 16(October 1949): 687-721.

_____. "Totemism in Portuguese Guinea." Translations on Africa,
#271 (1965): 20-41.

Santos, Eduardo dos. "Catolicismo, protestantismo, e islamismo
na Guiné Portuguesa." Ultramar, VIII, 4(April-June 1968):
112-24.

Santos Lima, A.J. "Organização económica e social dos Bijagós."
Centro de Estudos da Guiné Portuguesa, 2(1947): 1-154.

Silva, Artur Augusto da. "Considerações sobre os direitos de
família e propriedade entre os fulas da Guiné portuguesa e suas
recentes transformações." Extraito do Boletim Cultural da Guiné
Portuguesa, 31 (1953): 405-415.

_____. "Usos e costumes jurídicos dos Felupes da Guiné."
Boletim Cultural da Guiné Portuguesa, XV, 57(January 1960):
7-52.

_____. Usos e costumes jurídicos dos Fulas da Guiné Portuguesa.
Bissau: Centro de Estudos da Guiné Portuguesa, 1958.

_____. "Usos e costumes jurídicos dos Mandingas." Boletim
Cultural da Guiné Portuguesa, XXIII, 90-91(April-July 1968);
XXIV, 93(January 1969).

Taborda, António da Cunha. "Apontamentos etnográficos sobre os
Felupes de Suzana." Boletim Cultural da Guiné Portuguesa, V,
18(April 1959): 187-224; 20(October 1950): 511-61.

Tadeu, Viriato A. Contos do Caramô, lendas e fabulas mandingas da Guiné Portuguesa. Lisbon: Agência Geral das Colonias, 1945.

"Les traditions orales du Gabu." Actes du Colloque international sur les traditions orales du Gabu, Ethiopiques (Dakar), No. 28, Special Issue (October 1981).

Valoura, Francisco. "O Balanta e a Bolanha." Boletim Cultural da Guiné Portuguesa, XXV (1970): 561-68.

Viegas, Luis António de Carvalho. "Os diferentes nucleos populacionais da Guiné Portuguesa e seu estado de civilização na vida familiar." Conferência Internacional dos Africanistas Ocidentais, vol. 5, Bissau (1947): 333-46.

8. LANGUAGE, LITERATURE, AND CRIOULO CULTURE

LANGUAGE

Barbosa, Jorge Morais. "Cabo Verde, Guiné e São Tomé e Príncipe: Situação linguística." Lisbon: Instituto Superior de Ciências Sociais e Política Ultramarina, 1966.

_____. Crioulos: Estudos linguísticos. Lisbon: Academia Internacional da Cultura Portuguesa, 1967.

Bella, L. de Sousa. "Apontamentos sobre a língua dos Balantas de Jabadá." Boletim Cultural da Guiné Portuguesa, I, 4 (October 1946): 729-65.

Bocandé, Bertrand de. "De la langue créole de la Guinée Portugaise. Notes sur la Guinée portugaise ou Sénégambie meridionale." Bulletin de la Société de Géographie de Paris, ser. III, XI (1849): 265-350; XII, 57-93.

Bull, Benjamin Pinto. Le Créole de la Guinée Bissau. Structures Grammaticales Philosophie et Sagesse à travers ses surnoms, ses verbes et ses expressions. Dakar: Faculté des Lettres et Sciences Humaines, 1975.

Cardoso, Henrique Lopes. "Pequeno vocabulário do dialecto 'Pepel.'" Boletim da Sociedade de Geografia de Lisbôa, XX, 10 (1902): 121-28.

Carreira, António Augusto Peixoto. "Alguns aspectos da influência da língua Mandinga na Pajadinca." Boletim Cultural da Guiné Portuguesa, XVIII, 71(July 1963): 345-84.

_____ and João Basso Marques. Subsídios para o estudo da língua Manjaca. Bissau: Centro de Estudos da Guiné Portuguesa, 1947.

Klingenheben, August. "Die Permutationen des Biafada und des Ful." Zeitschrift fur Eingebornen-Sprachen, XV 3(1924): 180-213; 4(1925): 266-72.

"Les langues ethniques de Guinée-Bissau: le créole et le portugais." Réalités africaines et langue française, 11 (June 1979): 8-42.

Lopes, Edmundo Armenio Correia. "O dinheiro nas línguas da Guiné." Mundo Português, XII (1945): 139.

_____. "Manjacos. Língua." Mundo Português, X (1943): 113-114.

Marques, João Basso. "Aspectos do problema da semelhança da língua dos Papéis, Manjacos e Brâmes." Boletim Cultural da Guiné Portuguesa, II, 5(January 1947): 77-109.

Montenegro, Teresa and Carlos de Morais. "Uma primeira interrogação em crioulo a cultural popular oral." Africa. Literature-Arte e Cultura, 2, 6 (October-December 1979): 25-32.

N'Diaye-Correard, Geneviève. Etudes FCA ou Balante (Dialecte Ganja). Paris: SELAF, 1970.

Quintino, Fernando R. Rogado. "Algumas notas sobre a gramática Balanta." Boletim Cultural da Guiné Portuguesa, VI, 21(January 1951): 1-52.

_____. "Conhecimento da língua Balanta, através da sua estrutura vocabular." Boletim Cultural da Guiné Portuguesa, XVI, 64(October 1961): 737-68.

Scantamburlo, Luigi. Gramática e Dicionário da Lingua Criol da Guiné-Bissau. Bologna, Italy: Editrice Missionaria Italiana, 1981.

Silva, Viriato Lopes Ramos da. "Pequeno vocabulário Português-Mandinga." Boletim da Sociedade de Geografia de Lisbôa, XLVII, 3-4(March-April 1929): 98-108; 5-6(May-June 1929): 142-51.

Westermann, Diedrich and M.A. Bryan. Languages of West Africa. Oxford University Press, 1952.

Wilson, William andre Auquier. The Crioulo of Guine. Johannesburg: Witwatersrand University Press, 1962.

LITERATURE

d'Almada, Carlos. "3 Poemas." Africa. Literatura-Arte e Cultura, 2, 10 (October-December 1980): 610-11. Poems by a Guinean.

Andrade, M. de. Antologia de poesia negra de expressão portuguesa. Lisbon: 1956.

_____. "Guiné-Bissau. Seminário sobre a metodologia da recolha das tradições orais." Africa. Literatura-Arte e Cultura, 1, 3 (January-March 1979): 300-305.

_____. Literatura africana de expressão portuguesa. Lisbon: 1967.

Antologia dos Jovens Poetas. Momentos primeiros da construção. Bissau: Conselho Nacional de Cultura, 1978. Anthology of poetry by young Guinean poets.

Barbosa, Alexandre. Guinéus: contos, narrativas, crónicas. Lisbon: Agência Geral do Ultramar, 1967.

Belchior, Manuel Dias. Contos mandingas. Porto: Portucalense Editora, 1968.

_____. Grandeza africana: Lendas da Guiné Portuguesa. 1963.

Boletim Cultural da Guiné Portuguesa. Published African oral literature.

Brocado, Maria Teresa. "Os 10 poemas de Vasco Cabral--Uma leitura." Africa. Literatura-Arte e Cultura, 2, 8 (April-June 1980): 367-376.

Cabral, Vasco. A luta é a minha primavera. Collection of Poetry. Lisbon: Africa Editora, 1981.

_____. "10 Poemas de Vasco Cabral." Africa. Literatura-Arte e Cultura, 1, 5 (July-September 1979): 525-534.

Cesar, Amandio. Contos portugueses do ultramar. I. Cabo Verde, Guiné e S. Tomé e Príncipe. Porto: Portucalense Editora, 1969.

Conduto, João Eleuterio. "Contos Bijagós." Boletim Cultural da Guiné Portuguesa, X (1955): 489-506.

Cooperativa Domingos Badinga. 'N sta li, 'n sta la. Bolama: Imprensa Nacional da Guiné-Bssau, 1979. Book of jokes and riddles published in Crioulo with Portuguese translation.

Os Continuadores da Revolução e a Recordação do Passado Recente.
  Bolama, Guinea-Bissau: Imprensa Nacional, n.d. [c. 1981].
  Collection of poems by Guinean youths.

Dickinson, Margaret. When Bullets Begin to Flower: Poems of
  Resistance from Angola, Mozambique and Guiné. Nairobi: East
  Africa Publishing House, 1973.

Ferreira, Joao. "Dois capítulos do romance inedito 'UANA.'"
  Africa. Literatura-Arte e Cultura, 1, 3 (January-March 1979):
  280-288. Two chapters by a Guinean novelist.

Ferreira, Ondina. "Djidius--pequena mongrafia." Africa. Literatura-
  Arte e Cultura, 1, 3 (January-March 1979): 263-267. Crioulo
  oral literature in Guinea-Bissau.

"Fiju di Mandipole." Africa. Literatura-Arte e Cultura. 2, 9
  (July-September 1980): 454-458. Oral literature of Guinea-
  Bissau.

Filipe, Daniel. O manuscrito na garraía. Lisbon: Guimaraes, 1960.

Gomes, A. "Notas sobre a música indígena da Guiné."
  Boletim Cultural da Guiné Portuguesa, V. 19(July 1950): 411-24.

Hamilton, Russell G. Voices From an Empire: A History of Afro-
  Portuguese Literature. Minneapolis: University of Minnesota
  Press, 1975.

"Joao de Barros--um pintor guineense." Africa. Literatura-Arte
  e Cultura, 1, 1 (July 1978): 40-42.

JUNBAI. storias de bolama e do outro mundo. Bolama, Guiné-
  Bissau: Imprensa Nacional, 1979. Stories and fables written
  in Crioulo as well as translated into Portuguese.

Lopes, Norberto. Terra ardentes: narrativas da Guiné. Lisbon:
  Editora Maritimo Colonial, 1947.

Martinho, Fernando J.B. "A Nova poesia da Guiné-Bissau."
  Africa. Literatura-Arte e Cultura, 1, 2 (October-December
  1978): 157-163.

Matenhas Para Quem Luta! Bissau: Conselho Nacional de Cultura,
  1979. Collection of Guinean poems.

Montenegro, Teresa e Carlos Morais. "Três provérbios em Crioulo--
  Uma aproximação à universalidade dos ditos." Africa. Literatura-
  Arte e Cultura, 3, 11 (January-June 1981): 19-26.

_____. "Uma primeira interrogação em crioulo a cultura popular oral." Africa. Literatura-Arte e Cultura, 2, 6 (October-December 1979): 3-13.

Moser, Gerald M. "The Poet Amílcar Cabral." Research in African Literature, 9, 2 (1978): 176-97.

_____. A Tentative Portuguese-African Bibliography: Portuguese Literature in Africa and African Literature in the Portuguese Language. University Park, PA: Pennsylvania State University Press, 1970.

Pina, F. Conduto de. Grandessa di no tchon. Lisbon: Author's edition, 1978. A novel in Crioulo by a Guinean.

Proenca, Helder. "5 Poemas." Africa. Literatura-Arte e Cultura, 2,6 (October-December 1979): 26-32.

Quintino, Fernando R. Rogado. "Música e dança na Guiné Portuguesa." Boletim Cultural da Guiné Portuguesa, XVIII, 72 (October 1963): 551-70.

_____. "A pintura e a escultura na Guiné Portuguesa." Boletim Cultural da Guiné Portuguesa, XIX (1964): 277-88.

Sequeira, José Pedro Lopes. "Uma palavra humana ligada ao trabalho proficuo de cada um." Africa. Literatura-Arte e Cultura, 1, 4 (April-June 1979): 439-441. Guinean poetry.

Simoes, João Gaspar. "A antologia da ficção cabo-verdeana." Diário de Noticias (January 1, 1961): 13-15.

So, Abdul Carimo. "Presença dos novos poemas e prosas de Abdul Carimo So." Africa. Literatura-Arte e Cultura, 2, 13 (April-June 1986): 65-66.

Torrado, António. "A propósito de um livro de histórias." Africa. Literatura-Arte e Cultura, 1, 4 (April-June 1979): 467-469. Guinean proposes book of tales.

CRIOULO CULTURE

Ferreira, Ondina. "Djidius--pequena mongrafia." Africa. Literatura-Arte e Cultura, 1, 3 (January-March 1979): 263-267. Crioulo oral literature in Guinea-Bissau.

Lyall, Archibald. Black and White Make Brown: An Account of a Journey to the Cape Verde Islands and Portuguese Guinea. London: Heinemann, 1938.

Marupa, M.A. Portuguese Africa in Perspective: The Making of a Multi-Racial State. 1973.

Montenegro, Teresa e Carlos Morais. "Três proverbíos em Crioulo--
    Uma aproximação à universalidade dos ditos." Africa. Literatura-
    Arte e Cultura, 3, 11 (January-June 1981): 19-26.

_____. "Uma primeira interrogação em crioulo a cultura popular
    oral." Africa. Literatura-Arte e Cultura, 2, 6 (October-
    December 1979): 3-13.

Mota, Avelino Teixeira da. "Contactos culturais luso-africanos na
    'Guiné do Cabo Verde.'" Boletim da Sociedade de Geografia de
    Lisbõa, LXIX, 11-12 (November-December 1951): 659.

Pattee, Richard. "Portuguese Guinea: A Microcosm of a Plural
    Society in Africa." Plural Societies, IV, 4 (Winter 1973): 57-64.

Tenreiro, Francisco. "Acerca de arquipélagos crioulos." Cabo
    Verde: Boletim de Propaganda e Informação, XII, 137
    (1960-61): 31.

9. HEALTH AND EDUCATION

Almeida, Fernando C.M. Tavares. "Serviços de Saúde e
    Assistência na Guiné Portuguesa." Ultramar, VIII, 4 (April-
    June 1968): 165-75.

Brandao, J. da Costa. "O ensino na Guiné Portuguesa." Ultramar,
    VII, 4 (April-June 1968): 146-64.

Child Mortality in Guinea-Bissau: Malnutrition or Overcrowding?
    Report of MISAS/SAREC team on project of child health and
    nutrition, October 1978-April 1980. Copenhagen, Denmark:
    Institute of Anthropology, 1983.

Costa, Damasceno Isac de. Relatório do Servico da Delegação de
    Saúde da vila de Bissau, respectivo ao ano de 1884. Lisbon:
    Typografia Guineense, 1887.

A Educação na Guiné-Bissau. Comissariado de Estado da Educação
    Nacional, Bissau: Imprensa Nacional, 1978.

"Education and production in Guinea-Bissau." Development and
    Dialogue, 2 (1978): 51-57.

Ferreira, Fernando S. da C. As tripanosomiases nos territórios
    africanos portuguêses. Centro de Estudos da Guiné Portuguesa,
    publication 9, 1948.

Freire, Paulo. Pedagogy in process. The Letters to Guinea-Bissau.
    New York: The Seabury Press, 1978.

Instituto Nacional de Estudos e Pesquisa. ANO 1. Relatório Anual de Actividades Out.84 a Out.85. Bissau: INEP, 1985.

Lopes, Carlos. Guiné-Bissau Alfabeto. Bologna, 1984.

Macedo, Francisco de. A educação na República da Guiné-Bissau. Braga: Editorial franciscana, 1978.

Mota, Avelino Teixeira da. "O Centro de Estudos da Guiné Portu-guesa." Boletim Cultural da Guiné Portuguesa, VIII (1953): 609-50; X (1955): 641-55.

Oliveira, Darcy de. "Guinée-Bissau: education et processus révolutionnaire." L'homme et la société, 1978: 197-217.

Oliveira, Rosiska e Miguel Darcy de. Guiné Bissau: reinventar a educação. Lisbon: Colecção Cadernos Livros, 1978.

Programa do ensino para as escolas das regioes libertadas. Conakry: PAIGC, n.d.

Regulamento das escolas do partido. Conakry: PAIGC, September 19, 1966.

Sena, Luiz de and Marie Claude Lambert. L'Education en Guinée-Bissau: situation et perspectives. Paris: IRFED, 1977.

Tavares, Estevao. L'enseignement en Guinée 'Portugaise.' Conakry: PAIGC, June 1962.

Tendeiro, João. Actualidade vetermária da Guiné Portuguesa. Bissau: Centro de Estudos da Guiné Portuguesa, publication 15, 1951.

_____. Tripanosomiases animais da Guiné Portuguesa. Bissau: Centro de Estudos da Guiné Portuguesa, publication 110, 1949.

Varela, João Manuel. "Para uma Universidade da Guiné-Bissau/ Capo Verde." Africa. Literatura-Arte e Cultura, 1, 1 (July 1978): 57-64.

10. AGRICULTURE, ECONOMICS, DEVELOPMENT

Almeyra, Guillermo M. "Development as an act of culture: a first-hand report on the experience of Guinea-Bissau." CERES, 11, 1 (1978): 23-28.

Andreini, Jean-Claude and Marie-Claude Lambert. La Guinée-Bissau d'Amilcar Cabral à la reconstruction nationale. Paris: Editions l'Harmattan, 1978.

Areal, Joaquim A. "Possibilidades industriais da Guiné." Boletim
Cultural da Guiné Portuguesa, IX, 36 (October 1954): 707-70.

Baptista, Manuel Martins. "Agricultura da Colónia da Guiné."
Boletim Geral das Colónias, L (February 1934): 49-64.

Bollinger, Virginia L. "Development Strategy's Impact on Ethnically-
Based Political Violence: A Theoretical Framework with Compara-
tive Applications to Zambia, Guine-Bissau and Moçambique."
Ph.D. Diss., University of Colorado at Boulder, 1984.

Cabral, Vasco. "Nécessités sociales et développement économique
planifié." Studia diplomatica, 31, 2 (1978): 153-170.

Centre de Recherches en Aménagement et en Développement (CRAD).
Développement Intègre de la Zone IV [Guinea-Bissau]. Région
de Volama. Rapport de la Phase I. Québec, Canada:
Université Laval/Montréal: Service Universitaire Canadien
Outre-mer (SUCO), 1981.

Dumont, René. "La Guinée-Bissau Peut Encore Echapper au sous-
développement." Le monde diplomatique, July 1979.

Felkai, Istvan. "Tenir la promesse faite aux paysans." Le monde
diplomatique, April 1983.

Ficheiro Nacional de Tabancas, Monografia do Sector de Biombo,
Região de Biombo. Bissau: Department of Regional Development, State Commission on Economic Coordination and Planning,
1980.

Fonseca, Jorge P. Concela de. "Alguns aspectos da colheita,
armazenamento e transporte do amendoim (mancarra) na Guiné
Portuguesa." Garcia de Orta, 2, 3 (1954): 287-309.

Geisslhofer, Hans. Planification villageoise en guinée-bissau.
Dakar: ENDA, 1981.

General Inventory of Animal Husbandry. Bissau: General Bureau
of Statistics and Planning, State Commission of Economic Development and Planning, 1975.

Goulet, Denis. Looking at Guinea-Bissau: a New Nation's Development Strategy. Washington, D.C.: Overseas Development
Council, 1978.

_____. "Political will: the key to Guinea-Bissau's alternative
development strategy." International Development Review, 19,
4 (April 1977): 2-9.

Harrell-Bond, Barbara. "Guinea-Bissau: Part III: Independent

Development." American University Field Staff Report No. 22
(1981).

Henkes, William C. Mineral Industry of Angola, Mozambique and
Portuguese Guinea. Washington: U.S. Bureau of Mines, 1966.

Hochet, Anne-Marie. "Analyse Socio-économique d'Une Tabanca de
la Région de Bafata." Bissau, 1977.

_____. Etude des Habitudes de Consommation et des Besoins en
Produits d'Importation des Populations Rurales de Guinée-Bissau.
Bissau: Ministry of Economic Coordination and Planning, 1981.

_____. Etudes socio-économiques de base sur la Guinée-Bissau,
5 vols. Bissau: Ministry of Economic Coordination and Planning,
1979.

_____. Paysanneries en attente guinée-bissau. Dakar: ENDA,
1983.

_____ and Seco Uldely. Les Ex-Royaumes Pepel du Tor et du
Biombo: Zones d'Emigration Temporaire: Situation Socio-
économique. Bissau: Commissariat of Economic Coordination
and Planning, 1980.

Horta, C.A. Picado. Análise estructural e conjuntural de económia
da Guiné. Bissau: 1965.

International Labour Office. Portugal, Portuguese Guinea, Legislative Decrees: Native Labour. Geneva: 1938.

Introdução à Geografia Económica da Guiné-Bissau. Bissau:
Commissariat of Economic Coordination and Planning, 1980.

Lavrencic, Karl. "New routes in Guinea-Bissau." West Africa
3479 (April 23, 1984): 880.

Macedo, Zeferino Monteiro de. A estatística ante o movimento
comercial da Província no período de 1939-1961. Bissau:
Repartição Provincial dos Serviços de Economica e Estatística
Geral, 1961.

Makedowsky, Eric. "Les Insufficances et les Erreurs de la Politique
Economique." L'Année Politique et Economique Africaine Edition
1981. Société Africaine d'Edition, 1981.

Marini, Emilio. "Desenvolvimento agrícola da Guiné Portuguesa."
Boletim Geral do Ultramar, ano 36, 422-23 (1960): 285-289.

Mendes, José-Luis Morais Ferreira. "Considerações sobre a
problemática da planificação e do desenvolvimento agrícola

na Guiné." Boletim Cultural da Guiné Portuguesa, 26, 101 (1971); 217-223.

_____. "Inquérito Agrícola--Região do Gabu." Boletim Cultural da Guiné Portuguesa, 26, 104 (1971): 785-799.

_____. Problemas e perspectivas do desenvolvimento rural da Guiné. Lisbon: 1968.

Mendonça, Pio Coelho de. "Elevação do nível de vida do trabalhador na Guiné Portuguesa." Boletim Cultural da Guiné Portuguesa, XI, 42 (April 1956): 111-30.

Ministério do Ultramar. "Missão de Inquérito Agrícolas de Cabo Verde, Guiné, São Tomé e Príncipe." Recenseamento agrícola da Guiné, 1960-61. Lisbon: Imprensa Nacional, 1963.

Pereira, Luísa Teotónio and Luís Moita. Guiné-Bissau. 3 Anos de Independência. Lisbon: CIDA-C, 1976.

Projecto do IV Plano de Fomento. II. Ultramar. Lisbon: Imprensa Nacional, Casa de Moeda, 1973.

Quina, Carolina. "Guinée-Bissau. Les enjeux du développement économique." Afrique Asie, 1013, 378 (July 27, 1986): 30-31.

Quintino, Fernando R. Rogado. "Das possibilidades do aumento da produção na Guiné." Boletim Cultural da Guiné Portuguesa, VI, 22 (April 1951): 365-70.

Recenseamento agrícola da Guine, 1960-61. Lisbon: Comissão para os Inquéritos Agrícolas no Ultramar, 1963.

"La République de Guinée-Bissau: Quelques données de base." Marchés tropicaux et mediterranéens, 1741 (March 1979): 733-735.

Reysen, van den, Placca, Bagirishya. Rapport de Mission en Guinée Bissau et aux Iles du Cap-Vert. Addis Abeba: United Nations, FAO/CEA, 1978.

Ribeiro, Maria Luisa Ferro. "Ilha de Santiago--Principais culturas e seu valor económico." Cabo Verde: Boletim de Propaganda e Informação, XIII, 153 (1961-62): 30.

Rudebeck, Lars. "Conditions of Development and Actual Development: Strategy in Guinea-Bissau." In Mai Palmberg, ed., Problems of Socialist Orientations in Africa. Uppsala: Scandanavian Institute of African Studies, 1978.

_____. "Development and Class Struggle in Guinea-Bissau." Monthly Review, 30, 8 (January 1979): 14-32.

_____. Problèmes de pouvoir populaire et de développement.
Transition difficile en Guinée-Bissau. Research Report no. 63.
Uppsala, Sweden: Scandanavian Institute of African Studies,
1982.

Sampaio, Mario. "The New Guinea Bissau: how long will it live?"
African Development (March 1974): 11-13.

Santareno, José Alberto Lemos Martins. "A agricultura na Guiné
Portuguesa." Boletim Cultural da Guiné Portuguesa, XII, 47 (July
1957): 355-84.

Santos, Jesus Nunes dos. "Alguns aspectos da economia da Guiné."
Boletim da Sociedade de Geografia de Lisbõa, LXV, 1-2 (January-
February 1947): 49-71.

Sardhina, Raul M. de Albuquerque and C.A. Picado Horta. "Perspectivas da agricultura, silvicultura e pecuária na Guiné."
Boletim Cultural da Guiné Portuguesa, XXI, 81 (January 1966):
24-306.

Schissel, Howard. "Guinea-Bissau/Cape Verde. Now the boat's
come in." West Africa, 3455 (October 31, 1983): 2510-12.

_____. "Improving productivity [in Guinea-Bissau]." West
Africa, 3405 (8 November 1982): 2883-87.

Silva, Artur Augusto da. "Ensaio de estudo da introdução na
Guiné Portuguesa, das cooperatives agrícolas." Boletim
Cultural da Guiné Portuguesa, IX, 34 (April 1954): 417-30.

Soler, Anita. "Guinée-Bissau: L'Irréparable?" Afrique Asie,
1013, 381 (September 7, 1986): 34.

Sumo, Honore de. "La Guinée-Bissau s'amare a l'Occident."
Jeune Afrique, 1351 (November 26, 1986): 36.

Tall, Moktar Matar. Rapport de Mission (31 Aout-9 Septembre
1983) Valuation du Potentiel Scientifique et Technique de la
Guinée-Bissau. Dakar: Centre de Recherches pour le
Développement International, 1983.

U.S. Bureau of Labor Statistics. Office of Foreign Labor and
Trade. Labor Conditions in Portuguese Guinea. Washington,
D.C.: Government Printing Office, 1966.

Veiga, Aguinaldo and L. Patrício Ribas. "Alguns aspectos da
estrutura económica da Guiné." Boletim Cultural da Guiné
Portuguesa, IV, 14 (April 1949): 289-305.

11. BY AND ABOUT AMILCAR CABRAL

BY AMILCAR CABRAL (arranged by date of publication)

"Algumas considerações ácerca das chuvas." Cabo Verde: Boletim de Propaganda e Informação, I, 1 (1949): 15.

"Em defasa da terra." Cabo Verde: Boletim de Propaganda e Informação, I, 2 (1949-50): 2; 6, 15; II, 14 (1950-51): 19; 15, 6; III, 29 (1951-52): 24.

"Apontamentos sobre poesia caboverdeana." Cabo Verde: Boletim de Propaganda e Informação, 28 Praia, 1952.

"Para o conhecimento do problema da erosão do solo na Guiné, I. Sobre o conceito de erosão." Boletim Cultural da Guiné Portuguesa, IX, 33 (January 1954): 163-94.

"A propósito de mecanização da agricultura na Guiné Portuguesa." Boletim Cultural da Guiné Portuguesa, IX, 34 (April 1954): 389-400.

"Acerca da utilização da terra na Africa Negra." Boletim Cultural da Guiné Portuguesa, IX, 34 (April 1954): 401-16.

"Queimados e pousios na Circunscrição de Fulacunda em 1953." Boletim Cultural da Guiné Portuguesa, IX, 35 (July 1954): 627-46.

"Acerca da contribuição dos 'povos' guineenses para a produção agrícola da Guiné." Boletim Cultural da Guiné Portuguesa, IX, 36 (October 1954): 771-78.

"Recenseamento agrícola da Guiné: estimativa em 1953." Boletim Cultural da Guiné Portuguesa, XI, 43 (July 1956): 7-243.

"A propos du cycle cultural arachide-mils en Guinée Portugaise." Boletim Cultural da Guiné Portuguesa. XIII, 50 (April 1958): 146-56.

"Feux be brousse et jachères dans le cycle cultural arachide-mils," Boletim Cultural da Guiné Portuguesa, XIII, 51 (July 1958): 257-68.

Memorandum enviado ao govérno português pelo Partido Africano da Independência. Conakry: PAIGC, December 1, 1960.

Discurso proferido pelo delegado da Guiné 'Portuguesa' e das ilhas de Cabo Verde, Amílcar Cabral, secretário geral do Partido

Africano da Independência. Cairo: PAIGC, March 25-31,
    1961.

"The Death Pangs of Imperialism." In Rapport général sur la lutte
    de libération nationale. Conakry: July, 1961.

Memorandum à Assembleia Geral da Organização das Nações Unidas.
    Conakry: PAIGC, September 26, 1961.

"Une crise de connaissance." Third Conference of African People,
    (Cairo). 1961.

(Under pseudonym Abel Djassi). The Facts About Portugal's Afri-
    can Colonies, introduction by Basil Davidson. London: Union
    of Democratic Control, 1961.

Un crime de colonialisme (Fondements juridiques de notre lutte
    armée de libération nationale). Extrait du rapport présenté par
    le camarade Amílcar Cabral, au Comité Spécial de l'ONU pour les
    territoires administrés par le Portugal. Conakry: PAIGC,
    1961.

Rapport général sur la lutte de libération nationale. Conakry:
    PAIGC, 1961.

Note ouverte au gouvernement portugais. Conakry: PAIGC,
    1961.

Déclaration sur la situation actuelle de lutte de libération en Guinée
    'Portugaise' et aux îles du Cap Vert. Conakry: PAIGC,
    January 20, 1962.

"Liberation Movement in Portuguese Guinea." Voice of Africa, II
    (March 1962): 32.

"La Guinée Portugaise et les îles du Cap-Vert." Voice of Africa,
    II (May 1962): 37, 39.

Le peuple de la Guinée "Portugaise" devant l'Organisation des
    Nations Unies: Présentée au Comité Spécial de l'ONU pour
    les territoires administrés par le Portugal. Conakry: PAIGC,
    June 1962.

"Guinée, Cap-Vert, face au colonialisme portugais." Partisans, II,
    7 (November-December 1962): 80-91.

La lutte de libération nationale en Guinée Portugaise et aux îles du
    Cap-Vert. Conakry: PAIGC, 1962.

Rapport aux Etats-Unis. Conakry: PAIGC, 1962.

Discours prononcé par chef de la délégation de la Guinée "Portugaise" et des îles du Cap-Vert, secrétaire générale du PAIGC.
Conakry: PAIGC, 1962.

Déclaration faite par M. Amîlcar Cabral du Parti Africaine de
l'Indépendance de la Guinée et du Cap-Vert (PAIGC) lors de
la 1420ème séance de la Quatrième Commission de 12 décembre
1962. N.Y.: PAIGC, 1962.

Déclaration à l'occasion du anniversaire des grèves de Bissao et du
massacre de Pigiuti. Conakry: PAIGC, 1962.

Déclaration du PAIGC sur l'évacuation par les autorités portugaises
des civils européens du sud. Paris: Comité de Soutien à
l'Angola et aux Peuples des Colonies Portugaises, February
1963.

"Solução pacifica para Guiné e Cabo Verde." Portugal Democrático,
VII (February-March 1963): 6.

Nous avons lutté par des moyens pacifiques. Nous n'avons eu que
les massacres et le génocide. Addis Ababa: PAIGC, May
1963.

Pourquoi nous avons pris les armes pour libérer notre pays.
Addis Ababa: PAIGC, May 1963.

"The War in Portuguese Guinea." African Revolution, I (June
1963): 103-108.

"A guerra na Guiné." Portugal Democrático, VIII (October 1963):
3.

"O PAIGC pede à ONU Auxîlio concreto." Portugal Democrático,
VIII (December 1963): 4.

"The Struggle in Guinea." International Socialist Journal, I
(August 1964): 428-46.

"The Struggle of Portuguese Guinea." Translations on Africa,
#77 (1964): 29-40.

Le développement de la lutte nationale en Guinée "Portugaise" et
aux îles du Cap Vert en 1964. Conakry: February 1965.

"La lutte du PAIGC." Remarques Africaines, VII (May 26, 1965):
19-22.

"Liberating Portuguese Guinea from Within." The New African,
IV (June 1965): 85.

"Contra a guerra colonial: mensagem de Amílcar Cabral ao povo da Guiné e de Cabo Verde." FPLN Boletim (August 1965): 14-15.

Intervention faite à la Première Conférence de la Solidarité des Peuples d'Afrique, d'Asie et d'Amérique Latine. Havana: January 1966.

"The Social Structure of Portuguese Guinea and its Meaning for the Struggle for National Liberation." Translations on Africa, #420 (August 24, 1966): 37-48.

"Portuguese Colonial Policy." Africa Quarterly, V, 4 (1966): 287-99.

Fondements et objectifs de la libération nationale. Sur la domination impérialiste. Conakry: PAIGC, 1966.

"L'arme de la théorie." Partisans, #26-27 (1966).

"Combattre et bâtir." La Nouvelle Revue Internationale (February 1967).

"Breve análisis de la estructura social de la Guinea 'Portuguesa.'" Pensamiento Crítico, 2-3 (March-April 1967): 24-48.

"Mankind's Path to Progress." World Marxist Review, X (November 1967): 88-89.

"Determined to Resist." Tricontinental Magazine, #8 (September-October 1968): 114-26.

"National Liberation and Social Structure." In William J. Pomeroy, ed., Guerrilla Warfare and Marxism: A Collection of Writings from Karl Marx to the Present on Armed Struggles for Liberation and Socialism. New York: International Publishers, 1968.

"Guinea (B): Political and Military Situation." Tricontinental, 37 (April 1969): 25-34.

"Guinea: The Power of Arms." Tricontinental Magazine, #12 (May-June 1969): 5-16.

Revolution in Guinea. An African People's Struggle. London: Stage One, 1969; reprinted by Monthly Review, New York, 1970, 1972.

The Struggle in Guinea. Cambridge: Africa Research Group, 1969.

National Liberation and Culture. (Speech delivered at Syracuse University under the auspices of The Program of Eastern

African Studies of the Maxwell School of Citizenship and Public Affairs.) February 20, 1970.

"Report on Portuguese Guinea and the Liberation Movement, Hearing before the Subcommittee on Africa of the Committee on Foreign Affairs, House of Representatives, 91st Congress, second session, Thursday, February 26." Washington: U.S. Government Printing Office, 1970.

"Our Army Is Our Whole People." Newsweek, LXXV (March 9, 1970): 38-39.

"PAIGC: Optimistic and a Fighter." Tricontinental Magazine, #19/20 (July-October 1970): 167-74.

"Report on Portuguese Guinea and the Liberation Movement." Ufahamu, I, 2 (Fall 1970): 69-103.

Sur les lois portugaises de domination coloniale. Conakry: PAIGC, 1970.

Sur la situation de notre lutte armée de libération nationale, janvier-septembre 1970. Conakry: PAIGC, 1970.

Libération nationale et culture. Conakry: PAIGC, 1970.

Guinée "Portugaise": le pouvoir des armes. Paris: François Maspero, 1970.

Message to the People on the Occasion of the Fourteenth Anniversary of the Foundation of the PAIGC. Conakry: PAGIC, 1970.

Revolution in Guinea. New York: Monthly Review Press, 1970.

The Eighth Year of Our Armed Struggle for National Liberation. Conakry: PAIGC, 1971.

A Brief Report on the Situation of the Struggle (January-August 1971). Conakry: PAIGC, 1971.

Sobre a situação da luta. Sobre alguns problemas práticos da nossa vida e da nossa luta. Conakry: PAIGC, August 9-16, 1971.

A consciência nova que a luta forjou nos homens e mulheres da nossa terra é a arma mais poderosa do nosso povo contra os criminosos colonialistas portuguesas. Conakry: PAIGC, September 1971.

"PAIGC Attacks." Tricontinental, 68 (November 1971): 38-39.

"A Brief Report on the Situation of the Struggle (January-August 1971)." Ufahamu, II, 3 (Winter 1972): 5-28.

Our People Are Our Mountains: Amílcar Cabral on the Guinean Revolution. Introduction by Basil Davidson. London: Committee for Freedom in Mozambique, Angola and Guiné, 1971.

"New Year's Address to the People of Guinea and Cape Verde." January 1972.

"PAIGC's Denunciation." Tricontinental Bulletin, #71 (February 1972): 44.

"Speech Given at the 32nd session of the United Nations Security Council, Addis Ababa." February 1972.

"Frutos de una lucha." Tricontinental 31 (July-August 1972): 61-77.

"The People of Guinea and the Cape Verde Islands in front of the United Nations, Speech at the 27th session of the United Nations General Assembly." October 1972.

"Identity and Dignity in Struggle." Southern Africa, V, 9 (November 1972): 4-8.

"Identity and Dignity in the National Liberation Struggle." Africa Today (Fall 1972): 39-47.

"Interview." In NLF: National Liberation Fronts, 1960/1970, Donald C. Hughes and Robert E.A. Shanab, eds. New York: Morrow, 1972, pp. 156-70.

Rapport bref sur la lutte en 1971. Conakry: PAIGC, 1972.

"Establishment of the Peoples National Assembly and the 1972 Election Results, 8 January." 1972.

Mensagem do ano novo. Conakry: PAIGC, January 1973.

"Support for the People's Legitimate Aspirations to Freedom, Independence and Progress." Objective: Justice, V (January-March 1973): 4-7.

"An Informal Talk by A. Cabral." Southern Africa, VI, 2 (February 1973): 6-9.

"Cinquante ans de lutte pour la libération nationale." Questions Actuelles du Socialisme/Socialist Thought and Practice, (March-April 1973): 98-110.

"The Struggle Has Taken Root." Tricontinental, 84 (1973): 41-49. (Press Conference in Conakry in September 1972.)

"Realidades." Tricontinental, 33 (1973): 97-109. Interview.

"Original Writings." Ufahamu, III, 3 (Winter 1973): 31-42.

"On the Utilization of Land in Africa." Ufahamu, III, 3 (Winter 1973): 32-35.

"The Contribution of the Guinean peoples to the Agricultural Production of Guinea. I. Cultivated Area." Ufahamu, III, 3 (Winter 1973), 35-41.

Return to the Source: Selected Speeches of Amílcar Cabral. New York: African Information Service and PAIGC, 1973.

Cabral on Nkrumah. Newark, NJ. PAIGC, 1973.

Revolutsiya v Guinee. Moscow: Glavnaya Redaktsiva Vostochnoi Literaturi, 1973.

"National Liberation and Culture." Transition, IX, 45 (1974): 12-17.

Alguns Princípios do Partido. Lisbon: Seara Nova, 1974.

"Culture and Nationalism." Transition, IX, 45 (1974): 12-17.

Unité et lutte. Paris: Maspéro, 1975. Vol. I: L'arme de la théorie; Vol. II: La pratique révolutionnaire.

Unity and Struggle: Speeches and Writings of Amilcar Cabral. New York: Monthly Review Press, 1980.

Princípios do partido e a prática política 1-6. In Cabral ka muri. Portugal: Department of Information, Propaganda and Culture of the Central Committee of the PAIGC, 1983.

Cabral, Maria H. and Amílcar Lopes Cabral. "Breves notas acerca da razão de ser, objectivos e processo de execução do recenseamento agrícola da Guiné." Boletim Cultural da Guiné Portuguesa, IX, 33 (January 1954): 195-204.

ABOUT AMILCAR CABRAL

Ahmed, Feroz. "Amilcar Cabral: editorial and interview." Pakistan Forum, III, 4 (January 1973): 3-4.

Andelman, David A. "Profile: Amílcar Cabral. Pragmatic

Revolutionary Shows How an African Guerrilla War Can Be
Successful." Africa Report, XV, 5 (May 1970): 18-19.

Andrade, Mário de. Amilcar Cabral. Essai de biographie politique.
Paris: Maspero, 1980.

_____. "Amilcar Cabral et la guerre du peuple." Afrique Asie
66 (23 September-4 October 1974): vii.

_____. "Amílcar Cabral: Profil d'un révolutionnaire africain."
Présence Africaine, #2 (1973): 3-19.

_____. "L'oeuvre de Cabral." Afrique-Asie, 75 (27 January
1975): 14-15.

_____ and Arnaldo Franca. "A cultura na problemática da
libertação nacional e do desenvolvimento a luz do pensamento
político de Amílcar Cabral." Raizes, I, 1 (January-April 1977):
3-19.

Bessis, Sophie. "Qui a Tué Amilcar Cabral?" Jeune Afrique,
1193 (November 16, 1983): 53-56, 61.

Bienen, Henry. "State and Revolution, the work of Amílcar
Cabral." Journal of Modern African Studies, XII (June 1974):
191-210.

Bockel, Alain. "Amilcar Cabral, marxiste africain." Ethiopiques,
5 (January 1976): 35-9.

Bragança, Aquino de. Amilcar Cabral. Lisbon: Initiativas Editori-
ais, 1976.

_____. "L'Assassinat de Cabral." Afrique-Asie, XXIV (February
19-March 4, 1973): 8-15.

_____. "The Plot Against Cabral." Southern Africa, (May 1973):
4-8.

"Cabral is Assassinated by Portuguese Agents." African World
(February 3, 1973): 1-16.

Cardoso, Carlos. "Os Fundamentos do conteúdo e dos objectivos da
Libertação Nacional no pensamento de A. Cabral." Conferência
Internacional sobre a Personalidade de A. Cabral, December
1984.

Chabal, Patrick. "Amilcar Cabral as revolutionary leader." Ph.D.
Thesis, Trinity College, University of Cambridge, August 1980.

_____. Amilcar Cabral. Revolutionary leadership and people's
war. Cambridge: Cambridge University Press, 1983.

_____. "The social and political thought of Amilcar Cabral: a reassessment." Journal of Modern African Studies, 19, 1 (March 1981): 31-56.

Chaliand, Gérard. "The Legacy of Amilcar Cabral." Ramparts, (April 1973): 17-20.

_____. "The PAIGC Without Cabral: An Assessment." Ufahamu, III, 3 (Winter 1973): 87-95.

Chilcote, Ronald H. "African Ephemeral Material: Portuguese African Nationalist Movements." Africana Newsletter, I (Winter 1963): 9-17.

_____. "Amilcar Cabral: A bibliography of his life and thought, 1925-1973." Africana Library Journal, 5, 4 (Winter 1974): 289-307.

_____. "The Political Thought of Amílcar Cabral." Journal of Modern African Studies, VI, 3 (October 1968): 378-88.

Clapham, Christopher. "The context of African political thought." Journal of Modern African Studies, 8, 1 (1970): 1-13.

Crimi, Bruno. "Amilcar Cabral prêt pour l'independance." Jeune Afrique 619 (18 November 1972): 12-16.

_____. "Les assassins de Cabral." Jeune Afrique (February 3, 1973): 8-12.

_____. "Autopsie d'un assassinat politique." Jeune Afrique, 604 (5 August 1972): 36-9.

_____. "La vérite sur l'assassinat d'Amilcar Cabral." Jeune Afrique 734 (31 January 1975): 18-21.

Dadoo, Yusuf. "Amilcar Cabral--outstanding leader of Africa's liberation movements." African Communist 53, 2 (1973): 38-73.

Davidson, Basil. "Amílcar Cabral--Death of an African Educationist." Times Educational Supplement, #3009 (January 26, 1973): 6.

_____. "Profile of Amílcar Cabral." West Africa, XXVII (April 1964).

Ferreira, Eduardo de Sousa. "Amílcar Cabral: Theory of Revolution and Background to His Assassination." Ufahamu, III, 3 (Winter 1973): 49-68.

Figueiredo, A. de. "Amílcar Cabral." Race Today (February 1973): 40.

Ignatiev, Oleg. Amílcar Cabral: filho de Africa. Lisbon: Prelo
    Editora, 1975.

_____. Três tiros da PIDE. Quem, porque e como mataram
    Amílcar Cabral. Lisbon: Prelo Editora, 1975.

Intelligence Report. "Amílcar Cabral: a commentary." Lisbon:
    Overseas Companies of Portugal, 1973.

Jinadu, L.A. "Some African Theorists of Culture and Modernization:
    Fanon, Cabral and some others." African Studies Review, 21,
    1 (April 1978): 121-138.

Kravcova, T.I. "Amilkar Kabral (1924-1973)." Narodny Azii Afriki,
    #3, (1974): 76-87.

Lopes, Carlos. "As dominantes teóricas no pensamento de A.
    Cabral." Revista Internacional de Estudos Africanos, 2 (June-
    December 1984).

Magubane, Bernard. "Amílcar Cabral: Evolution of Revolutionary
    Thought." Ufahamu, II, 2 (Fall 1971): 71-87.

Marcum, John A. "Guinea Bissau: Amílcar Cabral; The Meaning of
    an Assassination." Africa Report, #18 (March 1973): 21-23.

McCollester, Charles. "The political thought of Amilcar Cabral."
    Monthly Review, 24, 10 (March 1973): 10-21.

Morgado, Michael S. "Amílcar Cabral's Theory of Cultural Revolu-
    tion." Black Images, III, 2 (1974): 3-16.

Moser, G.M. "The Poet Amilcar Cabral." Research in African
    Literature, 9, 2 (1978): 176-97.

Nyang, S. "The political thought of Amilcar Cabral: a synthesis."
    Odu, 13 (January 1976): 3-20.

Opuku, K. "Cabral and the African revolution." Présence Afri-
    caine, 105-6 (1978): 45-60.

PAIGC. "Amílcar Cabral: O homen e a sua obra." July 1973.

_____. "Palavras de ordem gerais do camarada Amílcar Cabral
    aos responsaveis do partido, november de 1965." Conakry,
    1969.

La pensée politique d'Amilcar Cabral. Montreal: SUCO, 1978.

Reed, Rick. "A Song of World Revolution: In Tribute to Amílcar
    Cabral." Institute of the Black World Monthly Report (February
    1973).

Segal, Aaron. "Amilcar Cabral: in memoriam." Third World, 2, 4 (April 1973): 7-8.

"Tributes to Amílcar Cabral." Ufahamu, III, 3 (Winter 1973): 11-29.

Vieyra, Justin. "Amílcar Cabral: liberté pour 350,000 Guinéens." Jeune Afrique, #230 (May 1, 1965): 23.

"Without Cabral." Economist, CSLVI (January 1973): 29+.

12. ON NATIONAL LIBERATION

"Allies in Empire: The U.S. and Portugal in Africa." Africa Today, 17, 4 (July-August 1970).

Amadou, Fode. "Cette année, un nouvel état souverain." Afrique Asie, 36 (6 August 1973): 31-2.

Anderson, P. "Portugal and the End of Ultra-colonialism." New Left Review, nos. 15 and 16, 2 parts, n.d.

Andrade, F.J.H. Rebelo de. "Armed Forces Activities in Portuguese Guinea." Ultramar, VII, 4 (April-June 1968): 176-200.

Andrade, Mario de. A guerra do povo na Guiné-Bissau. Lisbõa: Livraria Sa da Costa Editoria, 1975.

_____. "Colonialisme, culture et revolution." In Colones portugaise: la victoire ou la mort. Havana: Tricontinental, 1970; 39-53.

Beetz, Dietmar. Visite in Guine-Bissau. Berlin: Podium, 1975.

Belchior, Manuel. Os Congressos do povo da Guiné. Lisbon: Editora Arcadia, 1973.

Bender, Gerald J. "Portugal and Her Colonies Join the Twentieth Century." Ufahamu, IV, 3 (1974): 121-62.

Bergersol, J. "Guinea-Bissau Begins to Reconstruct." African Development, (October 1974): 18-19.

Biggs-Davison, John. Portuguese-Guinea: Nailing a Lie. London: Congo Africa Publications, 1970.

Bosgra, S.J. and C. Van Krimpen. Portugal and Nato. Amsterdam: Angola Comité, 1970.

Bouabid, M. "Guinée Bissau: l'heure de la reconstruction." Révolution africaine, 555, 11-17 (October 1974): 20-27.

Bragança, Aquino de. "Eloge d'une bourgeoisie africaine
     (l'expérience révolutionnaire de Guinée-Bissau)." In
     Problèmes actuels de l'unité africaine. Algiers: SNED, 1973;
     512-24.

_____. "Guinée-Bissau: les vérités sur les négociations."
     Afrique Asie 58 (10 June 1974): 16-18.

_____. "La longue marche d'un révolutionnaire africain."
     Afrique-Asie, XXIII, 5 (February 18, 1973): 12-20.

Cabral, Vasco. "Foreign Capitalist Interests in the So-Called
     Portuguese Guinea and the Islands of the Green Cape." In
     Peace and Socialism--Al Tali'a Seminar: Africa; National and
     Social Revolution, (Cairo, October 24-29), II, ref. #36 (1966).

_____. "Guinea-Bissau." World Problems of Marxism, Peace and
     Socialism Review (February 1974): 113-16.

_____. Intervention du camarade Vasco Cabral, membre du
     Comité Executif de la Lutte de PAIGC, au symposium en
     mémoire d'Amílcar Cabral. Conakry: PAIGC, January 1973.

_____. "Speech of the Delegation of 'Portuguese' Guinea." In
     Peace and Socialism--Al Tali'a Seminar: Africa; National and
     Social Revolution, (Cairo, October 24-29), II, ref. #42 (1966).

Campbell, Bonnie. Libération nationale et construction du socialisme
     en Afrique (Angola, Guinée-Bissau et Mozambique). Montréal:
     Editions Nouvelles Optique, 1977.

Cesar, Armandio. Guiné 1965: contra-ataque. Braga: Editoria
     Pax, 1965.

Chabal, Patrick. Amilcar Cabral. Revolutionary leadership and
     people's war. Cambridge: Cambridge University Press, 1983.

_____. "Guinée-Bissau, Cap Vert: histoire et politique." Le
     Mois en Afrique: Revue d'études politiques et économiques
     africaines, 190-191 (October-November 1981): 119-31.

_____. "National Liberation in Portuguese Guinea, 1956-1974."
     African Affairs, 80, 318 (January 1981): 75-99.

Chaliand, Gérard. Armed Struggle in Africa: With the Guerrillas
     in "Portuguese Guinea." New York: Monthly Review Press,
     1969.

_____. Guinée "Portugaise" et Cap Vert en lutte pour leur
     indépendance. Paris: François Maspero, 1964.

_____. "The PAIGC without Cabral." Ufahamu, 3, 3 (Winter 1973): 87-95.

Chilcote, Ronald H. "Development and Nationalism in Brazil and Portuguese Africa." Comparative Political Studies (January 1969).

_____. "Guine-Bissau's struggle: past and present." Africa Today, 24, 1 (January-March 1977).

_____. "Nationalist Documents on Portuguese Guinea and Cape Verde Islands and Mozambique." African Studies Bulletin, X, 1 (April 1967): 22-42.

_____. "Struggle in Guinea-Bissau." Africa Today, #21 (Winter 1974): 57-62.

Comité de Soutien à l'Angola et aux Peuples des Colonies Portugaises. Guinée "Portugaise" et îles du Cap-Vert, l'an deux de la guerre de Guinée, janvier-décembre, 1964. Paris: 1965.

_____. La lutte continue, janvier-avril, 1964. Paris: 1964.

Cornwall, Barbara. The Bush Rebels: A Personal Account of Black Revolt in Africa. New York: Holt, Rinehart and Winston, 1972.

Crimi, Bruno. "Guinée-Bissau: naissance d'un état." Jeune Afrique, 666 (13 October 1973): 24-8.

Cruz, Luis Fernando Diaz Correia da. "Alguns aspectos da subversão na província portuguesa da Guiné." Ultramar, VIII, 4 (April-June 1968): 125-47.

Davidson, Basil. Growing from Grass Roots. The State of Guinea Bissau. London: Committee for Freedom in Mozambique, Angola and Guiné, n.d.

_____. "Guinea-Bissau and the Cape Verde Islands: The Transition from War to Independence." Africa Today (Fall 1974): 5-20.

_____. "Guinea-Bissau Builds for Independence." New World Review, XLI, 2 (1973): 36-42.

_____. "Guinée-Bissau: naissance d'une démocratie africaine." Le Monde Diplomatique, 247 (October 1974): 34-6.

_____. "An Independent Guinea-Bissau: Political Foundations." West Africa (January 29, 1973).

_____. The Liberation of Guiné: Aspects of an African Revolution. Harmondsworth: Penguin, 1969.

_____. "Liberation Struggles in Angola and 'Portuguese' Guinea." Africa Quarterly, X, 1 (April-June 1970): 25-31.

_____. No Fist Is Big Enough to Hide the Sky. The Liberation of Guinea-Bissau and Cape Verde. London: Zed Press, 1981.

_____. "Notes on a Liberation Struggle." Transition, IX, 45 (1974): 10-21.

_____. "Practice and Theory: Guinea-Bissau and Cape Verde." In Barry Munslow, ed., Africa. Problems in the Transition to Socialism. London: Zed Books, 1986; 95-113.

_____. "The Prospect for Guinea-Bissau." Third World (April 1973): 3-6.

_____. "A Report on the further liberation of Guinea." The Socialist Register (1973): 283-301.

_____. "Revolt of 'Portuguese' Guinea." Tricontinental Magazine, #8 (September-October 1968): 88-91.

_____. "Victory and Reconciliation in Guinea-Bissau." Africa Today, XXI (Fall 1974): 5-22.

Davis, Jennifer. The Republic of Guinea-Bissau: Triumph Over Colonialism. New York: The Africa Fund, n.d.

Decisão. Conakry: PAIGC, August 30, 1970.

Dias, H. "'Portuguese' Guinea." Portuguese and Colonial Bulletin, V, 6 (December 1965-January 1966): 300.

Dias, José Manuel de Braga. "Mudança Sócio-Cultural na Guiné Portuguesa." Disertação, Universidade Técnica de Lisboa, Instituto Superior de Ciências Sociais e Política Ultramarina, Lisbon, 1974.

Diggs, Charles C., Jr. "Text of the proclamation of the state of Guinea-Bissau by the people's national assembly." Issue; a quarterly journal of africanist opinion, 3, 3 (1973): 28-32.

Duarte, Abilio Monteiro. "Aiding the Struggle in 'Portuguese' Guinea." Revolution, I (August-September 1963): 44-47.

_____. "On the Question of Territories under Portuguese Domination." United Nations General Assembly Document A/AC.109/PV.966, 29 march, 1974, 53 pps.

_____. "'Portuguese' Guinea." Information Bulletin (World Marxist Review), #42 (May 13, 1965): 53-54.

Duffy, J. "Portugal in Africa." Foreign Affairs, XXXIX (April 1961): 481-93.

Ehhmark, Anders and Per Wastberg. Angola and Mozambique: The Case Against Portugal. New York: Roy Publishers, 1963.

Felgas, Helio. A luta na Guiné. Lisbon: 1970.

_____. Os movimentos terroristas de Angola, Guiné, Moçambique (Influencia externa). Lisbon: 1966.

Fernandez, Gil. "Talk with a Guinean Revolutionary." Ufahamu, I, 1 (Spring 1970): 6-21.

_____. "We Are Anonymous Soldiers of U.N." Objective: Justice, IV, 1 (January-March 1972): 48.

Frente de Libertação da Guiné e Cabo Verde, Partido Africano da Independência. Message to the Portuguese Colonists in Guiné and Cape Verde. Conakry: October 1960.

Frente de Luta pela Independência Nacional de Guiné Bissau. Charte préambule. Dakar, 1962.

Galtung, Ingegerd. Reports from so-called liberated Portuguese Guinea-Bissau. Morgenbladet, Oslo, n.d.

"Guerre et paix en Guinée-Bissau: Naissance d'une Nation." Afrique-Asie, 66 (September 23-October 6, 1974).

"Guinea-Bissau: Along the People's Paths." Tricontinental Bulletin, #70 (January 1972): 43-47.

"Guinea-Bissau: La Victoire Reconnue." Afrique Asie, 65 (9-22 September 1974): 22-23.

Guinea-Bissau: Toward Final Victory. Selected Speeches and Documents from PAIGC (Partido Africano da Independência da Guiné e Cabo Verde). Richmond, B.C., Canada: LSM Press, 1974.

Guiné-Bissau: 3 Anos de Independência. Lisbon: Africa in Struggle Series, Anti-Colonial Center for Information and Documentation, CIDA-C, 1976.

"Guinea-Bissau's Liberation Struggle." Race Today, III, 11 (November 1971): 377-75.

Guinée e Cap-Vert. Libération des colonies portugaises. Algiers: Information CONCP (Conférence des Organisations Nationales des Colonies Portugaises), 1970.

Guinée, Peter. Portugal and the EEC. Amsterdam: Angola Comité in cooperation with the Programme to Combat Racism of the World Council of Churches, Geneva, 1973.

Gupta, Anirudha. "African Liberation Movements: A Bibliographical Survey." Africa Quarterly, X, 1 (April-June 1970): 52-60.

Hadjor, Kofi B. "The Revolution in Guinea-Bissau." Africa, (April 1974): 12-14.

Henrikson, Thomas. "People's war in Angola, Mozambique, and Guinea-Bissau." Journal of Modern African Studies, 14, 3 (1976): 377-99.

Hoti, Ukson. "The Liberation Struggle in the Portuguese Colonies." Review of International Affairs (November 5-20, 1972): 30-31.

Hubbard, Maryinez L. "Culture and History in a Revolutionary Context: Approaches to Amílcar Cabral." Ufahamu, III, 3 (Winter 1973): 69-86.

Ignatyev, Oleg Konstantinovich. Along the Paths of War: War Diaries from Three Fronts of Guinea. Moscow: Political Literature Publications, 1972.

"L'Independence du Cap-Vert: Un nouveau pays vers l'unité avec la Guinée-Bissau." Afrique-Asie, no. 86 (1975).

Infante, M. "La Guinée-Bissau all'ora dell'independenza." Politica Internazionale, 10 (October 1973): 54-56.

International Union of Students. Report of a Visit to the Liberated Areas of Guinea-Bissau. Helsinki: National Union of Finnish Students, 1971.

Ivekovic, I. "Guinée-Bissau: naissance d'une indépendance." Questions actuelles du Socialisme, 25, 7-8 (July-August 1975): 141-156.

Lawrence, Ken. "PIDE & SDECE: Plotting in Guinea." In Ellen Ray et al., Dirty Work: the CIA in Africa. London: Zed Press, 1980; 140-145.

Lefort, René. "Avec les nationalistes de Guinée portugaise." Le Monde, #6-7 (November 1970).

"Liberation Movements in Portuguese Guinea (PAIGC) Totes Up

1964 Achievements." Translations on Africa, 220 (1964): 5-10.

Liberation Support Movement. "Sowing the First Harvest: national reconstruction in Guinea-Bissau." Oakland, CA: 1978.

Lipinska, Suzanne. "Deux semaines dans le maquis de la Guinée-Bissao." Africasia, #16-18 (1970).

Lobban, Richard. "The Fall of Guiledge." AFRICA Magazine, August 1973, no. 24, Paris.

_____. "Guinea-Bissau: A New Era." New World Review, January-February 1975.

_____. "Guinea-Bissau: 24 September and Beyond." Africa Today 21, 1 (1974): 15-24.

_____. "Interview with President Luis Cabral." Southern Africa, VIII, 9 (1975): 12-14.

_____. "The Progress of the War in Guinea-Bissau." Southern Africa, August 1973.

Lopes, Carlos. Etnia, Estado e Relações de Poder na Guiné-Bissau. Lisbon: Edições 70, 1982.

_____. Guinea Bissau: From Liberation Struggle to Independent Statehood. London: Zed Press, forthcoming.

_____. "A Transição Histórica na Guiné-Bissau; do Movimento de Libertação Nacional ao Estado." Mémoire. Geneva: Institute Universitaire d'Etudes du Développement, November 1982.

Magarido, Alfredo see Margarido, Alfredo

Makedonsky, Jeanne. "L'épineuse décolonisation de la Guinée-Bissau." Revue française d'Etudes politiques Africaines, 9, 105 (September 1974): 43-55.

Makedowsky, Eric. "Le PAIGC seul maitre à bord." Afrique et Monde (August 13, 1974).

Malatu, G. "Viva Guinea Bissau." Africa, 38 (October 1974): 11-16.

Marcum, J. "Three Revolutions." Africa Report, 12, 6, November 1967.

Marcum, John A. The Politics of Indifference: Portugal and Africa,

A Case Study in American Foreign Policy. Syracuse University:
Program of Eastern African Studies, 1972.

Marcus, J. "A New Departure in Luso-America Relations." Africa
Today, 16, 1 (February-March 1969).

Margarido, Alfredo. "Guinée et Guinée-Bissau: Bilan provisoire
de la tentative d'invasion de novembre." Revue Française
d'Etudes Politiques Africaines, #63 (March 1971): 18-20.

_____. "Partis politiques africains sous domination portugaise."
Revue Française d'Etudes Politiques Africaines (July 1968): 44-68.

_____. "Les partis politiques en Guinée portugaise, en Angola,
et aux îles du Cap Vert." Mois en Afrique, #9 (July 1966).

Maria, Victor. "La Guinée 'portugaise.'" Voices of Africa, II
(March 1962): 34-35.

Martelli, George. "Progress in Portuguese Guinea." Geographical
Magazine (June 1967): 128-37.

Matteos, Salahudin Omawale. "The Cape Verdeans and the PAIGC
Struggle for National Liberation." Ufahamu, III, 3 (Winter
1973): 43-48.

McCollester, Charles. "The Political Thought of Amílcar Cabral."
Monthly Review, XXIV, 10 (March 1973): 10-21.

Mendy, Justin. "The Struggle Goes On." Africa Report (March-
April 1973): 24.

Miranda, Nuno de. "Defesa de Portugal." Cabo Verde: Boletim
de Propaganda e Informação, XIII, 147 (1961): 6.

Moolman, J.H. "Portuguese Guinea: The Untenable War." Africa
Institute Bulletin, XII, 6 (1974): 243-60.

Movimento de Libertação da Guiné e Cabo Verde. Proclamação.
Conakry: November 1960.

"Naissance d'un nouvel état africain: la République de Guinée-
Bissau." Présence Africaine, IV (1974): 248-301.

Neto, João Baptista Nunes Pereira. "Movimentos Subversivos da
Guiné, Cabo Verde e São Tomé e Príncipe." Cabo Verde, Guiné,
São Tomé e Príncipe. Lisbon: 1966.

Ngwube, Douglas. "Guinea-Bissau: Decisive Phase." Africa
(June 1974): 23-24.

Obichere, Boniface I.   "Reconstruction in Guinea-Bissau: From Revolutionaries and Guerrillas to Bureaucrats and Politicians." Current Bibliography on African Affairs, XIII (1975).

O'Brien, J.   "Tribe, class, nation: revolution and the weapon of theory in Guinea-Bissau." Race and Class, 19, 1 (1977): 1-18.

Ogawa, Tadahiro. Nô Pintcha. Tokyo: Taimatsu-Sha, 1972.

PAIGC.   [Arranged by date.]   "Estatutos dos Pioneiros do Partido." Conakry: n.d.

_____. "Statuts et programme." Conakry: 1962.

_____. Communiques. "Le Peuple de la Guinée 'portugaise' devant l'ONU." New York: 1962.

_____. Communiques. Extraits de quelques articles de l'organe du Partido Africano da Independência de la Guinée 'Portugaise' et des îles du Cap-Vert. Conakry: April 1963.

_____. Communiques. Développement de la lutte de libération nationale: l'action du PAIGC. Algiers: 1963.

_____. Communiques. Le développement de la lutte de libération nationale en Guinée 'portugaise' et aux îles du Cap Vert en 1964. Conakry: 1964.

_____. Communiques. Le PAIGC à la conférence des chefs d'état et de gouvernement des pays non-alignés le Caire, octobre 1964. Conakry: 1965.

_____. Lei da justiça militar de 19 de Setembro de 1966, com as modificações introduzidas pelo Bureau Político do Partido, na reunião de 20a 23 de dezembro de 1966. Conakry: 1966.

_____. Statuts de l'Institut Amitié. Conakry: 1969.

_____. O nosso livro, primeira classe. Uppsala: 1970.

_____. Regulamento de disciplina interna. Quembra: 1970.

_____. Regulamento interno dos internatos das regiões libertades, Conakry: September 1971.

_____. Manual Político. Vol. 1. Conakry: 1972.

_____. O nosso livro, quarta classe. Uppsala: 1972.

_____. Projecto da revisão de lei da justiça militar. Conakry: 1972.

_____ [and United Nations]. Resolution adoptée par le Comité
Spécial à sa 854ème séance, le 13 avril 1972 à Conakry (Guinée).
AF/109/63, 1972.

_____. Message du Comité Exécutif de la Lutte du PAIGC.
Conakry: January 1973.

_____. Biographies sommaires des membres du Secrétariat Perma-
nent du Comité Exécutif de la Lutte, 24 July. Conakry: 1973.

_____. Proclamação do Estado da Guiné-Bissau, Adopted by the
Peoples National Assembly, 24 September 1973. Boé, Guiné-
Bissau: 1973.

_____. Sobre a situação em Cabo Verde. Lisbõa: 1974.

Pereira, Aristides. Communiqué. Conakry: PAIGC, October 2,
1972.

_____. "Guinée 'portugaise': dernier quart d'heure?"
Révolution africaine, 99 (19 December 1962): 7.

Pineau, Guy. Le PAIGC et la Lutte de Libération Nationale en
Guinée Bissau et aux Iles du Cap Vert. Mémoire. Université
de Paris, October 1972.

Pinto, Cruz. "Guinea-Bissau's Liberation Struggle Against Portuguese Colonialism." Freedomways, #3 (1972).

"La politique étrangère de Guinée-Bissau." La Révolution Africaine,
October 1974.

Portuguese Colonies: Victory or Death. Havana, Cuba: Tricontinental, 1971.

"Portuguese Guinea: More War Than Most." Africa Confidential, 3
(February 2, 1968).

"Le Problème des réfugiés de la Guinée-Bissau en Casamance."
Sénégal d'aujourd'hui, 12 (October 1964): 11-17.

Rodrigues, Manuel M. Sarmento. No Governo da Guiné. Discursos
e afirmações. Lisbon: Agência Geral do Ultramar, 1949.

_____. A Nossa Guiné. Lisbon: 1972.

Rodrigues, Paulo Madeira. 4 Paises Libertados. Portugal, Guiné-
Bissau, Angola, Moçambique. Lisbon: Livraria Bertrand, 1975.

Rubio Garcia, L. "El caso de Guinea-Bissau: uma descolonizacion
vista como fenômeno cultural." Revista de Política internacional,
139 (May-June 1975): 169-190.

Rudebeck, Lars. Guinea-Bissau: A Study of Political Mobilization. Uppsala: Scandinavian Institute of African Studies, 1974.

_____. "Political Mobilisation for Development in Guinea-Bissau." Journal of Modern African Studies, 10, 1 (1972): 1-18.

Rurihose, N. "La reconnaissance de la Guinée-Bissau et le droit international." Etudes zairoises, 3 (December 1973): 73-89.

Sampaio, Mário. "The New Guinea-Bissau: How Will It Survive?" African Development (March 1974): 11-13.

Schilling, Barbara (ed.). Angola, Guinea, Mozambique. Dokumente und Materialien des Befreiungskampfes des Volker Angolas, Guinea und Mozambique. Frankfurt-am-Main: Verlag Marxistische Blatter, 1971.

Sevilla-Borja, H. et al. "U.N. General Mission to Guinea (Bissau)." Objective: Justice, #4 (July-September 1972): 4-15.

"The Situation of Portuguese Guinea Refugees in the Casamance Region of Senegal." Translations on Africa, 108 (1964): 17-21.

Spínola, António de. Por uma Guiné melhor. Lisbon: Agência Geral do Ultramar, 1970.

_____. Portugal e o futuro. Lisbôa: Arcadia, 1974.

_____. O problema da Guiné. Lisbon: Agência Geral do Ultramar, 1970.

Sun of Our Freedom: The Independence of Guinea Bissau. Chicago: Chicago Committee for the Liberation of Angola, Mozambique and Guinea, 1974.

Tavares, Estevão et al. Déposition des ex-détenus par la police politique portugaise (PIDE) à Bissau, en Guinée "Portugaise." Conakry: PAIGC, 1962.

União Democrática das Mulheres da Guiné e Cabo Verde." Status, Conakry, n.d.

União Nacional dos Trabalhadores da Guiné. 1962 Estatutos. Conakry: August 1962.

United Nations. [Arranged by date.] "Security Council's Attention Drawn to Situation in Portuguese Territories, with resolution." United Nations Review, X (April 1963): 9-11.

_____. "Questions Relating to Africa: Communications Concerning Portuguese Guinea." Yearbook of the United Nations, (1964): 120-121.

_____. "Statement on Territories Under Portuguese Administration." U.N. Monthly Chronicle V (July 1968): 32-42.

_____. "Adoption of General Assembly Resolution on Territories Under Portuguese Administration." U.N. Monthly Chronicle, VI (December 1969): 23-33.

_____. "Security Council Condemns Portugal and Demands Compensation." U.N. Monthly Chronicle, VI (January 1971): 3-19.

_____. "Report of the U.N. Special Mission to Guinea (Bissau)." Objective: Justice, September 1972.

_____. "Working Paper on Guinea (Bissau) and Cape Verde, Special Committee on the Situation with Regard to the Implementation of the Declaration on the Granting of Independence to Colonial Countries and Peoples." United Nations General Assembly, 24 May 1973.

_____. "UN Special Mission to Guinea-Bissau." Third World, 2, 4 (April 1973): 9-19.

_____. "Statement of the President of the U.N. General Assembly on the Implementation of the Declaration on the Granting of Independence to Colonial Countries and Peoples." U.N. General Assembly, 29th session, October 3, 1974.

United States. Congress. House Committee on Foreign Affairs, Subcommittee on Africa. Report on Portuguese Guinea and the Liberation Movement. Washington, D.C.: Government Printing Office, 1970.

Urdang, Stephanie. Fighting Two Colonialisms: Women in Guinea-Bissau. New York: Monthly Review Press.

_____. A Revolution Within a Revolution: Women in Guinea-Bissau. Somerville, MA: New England Free Press, n.d.

_____. "Towards a Successful Revolution: The Struggle in Guinea-Bissau." Objective: Justice (January-March 1975): 11-17.

Valimamad, E.D. "Nationalist Politics, War and Statehood: Guinea-Bissau, 1953-1973." Ph.D. Thesis, St. Catherine's College, Oxford, 1984.

Venter, Al J. Portugal's Guerrilla War: The Campaign for Africa. Cape Town: John Malherbe Party, Ltd., 1973.

_____. "Portugal's War in Guinea-Bissau." Munger Africana Library Notes, #19, California Institute of Technology, April 1973, 202 pps.

Wallerstein, Immanuel. "The Lessons of the PAIGC." Africa Today (July 1971): 62-68.

World Council of Churches. Program to Combat Racism. A Profile of PAIGC. Geneva: World Council of Churches, 1970.

Zartman, I. William. "Guinea: The Quiet War Goes On." Africa Report, XII, 8 (November 1967): 67-72.

13. POST-INDEPENDENCE POLITICS

Aaby, Peter. The State of Guinea-Bissau. African Socialism or Socialism in Africa? Uppsala: Scandanavian Institute of African Studies, 1978.

Almeyro, Guillermo. "Sobre el caracter del Estado en Guinea Bissau y Mozambique." Revista Coyocan (1978): 87-111.

Alves, Fernando. "Lionel Vieira: um embaixador pouco diplomatica." Africa (Portugal) (June 6, 1986).

Andreini, Jean-Claude and Marie-Claude Lambert. La Guinée Bissau d'Amilcar Cabral à la reconstruction nationale. Paris: l'Harmattan, 1978.

"Another Purge of the Left." West Africa, 3389 (July 19, 1982): 1906.

Autra, Traore Ray. "Comment les Soussou du Sénégal appellent les ressortissants de la Guinée Bissau et des Îles du Cap Vert." Notes Africaines, 162 (Abril 1979): 42-44.

Benoist, Joseph-Roger de. "Guinée-Bissau, le socialisme du bon sens." Croissance des jeunes nations, 168 (February 1976): 14-18.

Bigman, Laura. "Revolutionary Democracy in Guinea-Bissau." Master's Thesis, Howard University, December 1980.

Bollinger, Virginia L. "Development Strategy's Impact on Ethnically-Based Political Violence: A Theoretical Framework With Comparative Applications to Zambia, Guinea-Bissau and Moçambique." Dissertation, University of Colorado at Boulder, 1984.

Cabral, Luis. "Há medo na Guiné-Bissau." Africa (Portugal) (June 11, 1986).

Chabal, Patrick. Amilcar Cabral. Revolutionary leadership and people's war. Cambridge: Cambridge University Press, 1983.

_____. "Coup for continuity?" West Africa (12 January 1981):
62-3.

_____. "The PAIGC: the dilemmas of continuity." West
Africa, 22/29 (December 1980): 2593-4.

_____. "Party politics behind Cabral coup." West Africa
(15 December 1980): 2554-6.

_____. "Party, State and Socialism in Guinea-Bissau."
Canadian Journal of African Studies, 17, 2 (1983): 189-210.

Conchiglia, Augusta. "Bissau: un sommet pour cinq." Afrique
Asie, 313 (January 16-29, 1984): 40.

"Constitution de la République de Guinée-Bissau." Présence
Africaine, 88, 4 (1973): 302-309.

Cunningham, James. "Nationalist development in Guinea-Bissau."
Ph.D. Thesis, School of Oriental and African Studies,
London.

Dash, Leon. "Guinea-Bissau's Leftist Leaders Seek New, Pragmatic
Directions." Washington Post (June 6, 1981): 14-15.

Davidson, Basil. "Guinea-Bissau's people's election." People's
Power, 6 (January-February 1977): 27-31.

_____. "Practice and Theory: Guinea-Bissau and Cape Verde."
In Barry Munslow, ed., Africa. Problems in the Transition to
Socialism. London: Zed Books, 1986; 95-113.

Decreane, Philippe. "Guinée-Bissau: La Mobilisation Permanente."
Le Monde (April 13 and 14, 1976).

Dia, Mam Less. "Guinée Bissau: Les Difficultés de l'Indépendance."
Le Soleil (Senegal) (July 11, 1975).

Dianoux, Huges Jean de. "La Guinée-Bissau et les îles du Cap
Vert." Afrique contemporaine, 107 (January-February 1980):
1-17.

_____. "La Guinée-Bissau et les îles du Cap Vert en 1979."
Mondes et Cultures, 39, 4-10 (1979): 731-762.

Duarte, António. "Plano sobre Saude Maria foi delineado no estadio
do Sporting." O jornal (Lisbon) (March 30, 1984).

"Eleições locais na Guiné-Bissau." Diario de Noticias (April 1,
1984).

"Events in Guinea-Bissau: A Chronology." People's Power (Spring 1981): 16-23.

Fauvet, Gil. "Cabral Displeased with Deputies." New African (August 1979): 22-23.

Felkai, Istvan. "Tenir la promesse faite aux paysans." Le Monde Diplomatique (April 1983).

Forrest, Joshua B. "Guinea-Bissau Since Independence: A Decade of Domestic Power Struggles." The Journal of Modern African Studies, 25, 1 (March 1987).

_____. "State, Peasantry and National-level Power Struggles in Post-Independence Guinea-Bissau." Ph.D. Dissertation, University of Wisconsin-Madison, 1987.

Foy, Colm. "'Nino' Affirms the Revolution." West Africa, 3497 (August 27, 1984): 1723.

Gacha, Manuele. "Eveil de la conscience nationale et stratégie révolutionnaire chez Amilcar Cabral." Revue française d'études politiques africaines, 129 (July 1976): 69-84.

Galli, Rosemary and Jocelyn Jones. Guinea-Bissau: Politics, Economics and Society. Boulder, CO: Lynne Reinner Publs., 1987.

Gaspar, Fernando. "Um reporter na zona proibida." Presso (June 13, 1986). Journalist expelled from Guinea-Bissau.

Gjerstad, Ole and Chantal Sarrazin. Sowing the First Harvest. National Reconstruction in Guinea-Bissau. Oakland, CA: LSM Press, 1974.

"Guinea-Bissau: Another Cabinet Reshuffle." West Africa, 3450 (September 26, 1983).

"Guinea-Bissau. Constitution Revision Panel." West Africa, 3421 (March 7, 1983): 631.

"Guinea-Bissau coup: Cabral out." Guardian (New York) (November 16, 1980).

"Guinea-Bissau. Death Sentences of 38 commuted." West Africa, 3431, (May 16, 1983).

"Guinea-Bissau. Foreign Minister Dropped in reshuffle." West Africa, 3493 (July 30, 1984): 1550.

"Guinea-Bissau: Ministers Out." West Africa, 3446 (August 29, 1983): 2030.

"Guinea Bissau. Party Congress Evokes Diverse Reaction." <u>Africa</u>
<u>News</u>, 28, 3 (January 18, 1982): 8-9.

"Guinea-Bissau Premier Said to Stage Coup." <u>The New York Times</u>
(November 16, 1980).

"Guinea-Bissau: Reality and ideology." <u>Africa</u>, 70 (June 1977):
62-63.

"Guinea-Bissau. The tale of another plot." <u>West Africa</u>, 3650
(November 18, 1985): 2406.

"Guinea-Bissau: Top party cadres expelled." <u>West Africa</u>, 3454
(October 24, 1983); 2478.

"Guinée-Bissau: deux ans déjà." <u>L'Observateur</u>, 123 (October
1975): 7-54.

"La Guinée-Bissau: le démarrage du nouvel Etat." <u>Afrique</u>
<u>contemporaine</u>, 86 (July-August 1976): 11-17.

Harrell-Bond, Barbara. "Guinea-Bissau: Part III: Independent
Development." American University Field Staff Report No. 22
(1981).

Jegou, Jacques. "L'Afrique lusophone dix ans après la mort
d'Amilcar Cabral." <u>Afrique contemporaine</u> (July-September
1983): 28-33.

Lopes, Carlos. <u>Etnia, Estado e Relações de Poder na Guiné-Bissau</u>.
Lisbon: Edições 70, 1982.

_____. <u>Guinea Bissau: From Liberation Struggle to Independent</u>
<u>Statehood</u>. London: Zed Press, forthcoming.

_____. "A Transição Histórica na Guiné-Bissau; do Movimento de
Libertação Nacional ao Estado." Mémoire. Geneva: Institut
Universitaire d'Etudes du Développement. November 1982.

Makedonsky, Jeanne. "Guinée-Bissau: premières élections du temps
de paix." <u>Africa</u>, 86 (December 1976): 49-54, 89.

Makedowsky, Eric. Untitled section on Guinea-Bissau in <u>L'Année</u>
<u>Politique et Economique Africaine Edition 1981</u>. Société Africaine
d'Edition, 1981; pp. 51, 149-151.

Moita, Luís. <u>Os congressos da FRELIMO, do PAIGC e do MPLA:</u>
<u>uma análise comparativa</u>. Lisbon: CIDA-C & Ulmeiro, 1979.

Munslow, Barry. "The 1980 Coup in Guinea Bissau." <u>Review of</u>
<u>African Political Economy</u> (May-September 1981): 109-113.

Obichere, B. "Reconstruction in Guinea-Bissau: from revolutionaries and guerillas to bureaucrats and politicians." Current Bibliography on African Affairs, 8, 3 (1975): 204-19.

Odou, Rene. "Guinée-Bissau: un coup d'état pour rien." Afrique nouvelle, 1637 (19-25 November 1980): 6-7.

PAIGC. [Arranged by date.] "Relatório do C.S.L." III Congresso do PAIGC. Bissau: Conselho Superior da Luta, November 15-20, 1977.

_____. "Ante-Projecto dos Estatutos dos PAIGC," Cadernos para o III Congresso. Bissau: Edição do Serviço de Informação e Propaganda do Secretariado-Geral do PAIGC, October 7, 1977.

_____. "III Congresso do PAIGC, Documentos do Trabalho." Bissau: November 15-20, 1977.

_____. "Teses para o III Congresso do PAIGC." Bissau: Secretariado do PAIGC, October 21, 1977.

_____. "Programa do Partido." Bissau: INACEP, 1979.

_____. "Mensagem sobre o estado da Nação." President Luis Cabral. Bissau: INGB, May 1979.

_____. "Programa Bienal 1980-1981." Revista ANG. Bissau: Comissariado de Informação e Cultura, 1981.

_____. "Anteprojecto do Programa e Estatutos do PAIGC." Cadernos do 1o Congresso Extraordinário. Bissau: Secção de Informação, Propaganda e Cultura do Secretariado do CNG do PAIGC, November 8-14, 1981.

_____. "Programa do Governo Provisório." Bissau: Conselho da Revolução, July 3, 1981.

Pereira, Luísa Teotonio and Luís Moita. Guiné Bissau 3 Anos de Independência. Lisbon: CIDA-C, 1976.

Rudebeck, Lars. "Development and Class Struggle in Guinea-Bissau." Monthly Review, 30, 8 (January 1979).

_____. Guinea-Bissau: Difficulties and Possibilities of Socialist Orientation. Uppsala: Scandanavian Institute of African Studies, 1978.

_____. Guinea-Bissau: folket, partiet och staten. Uppsala: Scandanavian Institute of African Studies, 1977.

_____. Problèmes de pouvoir populaire et de développement.

Transition difficile en Guinée-Bissau. Uppsala: Scandanavian
Institute of African Studies, 1982.

Sarrazin, Chantal and Ole Gjerstad. Sowing the First Harvest.
National Reconstruction in Guinea-Bissau. Oakland, CA: LSM
Information Press, 1978.

Sigrist, Christian. "Probleme des demokratischen Neuaufbaus in
Guine-Bissau und den Kapverden." Revue de la société Amilcar
Cabral, (Université de Bielefeld), 2, 1977.

Silva, Babtista da. "Guiné-Bissau. O instável poder." Terceiro
mundo, 84 (December 1985); 32-35.

"Six Are Executed in Guinea-Bissau." The New York Times (July
22, 1986).

Soler, Anita. "Guinée-Bissau: L'Irréparable?" Afrique Asie,
1013, 381 (September 7, 1986): 34.

"Spécial Guinée-Bissau: 1er Congrès Extraordinaire du PAIGC 6-14
November 1981." ECO Magazine, Mensuel africain d'information
et politique (Bénin), 42 (December 1981): 17-24.

Sumo, Honore de. "La Guinée-Bissau s'amare a l'Occident; le
Congrès du PAIGC confirme l'orientation libérale et ramanie les
instances dirigeantes du parti." Jeune Afrique, 1351 (November
26, 1986): 36.

"Trouble à la frontière entre le Sénégal et la Guinée-Bissau." La
Presse (Tunisia) (March 14, 1973).

Vasconcellos, Tania. "Bissau: la chute de Saude." Afrique-Asie,
1013, 319 (April 9 to 23, 1984): 28.

_____. "Guinée-Bissau: épuration au Parti." Afrique Asie,
1013, 326 (July 29, 1984): 32.

Vieira, João Bernardo, [President]. Speech in O Militante, publication of the Secretariat of the Central Comittee of the PAIGC,
Special/Congress, Bissau, November-December 1981.

"Vitor Saude Maria saiu da Embaixada." Diario de Noticias
(March 27, 1984).

Washington, Shirley. "Some Aspects of post-war reconstruction in
Guinea-Bissau." Ph.D. Dissertation, Howard University, 1978.

APPENDIX A:

THE PAIGC PROGRAM

I. Immediate and Total Independence

1. Immediate winning, by all necessary means, of the total and unconditional national independence of the people of Guinea and the Cabo Verde Islands.

2. Taking over of power, in Guinea by the Guinean people and in the Cabo Verde Islands by the people of Cabo Verde.

3. Elimination of all relationships of a colonialist and imperialist nature; ending all Portuguese and foreign prerogatives over the popular masses; revision or revocation of all agreements, treaties, alliances, concessions made by the Portuguese colonialists affecting Guinea and the Cabo Verde Islands.

4. National and international sovereignty of Guinea and the Cabo Verde Islands. Economic, political, diplomatic, military, and cultural independence.

5. Permanent vigilance, based on the will of the people, to avoid or destroy all attempts of imperialism and colonialism to reestablish themselves in new forms in Guinea and the Cabo Verde Islands.

II. Unity of the Nation in Guinea and the Cabo Verde Islands

1. Equal rights and duties, firm unity and fraternal collaboration between citizens, whether considered as individuals, social groups or as ethnic groups. Prohibition and elimination of all attempts to divide the people.

2. Economic, political, social and cultural unity. In Guinea this unity will take into consideration the characteristics of the various ethnic groups at the social and cultural levels, regardless of the population in these groups. In the Cabo Verde Islands, each island or group of identical and close islands will be able to have certain autonomy at the administrative level, while remaining within the framework of national unity and solidarity.

3. The return to Guinea of all emigrés who wish to return to their country. The return to the Cabo Verde Islands of all emigrés or transported workers who wish to return to their country. Free circulation for citizens throughout the national territory.

III. Unity of the Peoples of Guinea and the Cabo Verde Islands

    1. After the winning of national independence in Guinea and
the Cabo Verde Islands, unity of the peoples of these countries
for the construction of a strong and progressive African nation, on
the basis of suitably consulted popular will.
    2. The form of unity between these two peoples to be estab-
lished by their legitimate and freely elected representatives.
    3. Equal rights and duties, solid unity and fraternal collabo-
ration between Guineans and Cabo Verdeans. Prohibition of all attempts to divide these two peoples.

IV. African Unity

    1. After the winning of national independence and on the
basis of freely manifested popular will, to struggle for the unity of
the African peoples, as a whole or by regions of the continent, always respecting the freedom, dignity and right to political, economic,
social and cultural progress of these peoples.
    2. To struggle against any attempts at annexation or pressure
on the peoples of Guinea and the Cabo Verdo Islands, on the part of
any country.
    3. Defense of the political, economic, social and cultural
rights and gains of the popular masses of Guinea and the Cabo
Verde Islands is the fundamental condition for the realization of
unity with other African peoples.

V. Democratic, Anti-Colonialist and Anti-Imperialist Government

    1. Republican, democratic, lay, anti-colonialist and anti-
imperialist government.
    2. Establishment of fundamental freedoms, respects for the
rights of man and guarantees for the exercise of these freedoms
and rights.
    3. Equality of citizens before the law, without distinction of
nationality or ethnic group, sex, social origin, cultural level, pro-
fession, position, wealth, religious belief or philosophical conviction.
Men and women will have the same status with regard to family,
work and public activities.
    4. All individuals or groups of individuals who by their ac-
tion or behavior favor imperialism, colonialism or the destruction of
the unity of the people will be deprived by every available means
of fundamental freedoms.
    5. General and free elections of the organizations in power,
based on direct, secret and universal voting.
    6. Total elimination of the colonial administrative structure
and establishment of a national and democratic structure for the
internal administration of the country.
    7. Personal protection of all foreigners living and working

in Guinea and the Cabo Verde Islands who respect the prevailing laws.

VI. Economic Independence, Structuring the Economy and Developing Production

1. Elimination of all relationships of a colonialist and imperialist nature. Winning of economic independence in Guinea and the Cabo Verde Islands.

2. Planning and harmonious development of the economy. Economic activity will be governed by the principles of democratic socialism.

3. Four types of property: state, co-operative, private and personal. Natural resources, the principle means of production, of communication and social security, radio and other means of dissemination of information and culture will be considered as national property in Guinea and the Cabo Verde Islands, and will be exploited according to the needs of rapid economic development. Co-operative exploitation on the basis of free consent will cover the land and agricultural production, the production of consumer goods and artisan articles. Private exploitation will be allowed to develop according to the needs of progress, on the condition that it is useful in the rapid development of the economy of Guinea and the Cabo Verde Islands. Personal property--in particular individual consumption goods, family houses and savings resulting from work done-- will be inviolable.

4. Development and modernization of agriculture. Transformation of the system of cultivating the soil to put an end to monocultivation and the obligatory nature of the cultivation of groundnuts in Guinea, and of maize in the Cabo Verde Islands. Struggle against agricultural crises, drought, glut and famine.

5. Agrarian reform in the Cabo Verde Islands. Limitation of the extension of private rural property in order that all peasants may have enough land to cultivate. In Guinea, taking advantage of the traditional agrarian structures and creating new structures so that the exploitation of the land may benefit the maximum number of people.

6. Both in Guinea and in the Cabo Verde Islands, confiscation of the land and other goods belonging to proven enemies of the freedom of the people and of national independence.

7. Development of industry and commerce along modern lines. Progressive establishment of state commercial and industrial enterprises. Development of African crafts. State control of foreign commerce and coordination of internal trade. Adjustment and stabilization of prices. Elimination of speculation and unfair profits. Harmony between the economic activities of town and countryside.

8. Budgetary balance. Creation of a new fiscal system. Creation of a national currency, stabilized and free from inflation.

VII. Justice and Progress for All

a. On the Social Level

1. Progressive elimination of exploitation of man by man, of all forms of subordination of the human individual to degrading interests, to the profit of individuals, groups or classes. Elimination of poverty, ignorance, fear, prostitution and alcoholism.

2. Protection of the rights of workers and guaranteed employment for all those capable of work. Abolition of forced labor in Guinea and of the exporting of forced or "contract" labor from the Cabo Verde Islands.

3. Fair salaries and appointments on the basis of equal pay for equal work. Positive emulation in work. Limitation of daily working hours according to the needs of progress and the interests of the workers. Progressive elimination of the differences existing between workers in the towns and those in the countryside.

4. Trade union freedoms and guarantees for their effective exercise. Effective participation and creative initiative of the popular masses at every level of the nation's leadership. Encouragement and support for mass organizations in the countryside and in the towns, mainly those for women, young people and students.

5. Social assistance for all citizens who need it for reasons beyond their control, because of unemployment, disability or sickness. All public health and hygiene organizations will be run or controlled by the state.

6. Creation of welfare organizations connected with productive activity. Protection of pregnant women and children. Protection of old people. Rest, recreation and culture for all workers, manual, intellectual and agricultural.

7. Assistance for victims of the national liberation struggle and their families.

b. On the Level of Education and Culture

1. Teaching centers and technical institutes will be considered as national property and as such run or controlled by the state. Reform of teaching, development of secondary and technical education, creation of university education and scientific and technical institutes.

2. Rapid elimination of illiteracy. Obligatory and free primary education. Urgent training and perfection of technical and professional cadres.

3. Total elimination of the complexes created by colonialism, and of the consequences of colonialist culture and exploitation.

4. In Guinea development of autochthonous languages and of the Creole dialect, creation of a written form for these languages. In Cabo Verde development of a written form for the Creole dialect. Development of the cultures of the various ethnic groups and of the

Cabo Verde people. Protection and development of national literature and arts.

5. Utilization of all the values and advances of human and
universal culture in the service of the progress of the peoples of
Guinea and Cabo Verde. Contribution by the culture of these peoples to the progress of humanity in general.

6. Support and development of physical education and sport
for all citizens of Guinea and the Cabo Verde Islands. Creation of
institutions for physical education and sport.

7. Religious freedom: freedom to have or not to have a religion. Protection of churches and mosques, of holy places and ob-
jects, of legal religious institutions. National independence for religious professionals.

VIII. Effective National Defense Linked to the People

1. Creation of the necessary means of effective national defense: army, navy and air force, linked to the people and directed
by national citizens. Those fighting for independence will form the
nucleus of national defense.

2. Democratic government within the armed forces. Discipline.
Close collaboration between the armed forces and the political leadership.

3. The whole people will have to participate in vigilance and
defense against colonialism, imperialism and the enemies of its unity
and progress.

4. Complete ban of foreign military bases on the national
territory.

IX. Proper International Policy in the Interests of the Nation, of Africa and of the Peace and Progress of Humanity

1. Peaceful collaboration with all the peoples of the world,
on the basis of principles of mutual respect, national sovereignty,
territorial integrity, non-aggression and non-interference in internal
affairs, equality and reciprocity of advantages, and peaceful co-
existence. Development of economic and cultural relations with all
peoples whose governments accept and respect these principles.

2. Respect for the principles of the United Nations Charter.

3. Non-adhesion to military blocs.

4. Protection for Guinean and Cabo Verdean nationals resi-
dent abroad.

GOVERNMENT OFFICIALS OF GUINEA-BISSAU
(as of July 1986)

President of the Republic
  and of the Council of State: João Bernardo Vieira

Vice-President of the Council
  of State: Iafai Camara

President of the Popular
  National Assembly: Carmen Pereira

Ministers of State:

Armed Forces:	Iafai Camara
Security and Public Order:	José Pereira
Justice:	Vasco Cabral
Presidential Affairs:	Tiago Aleluia Lopes
Rural Development and Fisheries:	Carlos Correia
Foreign Affairs:	Júlio Semedo
Planning:	Bartolomeu Pereira
Commerce and Tourism:	Manual dos Santos
Finance:	Victor Freira Monteiro
Information and Telecommunications:	Mussa Djassi
Natural Resources and Industry:	Filinto Barros
Social Infrastructure:	Avito da Silva
Civil Service, Labor and Social Security:	Henriqueta Bodinho Gomes
Public Health:	Alexandre Nunes Correia
Education, Sport, and Culture:	Fidelis Cabral de Almada
Resident for the Northern Province:	Mario Cabral
Resident for the Southern Province:	Luís Oliveira Sanca
Resident for the Eastern Province:	Malam Bacai Sanha

Appendix B   210

Secretaries of State:

Presidency: Bernardino Cardoso
Fisheries: Abubacar Balde
Information: Agnelo Regalla
Natural Resources: Pio Correira
Tourism and Handicrafts: Alberto Lima Gomes
Transport: Mário Ribeiro
Education: Manual Rambout Barcelos
War Veterans: Joaquim Furtado

Other Important Officials:

Governor of the National
    Bank: Pedro Godinho Gomes
President of the Supreme
    Court of Justice: Rui das Merces Barreto
Commander of the Police: Lourenço Gomes
Secretary General of the
    Union of the Women of
    Guinea-Bissau: Francisca Pereira
Chief of Staff of the Popular
    Armed Forces: José Marc Vieira

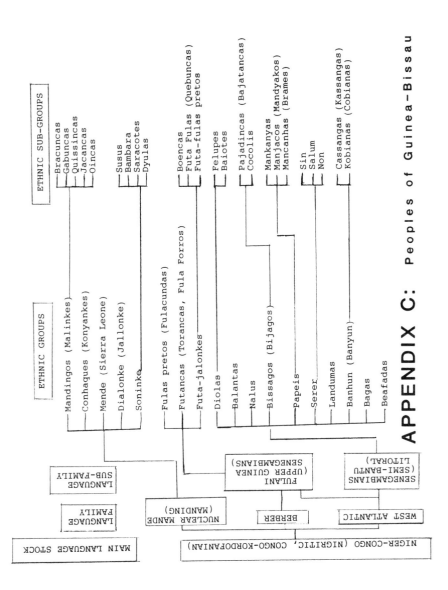

APPENDIX C: Peoples of Guinea-Bissau

MAIN LANGUAGE STOCK

NIGER-CONGO (NIGRITIC, CONGO-KORDOFANIAN)

LANGUAGE FAMILY

- NUCLEAR MANDE (MANDING)
- BERBER
- WEST ATLANTIC

LANGUAGE SUB-FAMILY

- FULANI (UPPER GUINEA SENEGAMBIANS)
- SENEGAMBIANS (SEMI-BANTU) LITTORAL)

ETHNIC GROUPS

- Mandingos (Malinkes)
- Conhaques (Konyankes)
- Mende (Sierra Leone)
- Dialonke (Jallonke)
- Soninke
- Fulas pretos (Fulacundas)
- Futancas (Torancas, Fula Forros)
- Futa-jalonkes
- Diolas
- Balantas
- Nalus
- Bissagos (Bijagos)
- Papeis
- Serer
- Landumas
- Banhun (Banyun)
- Bagas
- Beafadas

ETHNIC SUB-GROUPS

- Bracuncas
- Gabuncas
- Quissincas
- Jacancas
- Oincas
- Susus
- Bambara
- Saracotes
- Dyulas
- Boencas
- Futa Fulas (Quebuncas)
- Futa-fulas pretos
- Felupes
- Baiotes
- Pajadincas (Bajatancas)
- Cocolis
- Mankanyas
- Manjacos (Mandyakos)
- Mancanhas (Brames)
- Sin
- Salum
- Non
- Cassangas (Kassangas)
- Kobianas (Cobianas)